D0016757

Blue Smoke and Mirrors

Blue Smoke and Mirrors

How Reagan Won and Why Carter
Lost the Election of 1980

Jack W. Germond and Jules Witcover

THE VIKING PRESS

NEW YORK

First published in 1981 by The Viking Press
625 Madison Avenue, New York, N.Y. 10022
Published simultaneously in Canada by
Penguin Books Canada Limited

Library of Congress Cataloging in Publication Data
Germond, Jack.
Blue smoke and mirrors.
Includes index.
1. Presidents—United States—Election—1980.
2. Reagan, Ronald.   3. Carter, Jimmy, 1924–
I. Witcover, Jules, joint author.   II. Title.
JK526   1980.G47   324.973′0926   81-50685
ISBN 0-670-51383-0   AACR2

Printed in the United States of America
Set in Video Caledonia

To Barbara, Mandi, and Jessie
And to Marian, Paul, Amy, and Julie

Look now how mortals are blaming the gods, for they say that evils come from us, but in fact they themselves have woes beyond their share because of their own follies.

—*The Odyssey*, Book I

Acknowledgments

A presidential election year nowadays seems endless. After months of preliminaries, a dozen or more candidates embark on a series of state party primaries and caucuses stretching from January into June, assaulting the public's attention with daily speeches, press releases, news conferences, and "media events." Then, after the two great national party conventions, the daily assault resumes, from Labor Day through Election Day, with a deadening repetition that in the end leaves both contestants and voters numb. Yet when the campaign is over and a president has been elected, relatively few episodes stand out as turning points in the election. In our efforts to isolate and examine these as clues to how in 1980 Ronald Reagan won the presidency, and why Jimmy Carter lost it, we are indebted to many people in the political community who took the time to be interviewed. These include President Ronald Reagan; Vice President George Bush; former President Gerald R. Ford; former Vice President Walter F. Mondale; 1980 presidential candidates John B. Anderson, Howard H. Baker, and Edward M. Kennedy; and leading members of all the campaign staffs, including the staff of former President Jimmy Carter. Only Carter and his campaign manager, Hamilton Jordan, each of whom is writing a book, refused to be interviewed, in spite of our repeated requests.

During the long campaign there were hundreds of campaign workers, political professionals, and voters who contributed to our understanding of the electoral process. All of them obviously cannot be mentioned here, but we especially thank the following: Douglas Bailey, James A. Baker, Bob Barrett, Charles Black, James S. Brady, Patrick Caddell, Hodding Carter, Gerald Carmen, Richard Cheney, Roger Craver, Walter Cronkite, John Deardourff, Sam Donaldson, Robert Garrick, David Garth, Peter Hart, Ruth Hinerfeld, Lawrence Horowitz, Tom Jarriel, David Keene, David Kennerly, Paul Kirk, Senator Paul Laxalt, Andrew Lack, James Lake, Drew Lewis, Paul Manafort, Charles Manatt, Tom Mathews, George McGovern, Ron McMahan, Edwin Meese, Richard Moe, Lyn Nofziger, Speaker of the House Thomas P. O'Neill, Jr., Carey Parker, Jody Powell, Gerald Rafshoon, Rick Robb, John Sears, Stuart Spencer, Greg Schneiders, Robert Shrum, John Siegenthaler, Stephen Smith, Terence Smith, Theodore Sorensen, Tom Southwick, Roger Stone, Robert S. Strauss, Robert Teeter, William Timmons, Edward Walsh, Curtis Wilkie, Richard Wirthlin, and Phil Wise.

JACK W. GERMOND
JULES WITCOVER

Washington, D. C.
April 1981

Contents

Introduction

It was scarcely more than twenty years ago, in his celebrated *The Making of the President 1960,* that Theodore H. White told the world about "the O'Brien Manual"—Lawrence F. O'Brien's "sixty-four-page black-bound book" that provided "the diagram of organization for every Kennedy campaign from beginning to end." If the voters had thought much about it, of course, they would have realized there was something more to a presidential election campaign than the candidate giving speeches at party rallies, shaking hands on street corners, and waving from motorcades. But most people hadn't thought much about it, and there was an inevitable loss of innocence in learning how Larry O'Brien had codified in such detail the steps required to build a successful campaign for John F. Kennedy. Winning the presidency was not, after all, just a matter of devoted young volunteers stuffing envelopes and passing out bumper stickers.

Given what was to follow, however, the 1960 campaign was the Stone Age of political manipulation. The technically masterful campaign of Richard M. Nixon in 1968, in which spontaneity was an enemy, was revealed in all its calculated deceptiveness by Joe McGinniss in *The Selling of the President 1968.* And in 1972, Nixon's added political weapon of incumbency brought new manipulative refinements. The President's managers controlled to an exceptional degree what their candidate said and did, where he went, what the television cameras were able to reveal of him, and the results were almost invariably self-serving. In 1976, too, the elevation to the White House of a peanut farmer, a one-term governor of a rural Southern state named Jimmy Carter, was seen as a marvel of "packaging" and media manipulation. Anything was deemed possible with the legerdemain of the magicians of the new political technology.

By 1978, when the candidates of both major parties began preparing in earnest for the presidential campaign of 1980, each had his own expert on public-opinion polls, his own direct-mail specialist to raise money and influence voters, his own consultant or consultants on television and radio advertising. And behind these most prized advisers, each candidate had a corps of others with particular skills—schedulers to plan campaign tours, "advance men" (many of them now women) to make the arrangements and assure crowds, field operatives to direct local and state efforts, specialists in telephone canvassing and literature distribution, researchers to develop the "right" positions on issues as well as uncover the vulnerabilities of the opposition.

This naturally expensive cadre of political professionals was no longer employed only by presidential candidates. House, Senate, and gubernatorial campaigns that used their services might cost a million dollars or more. In 1978 one candidate for governor, William Clements in Texas, spent $9 million, and in 1979, in Louisiana alone, six gubernatorial candidates spent a total of $30 million. Even campaigns for mayor and county commissioner reached a level of sophistication at which pollsters and advertising consultants could be profitably employed. But the leading consultants flocked to the presidential campaigns, where the stakes were highest and the rewards, money, and recognition were greatest.

To some extent, the increased reliance on specialists was simply the effect of improved techniques and changes in the rules of the game. The new limits on campaign contributions in federal elections, enacted in 1974, obliged a candidate to find a large population of small contributors; the use of direct-mail advertising was an obvious way to do this. Computer technology made these mailing campaigns more effective and analyses of the public mood far more sophisticated than they had been a decade earlier. The function of the consultants also grew because of changes in the political culture. Fewer voters took an active part in either the Republican or the Democratic parties. The political boss or union leader, the governor or mayor who could really deliver votes, was now a rarity. Neither party identification nor ideological leaning was reason enough in itself for casting a particular vote.

But the most important change over those two decades since 1960 was that television had assumed a dominant, central position in the very life of the country. Along with such innovations as fast-food restaurants, the national networks had become a homogenizing force in American society. Whether voters lived in Sarasota or Butte, in Bangor or San Diego, they were all fed the staples of their diet of political news from the same sources— Walter Cronkite and John Chancellor and Frank Reynolds. Newspapers might provide greater detail and more analysis and commentary, but the raw material for most Americans was what they heard and saw on the evening news broadcasts.

Thus the aim of the new political technology was to control the images on those millions of television screens every night— to present the candidates not necessarily as they really were but as they would prefer to be seen. Advertising was tailored to touch the popular nerves the pollsters had identified. And in exploiting what the politicians called "the free media"—meaning television news coverage—the imperative was to create, each day of the campaign, a "visual" that would express the things that concerned most voters.

As the presidential campaign of 1980 began, the cliché had taken hold that American politics, as a result of this refinement of the art of measuring and shaping public opinion, had become a prisoner of technology. In this new discipline, the high priests were said to be the pollsters who gathered the basic data on which all else was predicated, but equally important were the new technocrats who made use of the data. Their "target areas" were no longer the old neighborhood precincts but rather the mass-media markets measured by the range of a television station's signal. The order of the day, in this view of the politics of 1980, was control and manipulation: control of the environment, of the candidate, of what the voters saw, heard, and—if possible—thought; manipulation of the nation's prime transmission belts of basic information, the news media—television especially. It was a nice, tidy concept, whose validity had been reinforced by the politics of the late 1960s and 1970s. Then, coldly efficient platoons of Nixon men all but banished free-form campaigning and substituted tightly planned agendas that dictated how television would cover their candidate.

As the 1980 campaign approached and it became clear that Ronald Reagan would be a serious contender for the Republican presidential nomination, the concept of controlled campaigning took full wing. Here, after all, was the ideal vehicle for the new technology—a motion-picture actor. Here was a man who had spent most of his adult life shaping perceptions of one fictional character or another in the eyes and minds of the public. What better raw material could the new technocrats, the new manipulators, hope to find? The formula for success was clear: assess the public mood, write an accommodating script, put it in the hands of the experienced actor/politician.

In the other party, of course, another crew of new technocrats was employing all the same techniques. Jimmy Carter's men did not have an actor to work with, but they had the power of the incumbency—the White House and all its trappings—with which to persuade the American people that only one man had all the information, and most of the wisdom and stability, to act in their best interests. It was all very simple.

But it was really not so simple at all. Unlike an antiseptic laboratory experiment, in which the environment and the subjects are all carefully controlled, political campaigns go forward in an atmosphere shaped by circumstance as much as by maneuver, and that was especially so in 1980. To be sure, this did not render the new technocrats powerless, but it did make them much, much less than omnipotent. Like surfers, they may master all the techniques, but so much depends on how the wave breaks—on how they and their candidates are then able to stay on its crest. With all their attendant skills and knowledge of their specialty, they must bend, and shift weight, and labor to stay afloat.

To some degree, the limits of the professionals' effectiveness in 1980 may have been simply a reaction by the voters against the manipulations of the past. The American people had found that the *reality* of Lyndon Johnson, Richard Nixon, and Jimmy Carter was quite different from what their campaigns had promised. It was not surprising, then, that the voters were more critical in 1980 in assessing political advertising and in recognizing exploitation of "the free media." Also, political and social trends were building that made voters more wary of their leaders and the professional manipulators in their employ. The shocks of the Vietnam war and then Watergate, and the disenchantment they bred with the effectiveness and credibility of government, encouraged pessimism and even resentment toward authority figures. Apathy toward the very act of voting became increasingly widespread. Carter as an "outsider" had tapped the public disillusionment in 1976, but even at that, barely more than one of every two voters cast a ballot for him, and only one of every four Americans old enough to vote. And in short order his performance in office only increased the disillusion.

Mistrust of government, and of presidents, dovetailed comfortably with a conservative trend that had made its serious entry into the national consciousness with the candidacy of Barry Goldwater in 1964 and had been sustained through the Nixon, Ford, and Carter years. The expanding American middle class soured increasingly on all government, labeling it as a coddler of those who didn't pay their way and as an intruder upon the individual's pursuit of happiness, measured as an ever-larger share of the economic pie. The conservative dogma that too much government was spending too much of the taxpayer's hard-earned money, and was the root cause of inflation, encouraged this public mistrust of politics and politicians. Also, challenges to American preeminence abroad further shook public confidence in the nation's political leaders and the professionals who labored to elect them, and then to keep them in office.

Finally, the new politics, like the old, was not immune to the unpredictable exigencies of a world in conflict. In 1980 unforeseen events were so dominant, compelling, and uncontrollable that they overwhelmed the professionals' efforts to shape and confine the presidential campaign and assure victory for the man of their choice. Even in the era of the new political technology, electing a president was not, and could not be, a science.

What follows is an attempt to chronicle and examine the manner in which this irrefutable fact of political life ruled the 1980 campaign for the presidency, and in the end contributed to the landslide victory of Ronald Reagan over Jimmy Carter.

Blue Smoke and Mirrors

1.
The "October Surprise"– in November

It was Saturday, November 1, 1980, and the ordeal was nearly over. In the last year, a dozen men had committed their ambitions, their energies, and their resources to pursuit of the most cherished prize in American politics—the presidency of the United States. Now, three days before the election, only two of them remained in serious contention—the Democratic incumbent, President Jimmy Carter, and the Republican challenger, Ronald Reagan—though a third, John Anderson, persevered as an independent.

In Houston, the President rose early, around six o'clock, put on shorts and running shoes, and proceeded in the company of similarly attired Secret Service agents, his military aide, Bob Peterson, and the White House physician, Dr. William Lukash, to jog for three miles. Then he showered, dressed, and embarked on one of his longest campaign days of 1980—a swing aboard Air Force One from Houston to Brownsville, Abilene, San Antonio, and Fort Worth, then north to Milwaukee, and finally to Chicago, just before midnight. The aim on this final weekend was to meet voters, yes, but more important, it was to exploit media markets—to bring Carter into those communications centers with television facilities that reached the widest possible audiences.

Meanwhile, in Grand Rapids, Michigan, Reagan started his public day with a large and enthusiastic outdoor rally. He was introduced by hometown hero Gerald Ford, the former President

1

whom Reagan had challenged unsuccessfully and who had then been beaten narrowly by Carter four years earlier. Reagan, with Ford at his side attacking his successor in the White House as a complete failure, flew on across Michigan to Battle Creek, Saginaw, and Pontiac, then south to Columbus, Ohio.

The campaign of 1980, like the one preceding it, had been a long, plodding affair. But now, on the final weekend, each of the two major party candidates was sprinting for the wire, campaigning all-out in the states regarded as the principal battlegrounds—Texas, Wisconsin, Illinois, Michigan, Ohio. There were other battlegrounds as well—Pennsylvania, Missouri, Washington, Oregon—where one or both of the candidates would campaign before election day.

Most of the public-opinion polls were indicating a very tight race, and in 1980 the news media had elevated polls—good, bad and indifferent—to a lofty position as clairvoyants. But the moods of the two campaigns suggested otherwise. The atmosphere in the Reagan entourage was gay, relaxed, confident, with only a single notable cloud hanging over it. This same night, half a world away, the parliament of Iran was to consider the fate of fifty-two American hostages held captive in Tehran for just three days short of a year. If the Iranians suddenly released the hostages, there was no telling what the political reaction at home would be. The Reagan camp was concerned that a relieved and grateful American electorate would somehow credit the incumbent President—and reward him with an emotional outpouring of votes, and reelection. So the buoyancy of this Saturday's swing through Michigan was tempered by that possibility, over which neither Reagan nor any of his advisers had the slightest control.

In the Carter entourage, the mood was determined, as the heavy schedule indicated. Carter's customary overweening confidence was absent, but the same factor that was causing quiet trepidation among the Reaganites traveling in Michigan was fanning cautious hope as the President and his party jetted across Texas and into the Midwest. Jimmy Carter, too, was at the mercy of events, but he understood from hard experience that it did not pay to rely on hopeful signals from Tehran. And so, on this final Saturday, he was campaigning like a man who knew that every vote was critical, that time was precious, and that no opportunity to rally support should be ignored.

It was approaching midnight when the President arrived at the Hyatt Regency Hotel outside O'Hare Airport in Chicago. He had been in seven cities in three states since rising to jog in Houston, and Sunday was to be another long day. He would campaign in Chicago and its suburbs, then go to Detroit for a large labor rally and on to Philadelphia for still another, both with Senator Ted Kennedy, his foe in the primaries who now was playing the good soldier for the Democratic Party cause.

As Carter prepared to go to his suite on the ninth floor, however, Marty Russo, a Chicago Democratic congressman, informed him that elsewhere in the hotel the Italian-American Sports Hall of Fame was holding a dinner honoring some famous sports figures. At about a quarter to twelve, the President of the United States suddenly appeared, unannounced, in the Rosemont Room, where the event was nearing its conclusion. The crowd of about five hundred festive diners in black tie and evening gowns stood and applauded the surprise guest as he took a hand microphone up front.

"I hope you'll forgive me for interrupting your banquet," President Carter said, "but I heard about all the famous people here tonight and I wanted to come and see them. As a matter of fact, I've been a great admirer and a fan of some of the great Italian-American athletes, the heroes that you are recognizing tonight. And I've come here not at all to talk about politics but to shake hands with some of these famous people. When I was a young naval officer just learning how to be a submarine engineer, one of my great heroes was Phil Rizzuto—and Mickey Mantle and Joe DiMaggio."

The crowd applauded again, although it must have come as a revelation to them that Mantle was an Italian-American. Carter reported that Tommy Lasorda, manager of the Los Angeles Dodgers, "is one of my mother's sweethearts," and that Miss Lillian "adopted the Dodgers many years ago and she's kind of a mascot of theirs. As a matter of fact, she's got a full Dodger uniform in Plains, including cleats, the gloves, and everything else."

While the audience conjured with that image, the President of the United States indicated he was beside himself with joy at being in such august company. "I would like to point out," he said, "that Andy Robustelli [a former New York Giants football player]—is he here tonight? I want to meet him too. . . . That's just great. And also Andy Varipapa [a bowling champion]. It's just unbelievable that I could have a chance to know him. Come on up, if you don't mind. I know you've already recognized him, but I want you to see me shake their hand." Again the crowd applauded.

Carter went on in this idolatrous vein for several more minutes, calling other sports heroes to come up so that *he*, a mere president, could shake *their* hands. "This is a very great thrill for me," he said, thanking the assemblage finally for giving him the chance "to meet these heroes of mine, and to share with you a moment of greatness with them for Italian-Americans, for all Americans, and for the greatest nation in the world."

With that hyperbole ringing in his astonished listeners' ears, Jimmy Carter repaired to his suite for the night. It was now past midnight, but he was not able to go directly to bed. Awaiting him on the ninth floor was Hamilton Jordan, his campaign manager. Jordan was the young, controversial political strategist who had masterminded Carter's successful run from obscurity to the White House in 1976, one of the new breed of political technocrats whose strength lay not in any acquaintanceship with politics at the ward level as of old, but with the world of polls and media markets and mass psychology. He had flown from Washington to be on hand if and when word came through that the Iranian parliament had taken some definite action that required a swift response—and a reassessment of the ramifications for the presidential election. Jordan's arrival at the hotel in Chicago had gone largely unnoticed, although television network correspondents with walkie-talkies that could tune in on the traveling White House radio frequency might have heard a cryptic alert to Phil Wise, the President's appointments secretary: "Wise, Wise. Base. Jordan requests Powell and Wise go to Deacon's room upon arrival." (Powell was Jody Powell, the President's press secretary; Deacon was Carter's Secret Service code name.)

The traveling press corps knew, of course, that the Iranian parliament was meeting this night, but the formal campaign schedule for the next day, Sunday, offered hope for a relatively late start. Candidates are always sensitive to the observance of the Sabbath, and if they campaign at all on a Sunday morning, it is usually by attending a church service. So it was supposed to be for Carter, at the Mercy Seat Baptist Church in Chicago, in what would be a thinly veiled effort to reinforce his support in the black community and generate a strong turnout among blacks on Tuesday. Since the service was scheduled to start at eleven o'clock, that meant, for the staff and accompanying press corps, a most cherished item on a campaign schedule—a late baggage call. (That is, bags did not have to be brought to the hotel lobby for pickup until 10:45 a.m.) Also, Daylight Saving Time for the year ended on this Saturday night, bringing a bonus of an "extra" hour. All of this meant two things to veteran campaigners—the options of a late night in the hotel bar or, for once, a decent night's sleep.

Some staff aides and reporters, exhausted from the long day, bypassed the first option or merely looked in for a quick drink, then went to bed. Others, though, stayed in the bar until closing, hoping they could still log in enough sleep before baggage call and departure to be functional the next day.

Not everyone with a stake in the campaign slept on this night, however. Back in Washington, at the Department of State, officials were at their posts awaiting the outcome of the long-delayed debate in the Majlis, the Iranian parliament, on the fate of the American hostages. Before the President had headed out on what was supposed to be his final campaign swing, he and his aides had decided that in the event of any substantial new development in Iran, he would fly back to Washington. "It just didn't make sense," Powell explained later, "if it was something you were going to have to work with, and not make one big decision but a series of decisions . . . to try to do that on the road."

Not lost in that decision, of course, was an awareness that such a sudden interruption of the campaign would certainly inject an element of high drama at the eleventh hour. Whether it would help or hurt the incumbent's chances depended, everyone realized, on the nature of the news.

This uncertainty, in fact, was the gist of the conversation at the dinner table of Gerald Rafshoon, Carter's advertising specialist,

at his home in Washington this night. Rafshoon was another of
the new political technocrats, as was his guest for dinner—Patrick Caddell, Carter's pollster.

The phone rang and Rafshoon answered. It was Paul Maslin,
one of Caddell's chief associates, reporting on a national survey just completed. "Is it good or is it bad?" Rafshoon asked anx-
iously.

"It's good," Maslin said.

Caddell took the phone, heard some numbers from his aide,
and told Rafshoon that the poll showed that Carter, after a dip
following his televised debate with Reagan in Cleveland four
days earlier, had come back. He was now running even, Caddell
said, or slightly ahead of the Republican candidate. This conclusion, as we shall see, ran contrary to polling being done simultaneously by the Reagan campaign. But Caddell swore by it, and
right or wrong, it controlled the thinking and strategy in the
Carter camp over this final weekend.

"We knew by Thursday night that we were a little shade less
than five points down from the debate," Caddell recalled later,
speaking in the now-familiar jargon. "From '76, the one thing we
knew was that whatever impact the debate had, it usually had
a half-life of about seventy-two hours. We'd seen that most pronounced in the second debate [in '76], where Ford stumbled so
badly, and yet most of the vote impact was gone relatively quickly on that. So it was our assumption that . . . we would get the
same kind of debate bounce by the weekend, and [we had to]
structure ourselves accordingly." The Carter strategists, he said,
persuaded the President to present himself over this final weekend as the struggling underdog, "because one thing we knew all
along was that we had to keep the focus on Reagan, and keep the
focus on a candidate choice [rather than issues], much as '76 had
been. That had always been the key factor in being able to win."
So it was considered advantageous to Carter to have Reagan perceived by the voters as slightly ahead—presumably as an induce-
ment to fence-straddling Democrats to come home to their party
because Carter really needed their votes.

The post-debate "bounceback" toward Carter, Caddell insisted, was in a pattern visible in the 1976 election as well as in the

1980 primaries: "every time one of the candidates started getting an edge on the other one, it was almost as though they stuck their nose out in front of the American public. . . . When one candidate began to move up ahead of the other, he began to slip." So that was another good reason to play the underdog. Also, he said, recent elections had been marked in the final week by "an incumbent party surge," and he clearly hoped that Carter would benefit from that.

Rafshoon was nevertheless uneasy. "We knew the hostage thing was going to happen that night," he said later. "I remember saying to Pat, 'I wish this hostage thing wasn't going to happen tomorrow.' Everybody was saying it was going to be good for us. I said, 'It's not going to be good, because it is just going to break the rhythm.' I mean, it looked like we were coming back. We were going to win the thing, and who needs it? It was just going to bring up everything." After dinner, Caddell went back to his office to work over the polling data and Rafshoon went to bed.

In Chicago, when Carter returned from the Italian-American sports dinner, the Iranian parliament's expected action was much on his mind and those of his advisers. So, although the hour was late and they had reason to expect that they would be called in the middle of the night with news, the President, Jordan, Powell, and Wise sat around for more than an hour, mulling over the possibilities. Before they all retired, the switchboard was alerted that a call from Warren Christopher, the deputy secretary of state directly in charge of diplomatic negotiations on the hostages, was expected and should be put through to Carter when it came.

For Ronald Reagan, the day's end was marked neither by any desperate quest for one more crowd to address nor by any late-night conference. The Republican candidate, staying overnight at the ancient Neil House, across the street from the Ohio state capitol in Columbus, had a quiet dinner in his suite with his wife, Nancy, and retired early. His ranking political aides on the trip—his own band of professionals—met in another part of the hotel, as was their nightly routine, to prepare for the next day's events.

There was some discussion of the impending decision from Iran, but there was no need to involve Reagan himself, because there was nothing he could say or do until the details of the parliament's action were known.

This placid Saturday evening did not mean, however, that Reagan's campaign was not also concerned about what might happen in Tehran. The staff consensus was indeed that if anything could deny Reagan victory now, it was only some major development concerning the hostages. Reagan's own polls, taken by Richard Wirthlin, one of the most able of the new breed, had shown him—in sharp contrast to Caddell's data—picking up strength even before the debate, and adding to it almost daily afterward. But as far back as the Republican convention in Detroit in July, Reagan's campaign manager, the former CIA man William Casey, had been warning darkly and apprehensively of an "October surprise" that Carter would engineer in the final days of the campaign to snatch victory from defeat.

A good part of Casey's warning was clever strategy—an attempt to condition the American people to wonder, if such an eleventh-hour surprise did come about, whether it was merely a political ploy by a desperate incumbent. There was, after all, a recent history of similar late-campaign foreign-policy gambits designed to affect presidential elections: President Lyndon Johnson's efforts in 1968 to negotiate a bombing halt of North Vietnam and peace talks to help the Democratic candidate, Hubert Humphrey, was one; Secretary of State Henry Kissinger's declaration in 1972 that "peace is at hand" to help the incumbent, Richard Nixon, was another. This time, though, many of the Reagan insiders really believed, and feared, that a breakthrough in the hostage situation might be the Reagan campaign's undoing at the very end. In the two or three days immediately after the debate, Reagan's press secretary, Lyn Nofziger, recalled later, "We were scared to death, we were really scared to death, because we didn't know how it would play" if a break occurred in the hostage affair. Stuart Spencer and Michael Deaver, the two principal political strategists on Reagan's campaign plane, would stay aboard at stops as the candidate went off to speak; using special telephones installed on the plane and plugged in the moment it taxied up to a terminal, they would gather late intelligence on the situation from various sources, including Henry Kissinger. In his 1976 campaign against President Ford, Reagan had painted Kissinger as a villain, but now he had become a highly valued foreign-policy kibitzer and confidant (as well as, many thought, a prospective Reagan administration job applicant). Kissinger was said to have "incredible" sources around the world and "all kinds of wires out," and according to one insider, "kept telling us, 'The hostages are coming out.'"

Spencer and Deaver, Nofziger said later, were on the phone to Ford and Kissinger "trying to figure out how we could start a backfire" if that happened. In fact, in anticipation of the worst—politically for Reagan—arrangements had already been made to shuttle both Ford and Kissinger onto network news shows to help put out the political fire. The Reagan campaign had also prepared new television and radio tapes that could be rushed to stations around the country and substituted for tapes for which the campaign had already bought air time. Also, half an hour of network television time had been purchased for Reagan for a conventional Election Eve broadcast. If necessary, he could himself suggest that Carter was playing politics with the hostages.

Until some definite information came out of Tehran, however, all this was mere contingency planning. Reagan's own instincts, Spencer said at the time, were "to leave it alone," because even if the hostages were being released, he thought it was too late to help Carter. The very timing, Spencer reasoned, would itself encourage public cynicism, and any overt action by Reagan or his supporters would risk a political backlash. Lounging in an anteroom in Pontiac, Michigan, late that Saturday afternoon as Reagan addressed his last rally of the day in a large airport hangar, Spencer leaned back in an easy chair, puffed on a cigarette, and said with a grin: "They can't hurt us in the last twenty-four hours."

Others in the Reagan camp, however, were not so sanguine. As Reagan slept in Columbus, a relatively sophisticated "hostage watch" was under way in the Reagan campaign operations center in Arlington, Virginia, just across the Potomac from Washing-

ton. Back during the Republican convention, when Casey had
first told reporters of his concern over an "October surprise," the
reporters inquired whether he had any plan to cope with it. To
their surprise—and some considerable incredulity—former CIA
man Casey said he did. He was setting up an "intelligence operation," he said, to keep "an incumbency watch" on Carter. It
would guard against any hanky-panky concerning the hostages
or any other foreign-policy matter whose manipulation might inject a real or phony atmosphere of crisis into the final days of the
campaign.

Nothing more was said about any such monitoring operation
thereafter. But Casey was true to his word. During the fall campaign the Reagan operation signed on a retired naval reserve admiral named Robert Garrick, essentially a public relations and
public information specialist. Garrick in turn recruited some old
military friends, mostly also retired, who lived at or near four air
force bases—Andrews in the Maryland suburbs of Washington,
McGuire in central New Jersey, Norton in San Bernardino, California, and March in Riverside, California. It was judged that if
there were to be any major movement of troops or materiel,
large numbers of transport planes would come in or out of one
or all of these bases. "We wanted to know," Garrick said in military parlance after the campaign, "what kinds of birds they
were, and how many," as a possible clue that something unusual
was happening, such as an exchange of supplies for the hostages.

In addition, during these final few days some people from the
political section of Reagan's campaign headquarters were sent to
Andrews, to the naval and other installations at Norfolk, Virginia,
and to a base in Mississippi, another Reagan source said, "to report in plane numbers and tail numbers" in an effort to keep
track of any movements toward Iran. Also, businessmen who had
sold goods to Iran but had never been paid when Iranian assets
were frozen by Carter kept an eye on planes in New York believed to be bearing their goods. Meanwhile, Republican congressmen were phoning Secretary of State Edmund S. Muskie to
keep abreast of latest developments and passing on whatever
they could learn to the campaign headquarters. At the same
time, sources described only as "outside government in the Arab
world" with contacts in the Iranian parliament provided intelli-

gence about the views and activities of various factions relating to the hostage situation. And, finally, a liaison was established with some of the families of the hostages, to learn what they were hearing and thinking.

Garrick's "hostage watch" at Reagan's campaign headquarters kept in touch with all these informants and also monitored all the wire services and television networks as well as the armed forces network, passing on what was learned to the campaign plane. On this Saturday night, Garrick said later, the campaign had in its possession a manifest of all the military spare parts that Iran had previously purchased from the United States but were being withheld as part of President Carter's response to the seizure of the hostages. The list had been culled from congressional hearings and other public sources. Just what use it was to the Reagan campaign was not clear, but the fact that the campaign went to the trouble of getting the data underscored its fixation about the "October surprise." Of the whole drill, Garrick said, "It was one of the things you do to try to get information, because you didn't get it any other way."

The "hostage watch" had been instructed to be "on full alert" for any information that might give the Reagan party in Columbus advance indication of what was going to happen over this critical weekend. The objective was to have Reagan prepared for any eventuality, and for his political strategists to devise the most effective response on the shortest notice. "You can't write a statement for that kind of thing in advance," Jim Brady, the press aide who eventually became the White House press secretary, said later. "You can war-game it, but it's a ground call, because you don't know the imponderables in advance." This Saturday night, in keeping with the military-like organization and lingo, Brady had "the watch" in Columbus. The operations center was instructed to call him at any hour to report anything notable going on in Tehran, or anywhere else where the Reagan "hostage watch" was functioning.

In Chicago the call from Christopher came through at 3:55 a.m. Central Standard Time. He woke the President, who had been asleep less than three hours, and quickly told him that the Iranian parliament had at last acted. Although the demands had not yet been officially transmitted, there were four major points: in return for the fifty-two Americans, the United States must pledge noninterference in Iranian affairs; free the Iranian assets in America that had been frozen; cancel all American public and private claims against Iran; and return to Iran the late Shah's wealth. On their face, these four demands seemed unacceptable, if only because the American government did not have the power to accede to the last two.

But it was no time, practical or political, for any precipitate rejection. The President would have to know more precisely what the Iranians were proposing, and he then would have to determine what the United States could and should do. Carter instructed Powell to prepare for the speediest possible return to Washington. Meanwhile, the President phoned Secretary of State Muskie at his home in Bethesda, Maryland, a Washington suburb, and told him to start briefing the congressional leaders as well as Reagan and Anderson on what had happened.

Although the Carter people had known that the President might well be returning to the White House, the scene at the Hyatt Regency was pandemonium nonetheless. Powell called his deputy, Rex Granum, and told him to round up a press pool— a small group of reporters from the networks, the wire services, and newspapers representing the entire press corps—to return with Carter on Air Force One. The reporters were phoned in their rooms and rousted out on the double.

At around the same time Jordan and Powell placed a conference call to Rafshoon, Caddell, and campaign chairman Robert Strauss, all at their homes in Washington. Jordan told them that Carter was returning, and that this group—the key political advisers—had better get together Sunday morning to consider the implications. They agreed to meet at Strauss's apartment at the Watergate in a few hours.

It was not yet five o'clock and still dark in Chicago when the President appeared outside the hotel. He was dressed in the same dark blue suit he had worn the night before, with a light tan raincoat over it. The motorcade, with a single police car at the front flashing its roof lights, sped away, leaving behind one member of the press pool notified late, Terence Smith of *The New York Times*. Smith hitched a ride in a network car and raced to the airport, vainly seeking the entrance to the proper military gate at the vast O'Hare complex. Then he came upon one of Carter's young press aides, Dale Leibach, with a walkie-talkie in his hand. Leibach hopped into the network car on the run and, all together, they barely made it to Air Force One. The President had already boarded. At 5:23 a.m. the plane took off with Chicago still in darkness, and without several ranking staff aides who either hadn't been notified in time or were too slow afoot.

As Air Force One roared toward Washington, other press aides who had stayed behind phoned the rest of the traveling press corps, rousing them from sleep, and told them simply: "The President is going back." They were to be ready to leave in an hour. No details of what had happened were offered. Curtis Wilkie of *The Boston Globe* said later: "I assumed the hostages were being sprung, because Carter had left Chicago so fast that people were left behind. I couldn't imagine he'd go back for anything less." Some reporters grilled Beth Lumpkin, of Powell's office, although it was Sunday morning and there were no deadlines to meet for hours. "Ed Walsh [of *The Washington Post*] asked a million questions," she recalled. "I finally hung up."

In all this, Powell said later, the only reason for the haste was that the President wanted to get to the White House as soon as possible. But reporters in Chicago were skeptical; Terry Smith thought the departure showed "extraordinary and exaggerated haste" under the predictable circumstances. Was the Carter campaign intentionally adding maximum drama to the situation, hoping that a sense of crisis would again induce the public to rally around the President? That had happened several times earlier in the campaign, on the occasion of any real or proclaimed development concerning the hostages.

Aboard Air Force One, Carter remained in his forward compartment during the entire flight. En route, Powell went back to the press pool and read a prepared statement from a yellow legal pad, as staff aides bustled up and down the aisles. The President would be consulting with his senior foreign-policy advisers, it said, and was returning "simply because of the greater access to his advisers and the advantages in communications afforded by the White House." The United States "will respond to the Iranian action in accordance with American law and the two principles that have guided our actions throughout, namely the national interest of this country and our concern for the safe and early release of the hostages."

Air Force One touched down at Andrews Air Force Base at 7:30 a.m. Eastern Standard Time, and a marine corps helicopter immediately whisked the President to the south lawn of the White House. There, Vice President Walter F. Mondale, who had been phoned in the early hours by Christopher, greeted him and they walked toward the Oval Office. As they did, a third figure came up quickly—Zbigniew Brzezinski, Carter's national security adviser—and handed the President a sheaf of papers, presumably the latest information on the Iranian demands.

(Bob Strauss, not one of Brzezinski's most devoted admirers, witnessed the scene on television later and was livid. After the election, in his customary colorful fashion, Strauss described his reaction: "Let me tell you the final straw for me, when I almost felt like throwing it in. We finally staged it: the President flies back on Sunday morning of the hostage thing. He's got this message, he comes back from the campaign, he helicopters in to the White House, and he takes a long stroll by himself, not even with his wife with him, so he'll look dramatic. Here's this man dealing with the issue. I'll be a dirty son of a bitch if in the middle of the television screen I'm looking at, and thinking how good it's looking, out runs Brzezinski, puts his arm around him, and hands him a paper. And the two of them walk off together talking about the paper. He [Brzezinski] put the negative touch on that, a great scene, a poignant scene. So he killed that morning. The news could have been good. It turned out to be a negative instead of a positive. That's the story of the campaign there."*)

*Strauss was convinced that Brzezinski was a political albatross, and he had repeated arguments with Carter about permitting the national security adviser to appear on network interview shows. Finally Strauss persuaded Caddell to test Brzezinski's public standing in a poll. Caddell dragged his feet until Strauss threatened to cut off campaign payments to him. Finally he made the test and reported that Brzezinski, according to Strauss, "set new records in five states, and his best negative was 68 percent negative." Strauss dutifully—and gleefully—reported the results to Carter, with Caddell present to back him up.

At just about the time the President was landing at Andrews, a well-rested Ronald Reagan was learning in Columbus of the night's developments. About three and a half hours earlier, Brady had gotten the first fragmentary information from the Reagan "hostage watch" manning the Reuters wire. It told him no more than what Carter now knew—that the Iranian parliament had at last set the four conditions for the hostages' release. Knowing not much could be done, Brady waited until about 5:30 a.m. and then phoned Ed Meese, Reagan's campaign chief of staff, in the hotel. Christopher had already called Meese, as the President had instructed.

At about 7:30, Mike Deaver went to Reagan's suite, woke him, and told him the news. The candidate and his wife had a leisurely breakfast, and then his staff people joined him. Considering the inconclusive nature of the situation, it was clear that Reagan's only course was the one he most preferred—"to leave it alone," at least for now. He would make no substantive comment. When questioned by reporters before leaving Columbus, he followed the script to the letter: "All I can tell you," he said, "is I think this is too sensitive to make any comment at all." In later Ohio stops that day he allowed himself to observe only that "we all want this tragic situation resolved. We want them home. It's my deepest hope and I know it's yours."

The President's meeting with his advisers at the White House began almost immediately after he arrived there and lasted nearly two hours. As it proceeded in the Cabinet Room, Carter's political group gathered, first at Strauss's apartment and later in the morning in the White House office of Jack Watson (who had succeeded Jordan as White House chief of staff when Jordan moved over to the campaign committee). "We tried to speculate both ways, whether it was going to be good or bad," Rafshoon recalled later. "It ranged all the way from, 'It's got to be good because all the attention is now on the hostage thing and nothing else,' to, 'It's bad because all the television networks are running these hostage specials showing a year of hostage captivity.' The thing that bothered all of us was that we always did well when the attention was on Ronald Reagan. It was letting him off the hook. Nobody was looking at him. I know when we saw all the specials Sunday night, with Khomeini coming on television telling the students 'We brought the Americans to their knees,' and 'We can give them back the hostages because we won,' it was bringing everything into focus to make the American people mad."

But Strauss, for one, thought the news might help Carter. "I thought we were behind," he said later. "We needed something, and I thought maybe this would be it."

A decision was made, at any rate, that the President should not let the day pass without reporting to the American people. The foreign-policy advisers considered what he should say, with counsel from the political group. "It probably would have helped," Rafshoon speculated later, "if you could have been able to say, 'I'm going to Andrews [Air Force Base] to meet the hostages.' Short of that, the only other thing that would have helped was if he had told the Iranians to shove it, if he got up and said, 'This is unsatisfactory. We're not going to be pushed around, and you can't blackmail us.' He couldn't do it, but it would have helped him politically. He didn't do it and it was to his credit. Because the next question was, what if they put the hostages on trial tomorrow?"

On the same point, another Carter insider said, "The cleanest political option was, frankly, to demagogue it, reject the thing outright, attack the Iranians for blackmail, and so on. Everyone knew that option existed. The game was, if you got the hostages back, that was a plus. Anything short of that had real dangers." Everyone also knew, this insider went on, that outright rejection "would be extremely irresponsible. No one really took the option seriously. . . . You pay a price just for being there [in the presidency]." Technically the Iranians' conditions were unacceptable, but at least they served as a basis for negotiations, and there was a feeling that Carter had to negotiate.

Strauss agreed. The political group told Carter that if he forcefully rejected the Iranians' demands, it would help him politically, "but he needed a positive response . . . for the hostages' sake." The President readily agreed.

After a break for lunch in the White House mess, during which time Muskie left to appear on a network interview show, the advisers convened again. Christopher and Jordan were dispatched down the hall to Mondale's office to write a statement for Carter to read on television later in the day. When the first draft was shown to the political people, Strauss objected, on the grounds that it made no mention of the political campaign drawing to a close—which, he argued, would look bogus under the circumstances. Jordan quickly wrote some additional passages incorporating the political references suggested.

As all this work was going on, Mondale departed for a flight to Chicago and then Detroit, where he joined Ted Kennedy for the labor rally the President was to have attended, and then on to Philadelphia with Kennedy for another event. (At Cobo Hall, in Detroit, Kennedy joked that Carter had called him earlier in the day and asked him to fill in for him. Kennedy said he told the President: "I've been trying to do that for a year." Declaring himself Carter's official substitute while Mondale stood on the same platform was, in the view of political insiders, a mild put-down; they thought it was possibly the first shot in Kennedy's campaign for the 1984 Democratic presidential nomination.)

While the men in the White House were grappling with this latest turn of events, Dick Wirthlin had already put his polltakers for Reagan into the field on Sunday morning, and the results were immediately reassuring. "Sunday morning the whole thing was opened up," he said later. "Our instinct was [that the Iranian news] was really juxtaposed too closely to the election at that juncture, and that it would be viewed as more political than simply a stroke of luck. We went out and we interviewed a thousand people Sunday morning. We asked them some very specific questions about the hostages, and confirmed that the vote still gave us a ten- or eleven-point lead." Wirthlin had another national sample taken in the afternoon and talked to other pollsters who were taking statewide surveys. By three o'clock, he said later, "I was convinced that the hostage situation was a complete wash."

In anticipation of the "October surprise," he said, the Reagan

campaign had set aside $200,000 for radio time in which to air
the specially prepared ads and to buy more last-minute television time for Reagan himself. "We were building all the contin-
gencies we could possibly think of," Wirthlin said, so as to be able
"to change the nature, thrust and scope of our campaign right
up until Monday night [Election Eve]. But once we made the decision that the hostage situation was washing, we just went back
to our original game plan."

It was after six o'clock in the East by the time the White House
and the television networks could work out a mutually satisfactory time for the President to make his statement. In Washington the football game between the Washington Redskins and the
Minnesota Vikings was interrupted for Carter—a circumstance
that might have been considered a political *faux pas* save for the
fact that the hapless Redskins were getting clobbered. The President, appearing somber and weary after two days with little
sleep, walked into the White House press room to make the
statement.

The Iranian proposal, he said, was "a significant development"
that appeared to offer "a positive basis" for achieving the twin
American objectives of obtaining the hostages' release while preserving American interests and honor. The American government was pursuing the release through diplomatic channels, but,
he added, "I know also that all Americans will want their return
to be on a proper basis, which is worthy of the suffering and sac-
rifice which the hostages have endured." This was a delicate way
of suggesting that Iran's demands were excessive and that efforts
would be made to negotiate them down. And this approach, of
course, indicated strongly that there was little or no chance that
there could even be an agreement struck, let alone actual release of the hostages, by the time voters started going to the polls
in less than thirty-six hours.

Carter then added the words Strauss and the other political
advisers had wanted: "We are within two days of an important
national election. Let me assure you that my decisions on this
crucial matter will not be affected by the calendar. We are in
contact with the bipartisan leadership of Congress, with Gover-

nor Reagan, with Congressman Anderson, and we will keep the American people informed. I wish I could predict when the hostages will return. I cannot. But whether our hostages come home before or after the election, and regardless of the outcome of the election, the Iranian government and the world community will find our country, its people, and the leaders of both political parties united in desiring the safe return of the hostages to their homes, but only on a basis that preserves our national honor and our national integrity." The purpose of these remarks, clearly, was to avoid any appearance that Carter was capitalizing politically on the new development, and to minimize any adverse reaction among voters who might be skeptical about the timing. But this in and of itself was a political move—disclaiming political motive for political purpose.

In any event the statement made clear that after all the anticipation and speculation about the political ramifications, the whole business was on hold. With no more to be said or done, Powell told reporters in the press room that, barring the unforeseen, the President would be out on the campaign trail again the next day—the last day of the presidential campaign of 1980.

It was in many ways appropriate that the election was approaching its climax in this manner. The "October surprise" that the Reagan campaign had anticipated with a trepidation bordering on paranoia had arrived—two days into November. For months, the Reagan forces had had visions of the stumping President, in the waning hours of the campaign, receiving a message about the hostages, dashing back to the White House, and then appearing on nationwide television to announce that they would be released, or even flying aboard Air Force One to Europe to greet them personally. Only the first part of these visions had been realized, but who could tell? The rest might yet be. And no one could say with certitude that the election would not at last turn on this dramatic eleventh-hour development, flooded into millions of American homes by the instant magic of television.

That the hostage situation had dominated politics in America throughout the year was indisputable. At first, and for months into the campaign, the Iranian crisis had been an undeniable political advantage for the President, unleashing patriotic support for him and effectively stifling criticism by his opponents, both Democratic and Republican. Indeed, it was a sign of Carter's political ingenuity that he was able to sustain a sense of genuine crisis in the public mind for so long.

But the longevity was not without its political price. A well-established American trait is impatience in a long-standing dispute; the failure to produce results is bound to take its toll—as the crescendo of opposition to the Vietnam war gives ample evidence. Back in April Carter's declaration of a "positive development" in the negotiations for release of the hostages, at a sudden early-morning press conference just as voting was starting in the presidential primary in Wisconsin, served more to fuel skepticism than to encourage optimism, especially when nothing happened. Shortly afterward polls for the first time registered greater disapproval than approval of Carter's handling of the hostage problem. One conducted for *Newsweek* by the Gallup organization showed 49 percent disapproving to only 40 percent still supporting his actions.

Within days of the failed effort to rescue the hostages by military means, an effort that came to an abrupt and embarrassing end in April, President Carter abandoned what reporters had dubbed his "Rose Garden strategy"—the political ploy of staying put in the White House and using the hostage situation as a rationale for not campaigning. Still, as long as Americans remained captive in Iran, the President's challengers were severely limited in criticizing his handling of the affair, since their remarks might somehow jeopardize the hostages' safety—or be subject to such a charge from Carter. And this remained true right up to this final weekend, when the belated "October surprise"—sprung by Iran, not by Carter—brought matters full circle.

One thing was already clear, however, no matter what the outcome of this latest development. For all the focus on the new political technocrats—the pollsters, the campaign consultants, the makers of slick television commercials, and the rest—it was an *event,* wholly unpredicted and entirely out of their control, that had dominated the year and the presidential campaign, to the last day. And as they grappled with this hard reality, the professionals had to deal with yet another factor that determined what they might do. Carter and Reagan, and their strategists, understood well that the days were over when the old big-city persuaders of "street money" and job promises won votes. In the current era of a television-oriented electorate, votes were to be won or lost largely by persuading voters of the merits of one candidate and/or the deficiencies of the other. Candidates and their professionals could persuade voters to support one individual or oppose another either by conveying the truth about him—the reality—or having what was said about him, true or false, be perceived as the truth. When the reality is advantageous, the candidate runs on it—"on his record." When it is disadvantageous, he tries to have it perceived in a better light, or he seeks to divert the voters' attention from it—usually by trying to shape or compound a negative perception of his opponent.

In 1980 Jimmy Carter's challengers all seized on the facts about his record at home and abroad and tried to hold him to them. And he, knowing the record would likely defeat him, sought to escape from it: to distort and tinker with the reality and to paint his opponents—first Edward Kennedy in the Democratic primaries, then Ronald Reagan in the fall campaign—as destructive, dangerous figures. In the end, however, the reality came back to confront him.

A week before Election Day, at the close of the televised debate with the President in Cleveland, Reagan reminded voters of Carter's record, summing up his case simply but effectively: "Are you better off than you were four years ago? Is it easier for you to go and buy things in the stores than it was four years ago? Is there more or less unemployment in the country than there was four years ago? Is America as respected throughout the world as it was? Do you feel that our security is as safe, that we're as strong as we were four years ago? And if you answer all those questions 'yes,' why I think your choice is very obvious as to who you'll vote for. If you don't think that this course that we've been on for the last four years is what you would like to see us follow for the next four, then I could suggest another choice that you have." That summation placed the reality of the record squarely before the voters.

And now, in his Sunday night television report to the nation, less than thirty-six hours before the first polls would open on the East Coast, Jimmy Carter was obliged to deal with the other major reality of 1980: the Americans seized in Tehran were completing a full year in captivity, and for all his alleged single-minded attention to their plight, he still could not express any real optimism that their release might be near.

Without serious dispute, the reality of the four years of President Carter's administration was not the stuff, in its unvarnished form, to justify electing the man to another term in office. His technocrats could measure the degree of public disaffection from him, but they could not eradicate it. The best they could hope to do was to soften it. Their job, then, was to divert public attention from Carter's record and to engage all-out in the contest of shaping perceptions—to persuade the voters that the record wasn't all that bad, that the bad news wasn't all Carter's fault, that the opposition would be much worse, for both ideological and temperamental reasons.

Long before the campaign of 1980 began, this task had been undertaken. In the summer of 1979 Jimmy Carter, faced with the fact that his administration was not curing the nation's ills, conducted an unprecedented presidential "retreat" in the Catoctin Mountains of Maryland. There, at Camp David, he and his advisers concocted a grand scheme to persuade the American people that they, not he, were at fault, and that he would have to wipe the slate clean, and make a new start.

2.
"Malaise"at the Summit

In June 1979 it was no longer possible, even looking out through the rose-colored windows of the White House, to rationalize President Carter's political weakness. It had reached the point, in Patrick Caddell's view, "that he had become almost irrelevant by the summer of '79 to what was indeed happening, to what was on people's minds."

In fact, Jimmy Carter's political troubles had begun almost as soon as he was elected in 1976. In violation of the traditional pattern, opinion surveys found his triumph over Gerald Ford had earned him almost no "halo effect"—that is, the warmth of feeling that voters usually give to a politician once they have elected him, whether or not they voted for him. On the contrary, a month after the election the figures on approval and disapproval were essentially unchanged from what they had been on Election Day. The voters were querulous and skeptical. They had expressed their dissatisfaction with things as they were by electing an obscure one-term governor of Georgia, and now they were waiting to be shown they had made the right decision. There was, in Caddell's phrase, no "automatic grant" of confidence or trust.

That seemed to change, for the moment, when Carter took that walk down Pennsylvania Avenue from the Capitol to the White House on Inauguration Day. But by the fall of 1977, the new President's reputation for ineptitude was well-established in Washington—built on many incidents, from the pointless wrangling with Congress over the "hit list" of water projects that Carter wanted scuttled, to the Bert Lance affair. And there was an epidemic of "little stories" about gaffes made by the Georgians on the presidential staff. Some of these were essentially trivial (at one point, for example, the White House failed to clear with the speaker of the House, Thomas P. (Tip) O'Neill, Jr., prospective appointments to federal posts of two Massachusetts Democrats—both considered potential political rivals of his son, Lieutenant Governor Thomas P. (Tommy) O'Neill III), but trivial or not they indicated a lack of political sensitivity. It was only a matter of time before that Washington judgment would ripple out across the country.

By April 1978, little more than a year into his term, it was obvious that had happened. Carter summoned his Cabinet and senior staff to a weekend of meetings at Camp David, inevitably labeled a "summit" by the press, with its penchant for cheapening the currency of language. Gerald Rafshoon, the Atlanta advertising man who had worked for Carter in 1976, was called back to the White House full-time, to begin planning tactics for improving Carter's relationship with the news media—little stratagems that soon became known as Rafshoonery. Anne Wexler, a veteran political professional, was also appointed to the White House staff and charged with dealing with those whom presidents always seem to call their "constituency groups" and whom their opponents call "special interests"—labor unions, racial and ethnic minorities, environmentalists, women's organizations, leaders of business and industry. She would take Jimmy Carter's case to them, and more to the point, enlist them to take that case to Congress and the public at large.

There was a moment of euphoria in that new beginning. Jody Powell and Hamilton Jordan talked enthusiastically about getting things "in shape" and hinted at changes in both operating methods and personnel to establish an image of Jimmy Carter as a firm, if never iron, hand at the controls. Others mused aloud about various sub-Cabinet-level officials who, they were convinced, sometimes accurately and sometimes not, were undercutting them with the Washington establishment. (The principal aides of Brock Adams, secretary of transportation, were a particular target, perhaps because several of them had worked in the 1976 campaign of Morris Udall, the most persistent of those Democrats who had competed with Carter for the nomination that year.) Jerry Rafshoon prescribed strong medicine: "We've got to kick some ass."

At times the talk was giddy. On one occasion, for example, some of the President's men speculated among themselves about whether Carter might be persuaded to fire Secretary of the Treasury Michael Blumenthal, who was notably unpopular with the White House staff, and make an example of him. After all, look what the firing of Douglas MacArthur had done for the "image" of Harry Truman! Wiser heads in the White House, including Powell's and Jordan's, understood that the parallel was not quite precise and recognized that, anyway, Carter could not be talked into doing it. But the speculation was nonetheless a measure of the unease in his administration. And it reflected the belief that the right public relations measures, call them Rafshoonery if you will, would put things right politically. It was just a question, everyone in the White House was saying, of "getting our story across" to the public.

But after that first "summit" of April 1978, nothing really changed in any substantive way. If the government was being managed in any strikingly different fashion, it was not apparent to the naked eye. The relationship between the White House and Congress did not improve materially. Gaffes were still committed, and "little stories" about them continued to make the rounds. (For example, when the prime minister of Japan was the guest of honor at a state dinner, the White House failed to invite Representative Norman Mineta of California, a Japanese-American, because they thought he was Italian.) Meanwhile, Carter himself became increasingly preoccupied with what proved to be the singular accomplishment of his administration, the negotiations between Anwar Sadat of Egypt and Menachem Begin of Israel on the Middle East.

By the early summer of 1979, in fact, there were no signs of any improvement in the President's position or of any effect of that first attempt at a new beginning. The late John Osborne, the perceptive White House watcher for *The New Republic*, summed it up this way: "What had been thought and said at the time to be a major turn in the Carter presidency, a significant change in the way the White House staff was to be managed and the Cabinet was to be monitored and overseen from the White House, had proven to be much less than Carter intended or desired." Thus it was that more than halfway through the Carter stewardship, and only seven or eight months from the opening of the campaign for reelection, the White House faced what Stuart Eizenstat, the President's adviser on domestic affairs, described in a memorandum to Carter as "the worst of times." Across the country gasoline lines were growing longer, and Carter's standing in the opinion polls was declining almost weekly—to the point that the approval rating for his performance in office was no better than it had been for Richard Nixon in the final days before his resignation. There was, it now seemed apparent, more involved here than simply "getting our story across." The pressures began to build within the administration for some more basic change in approach.

Pat Caddell, poring over the poll results from the field, was a particular goad. In April 1979 he met first with Rosalynn Carter and then with the President himself to tell them of his findings: almost half the voters were pessimistic about the future, a significant increase even from the previous post-Watergate high point of 30 percent in 1975. The phenomenon of declining public confidence was not a new one; it had been observed in survey research for several years. Nor was it necessarily fatal to a politician. On the contrary, as Caddell later observed, "Carter himself had in part been a by-product of some of those instincts. Otherwise there was not much reason to send him, given his message and given his professed lack of experience, to be President in 1976." But Carter's hold on the public was "that he had promised the people he would be a different kind of President." It was essential to regain that role—in short, to return to the techniques and the themes that had elected him in the first place.

What the staff and the President found most difficult to face, however, was the fact that so much of the responsibility for the failure lay not in the mechanics of the Cabinet or the White

House staff but in Carter himself. Although he had been a superb campaign politician, Carter resisted the idea that politics should be a major ingredient of his performance in office. And this was a centrally important factor.

Robert Strauss, surely one of the Democratic Party's most insightful politicians, discovered as much while he was serving as Carter's special ambassador for trade negotiations. If he telephoned the White House for an appointment to discuss international trade with the President, some time was almost always available that same day. On the other hand, if he said he wanted to discuss a sensitive political question, the message would come back from the appointments secretary (first Tim Kraft, later Phil Wise) that the President wondered if that couldn't be postponed for a day or two. Lesser figures who raised questions about the political effect of this or that decision found themselves cut off curtly. "Let's move on," Carter would say. Members of Congress were lectured on doing what was "right" rather than worrying so much about politics. And a member of the Cabinet told us of the President using that same approach when he was soliciting the help of an influential congressional subcommittee chairman on an important bill. Carter resisted not only spending time and effort on politics, but even the inference that there was political content in his decisions. Once he complained pointedly about a column we had written eighteen months earlier discussing the political benefits he could realize from the emphasis he placed on human rights in foreign policy.

"Having gotten elected," one adviser said later, "he could compartmentalize [politics] and lay that part of it aside and begin to deal as the engineer with what's on the plate, what's on the agenda." Implicit in this attitude, of course, was his faith that once the job was done well enough, the story would get across and the political benefit would follow. Within the political community, however, Carter's distaste for politics was interpreted as both offensive to other politicians and pitiably naïve. There is little confidence among politicians that merit provides its own reward.

By June 1979, moreover, it was no longer possible for even those closest to the President to imagine that things would work themselves out. Caddell, with some support from Jody Powell and Rosalynn Carter, argued with forceful earnestness for the President to return to the themes that had won him election in the first place, to identify himself with those "instincts" in the electorate. He dispatched memoranda to the White House and commended to Carter's reading list such books as Christopher Lasch's *The Culture of Narcissism* and James MacGregor Burns's *Leadership*.

Meanwhile, Eizenstat and Rafshoon, with some support from Hamilton Jordan, argued for the kind of structural changes that might impose both greater order and greater discipline on the administration. At one point the pressure for Carter to appoint a "chief of staff" (Jordan was always the only realistic possibility) had reached the point that the Carters met to discuss it with the inner circle of advisers: Jordan, Powell, Eizenstat, Kraft, congressional liaison chief Frank Moore—and Vice President Walter Mondale and his chief of staff, Richard Moe. It was assumed then that it would be done, eventually, but President Carter was still reluctant and occupied elsewhere. Nothing forced the issue until the final days of the month, when the lines at the gasoline stations were reaching their longest and Carter himself was off in Tokyo for a meeting on international economic issues.

The Carters had been planning, after a stop in Seoul, to break their homeward trip in Hawaii and rest for a few days there. But now Jordan and Powell were arguing that it would be politically foolhardy to be lolling on the beach while so many Americans (read, voters) were fuming on those gasoline lines. So Carter abruptly canceled the vacation and flew back to Washington on July 1. It was agreed at once that he should give a televised speech about the energy crisis, outlining a new policy. Eizenstat, in a memorandum that quickly found its way into *The Washington Post*, suggested that it was possible to convert these "worst of times" to Carter's advantage. Because of the gasoline shortages the President could be assured of national attention and could use the occasion to single out a new "enemy"—the Organization of Petroleum Exporting Countries—while simultaneously signaling a new beginning for himself. Hendrik Hertzberg, the chief speechwriter for the President, was already preparing a draft, and on July 3 it was flown to Camp David only a few hours after the Carters' own helicopter had taken them there. Caddell, too, sent along some reading—a 107-page memorandum dealing with the broader thematic questions he was convinced Carter most needed to address. The networks were told that the President would appear Thursday night, July 5.

There was, however, a basic problem: What would the President say? Although Carter had new proposals to offer, they were neither substantively so innovative nor politically so attractive that they would solve either the energy problem or Carter's own political difficulties. It may have been an exaggeration to say, as one White House official did, that "there was neither a policy nor a speech" at that point, but there was some obvious truth in it. The President simply wasn't ready to deliver what he now had promised.

On July 4, the day before he was scheduled to speak, Carter and his wife decided it would be a mistake to go ahead. It was turning out, after all, to be just another speech about energy, and the President knew that if that was all it was, he was likely to be tuned out at best and savaged at worst. He telephoned Mondale, Rafshoon, and Jordan and told them he was calling it off. Powell was ordered to notify the networks and the news media. "If I give this speech," he told Powell in another call, "they'll kill me."

The remark showed a shrewd insight into his own position, something that Jimmy Carter didn't always manage. It had become increasingly apparent that he was losing the nation's attention. He had given four speeches about energy already, the first a fireside chat in April 1977, and the television audience had declined from something over eighty million to about thirty million. Moreover Carter was having trouble communicating effectively even with those who *did* listen. He was proving to be one of the least vivid figures in American politics, and that was true even among those with a direct stake in what he had to say. A Democratic senator sympathetic to Carter described what happened among his colleagues when, for example, the President scheduled a press conference while the Senate was in session. "We all go into the cloakroom and they turn on the set so we can watch," he said, "but inside ten minutes or less we're all gossiping among ourselves and ignoring him. Hell, if we don't listen, who will?" It was a condition of life that plagued the President for the rest of that year and throughout his reelection campaign.

The cancellation of the speech sent tremors of uneasiness through the country and abroad—so much so, in fact, that Carter's original intention to offer no explanation at all had to be modified. The press and American allies were assured that the President was "all right" and they could "relax"; it was simply a matter of broadening the agenda. Carter now, we were told, would look at the whole range of economic issues, and perhaps more—perhaps there might even be a few juicy changes in the high ranks of the administration. The explanations were accepted more or less at face value, but still, the cancellation of the speech was peculiar enough to cause apprehension—and a great deal of speculation. Carter had created a "situation," and now he had to find a way out. And, it was hoped, one that would not bring more derision down on his head.

On July 5 the President and Rosalynn Carter held two meetings at Camp David with most of those who had been closest to him. Mondale, Powell, Jordan, Rafshoon, Caddell, and Eizenstat were there; only Charles Kirbo, the Atlanta lawyer who had functioned as a kind of one-man kitchen cabinet for Carter, was missing. By all accounts* there was a clear clash of approaches. On the one hand, Pat Caddell—with support from Powell and to a lesser degree Rafshoon and Jordan—argued vehemently that the President must use the opportunity to reestablish his connection with the voters by dealing primarily with those issues of national confidence that Caddell had identified in his survey data. On the other, Fritz Mondale, supported by Eizenstat, took a more pragmatic and politically conventional approach. He was scornful of what he considered "some of this social psychology stuff that was floating around"—meaning both Lasch's book and Caddell's analysis of what needed to be done. The Vice Presi-

*The best contemporary report is that written by Elizabeth Drew in *The New Yorker* of August 27, 1979.

dent seized on one suggestion in Caddell's memorandum (one of many, Caddell said later)—that a constitutional convention might be called to focus the nation on its goals. It was the worst idea he had ever heard, Mondale said, because it could create a wide-open situation that would put the country in real peril.

Mondale was, like his mentor Hubert Horatio Humphrey, an essentially optimistic politician as well as an extremely pragmatic one. What he was finding among the voters, he argued, was not some yearning for new themes but, rather, a totally understandable concern about inflation and unemployment and energy. What the people needed was a reason to believe that Carter was capable of dealing with those problems effectively. "I felt very strongly," he said in a subsequent interview, "that the American people had to be approached in a positive, hopeful way."

The discussion went on most of the afternoon and, after a break, again in the evening, this time to focus more directly on questions of personnel and program. Carter himself presided over both meetings, taking notes and asking opinions but revealing little about his own intentions. The context pressed in on all those present, but Carter himself was sarcastic about the implications of having "denied" his public another speech on energy. "Oh, well, they're all waiting out there for another energy speech," he told Rafshoon. "I'm sure they're going to be disappointed." Yet his advisers clearly understood how unsettling the delay had been.

It is clear in retrospect that Carter might have saved the situation right then simply by getting on his helicopter and flying back to the White House. He could have explained, with minimal damage, that he simply wanted a better speech and had postponed the original one. But this would have been to admit that "damage control" was the most he could hope to achieve, that it was not realistically possible to make some more fundamental change in his presidency and, not incidentally, in his political prospects. So Carter and his advisers allowed themselves to be drawn more and more into what amounted to a contrived crisis, perhaps deluded by the splendid isolation of Camp David into believing that they could see things more clearly than the others at sea level. "The die had been cast without necessarily knowing exactly what it was we were going to do," said one of those who participated in the meetings. "I mean, we had thrown the pontoon bridge across the Rubicon, once the speech was canceled, without any particular idea of . . . exactly what we were going to take across the river."

Carter had been scheduled to fly to Louisville that weekend to speak to the National Governors' Conference, but that date had been canceled along with the televised speech. So now he decided to make amends by inviting a delegation of governors to Camp David—one Republican, Otis Bowen of Indiana, because he was chairman of the group that year, and seven Democrats: James Hunt of North Carolina, Julian Carroll of Kentucky, Ella Grasso of Connecticut, Hugh Carey of New York, Brendan Byrne of New Jersey, George Busbee of Georgia and Dixy Lee Ray of Washington. (The Democrats were important because, at the same time, White House agents were trying to engineer a resolution endorsing Carter for reelection they hoped the Democrats at Louisville would support. As matters turned out, it was approved 21-0, with four abstentions.)

It all semed routine enough, but once the governors had been to Camp David, political dynamics began to take over. "Once you got into sort of having people up," said Powell, "you can't make an arbitrary decision. You've got to think about who you're leaving out." As it happened, almost no one was left out. Over the next eight days almost 150 of these ad hoc consultants were flown up to the mountain—old Washington hands, mayors, members of the House and Senate with presumed expertise on energy and economic issues, more governors, mayors, labor leaders, economists, businessmen, preachers, state legislators, county officials. The President, explained Mondale, "wanted to spend some time freshly reviewing where he was."

The guests were, unsurprisingly, positive about their talks with the President, but this was dangerously misleading. It was flattering to be asked to advise a president of the United States, and that was clearly reflected in many of the comments, but some of the guests, politically more sophisticated, were vaguely disturbed by the crisis atmosphere and by Carter's self-deprecatory manner. Governor Richard Riley of South Carolina, one of the

President's most devoted allies, found it all "a bit bizarre." Others couldn't see anything that could be accomplished by such an exercise.

They recognized, of course, that there was very little either fresh or special in the advice they could bring to Camp David. On the contrary, what was striking to many of them was that Jimmy Carter was hearing nothing he might not have learned from reading the newspapers and listening to other politicians for the past eighteen months or longer. Much of what they said focused on the way the President was being perceived. "I think he believes, as I do," said the well-known Washington lawyer Clark Clifford, "that he's not getting across to the people." Bill Clinton, the young governor of Arkansas and a Carter loyalist, told the President *his* constituents back home had a less clear picture of him after two and a half years in office than they had had when he was a candidate in the 1976 campaign. There were repeated suggestions that James Schlesinger, the secretary of energy, was a political liability—but that was something Schlesinger himself had acknowledged long before. (Indeed, he already had offered to resign and made plans to do so.) And there were many recommendations, particularly from old Washington hands, that Carter impose sterner discipline on his staff in the White House. On too many issues the administration was speaking with several voices.

Carter himself was not forthcoming about his plans, even with those closest to him. "The President never tipped his hand about what he was going to do," said one intimate. "He played it close to the vest, and he was spending a lot of time there on his own." Back at the White House, those who had been left behind were disturbed because it was soon apparent to them that senior advisers who *were* included had been instructed not to share their information even with their deputies. Moreover, the public nature of the whole "retreat" at Camp David, and the extraordinary attention it was being given in the news media, seemed to delineate in unmistakable terms the difference between those in the inner circle and those outside it. Jack Watson, who was later to replace Jordan as chief of the White House staff, was not brought to Camp David until the final day of the conferences, almost as an afterthought; the same was true of Anne Wexler.

But the insiders who shuttled back and forth from Washington to Maryland shared the anxiety. The ridicule in the press and among politicians on Capitol Hill was growing more pointed as the whole process took on more and more of the flavor of "Rafshoonery." On one occasion the Carters went with no advance notice to Carnegie, Pennsylvania, and on another to Martinsburg, West Virginia, for meetings with "ordinary people" who had been brought together for that purpose by Caddell. Carter was obviously trying to recapture his beginnings as an unknown candidate back in 1975, when he had spent five days a week for fifty weeks in just such meetings.

What was missing was any bolt of lightning to illuminate a new road out of this plastic crisis. "They got up there," said one White House official, "and they didn't know how to get out." So what Carter did is what Presidents always do in those circumstances: He scheduled a new date, July 15, for his speech, and did so before he had fully resolved what he planned to do with the television time or, more to the point, with his administration.

To set the stage, and perhaps to assure a more attentive if not necessarily more sophisticated reading of his intentions, Carter invited eighteen editors, columnists, and television anchormen for lunch on July 13. The conversation would be conducted on "deep background," meaning that the journalists could report on what Carter said he thought and intended, to the extent that he revealed his thoughts and intentions, without quoting him directly.*

It was a strange session. The visitors were flown to Camp David shortly before noon, then driven in vans to Laurel Lodge and given drinks while they waited for the Carters, who had gone off

---

*The eighteen included: anchormen Walter Cronkite of CBS, John Chancellor of NBC, Frank Reynolds of ABC, and Jim Lehrer of PBS; editorial page editors Edwin Yoder of *The Washington Star*, Meg Greenfield of *The Washington Post*, Max Frankel of *The New York Times*, and Anthony Day of *The Los Angeles Times*; columnists David Broder of *The Washington Post*, Hugh Sidey of *Time* magazine, Tom Wicker of *The New York Times*, Jack W. Germond of *The Washington Star*, Joseph Kraft and Carl Rowan of the Field Newspaper Syndicate, James J. Kilpatrick of the Washington Star Syndicate; and editors Marvin Stone of *U.S. News and World Report*, John McCormally of the *Burlington* (Iowa) *Hawkeye*, and Brandt Ayres of the *Anniston* (Alabama) *Star*.

that morning to take the public pulse in Martinsburg. When the President and his wife arrived they talked in tones of wonder about what they had heard: people were concerned about inflation and energy, Rosalynn Carter told one clutch of journalists, but were so willing to make sacrifices. What the Carters seemed to be saying was that they had now learned at first hand, and just that morning, what everyone had been telling them for so long. One of those listening put aside his Bloody Mary and wrote in his notebook, perhaps uncharitably: "She acts like they've 'rediscovered America.'"

At the luncheon itself Rosalynn Carter sat at her husband's side at the head of the table, frequently offering her own views, sometimes completing his arguments in mid-thought. The visitors who were there that day had long since become accustomed to Rosalynn Carter's position in the White House, but her prominence at that luncheon seemed to contribute to the defensive atmosphere. Sitting at the table, scribbling notes on big white pads that had been placed at each seat, the guests could not but wonder what the hell was going on.

Carter himself seemed ambivalent, at once chastened by the criticism he had heard over the previous week and characteristically confident he could put things right, now that he had been through this process. Just what he intended to do, other than give a speech, was unclear, however. "He had begun to change at this point, too," an adviser said much later. "I'm not sure by this point on that Friday that he had not begun to worry about how big a thing he had gotten himself into."

The speech itself, when it finally was delivered, was a curious structure of disparate elements. It attempted to blend the lessons the President had learned at Camp David with the advice of Pat Caddell, to deal with *his* themes, and of Stuart Eizenstat, to deal with the specifics of his administration's energy program. In a studied attempt to be disarming, Carter quoted several of his adviser-critics. "This from a Southern governor: 'Mr. President, you are not leading this nation—you're just managing the government.'" "'You don't see the people enough any more.'" "'Some of your Cabinet members don't seem loyal. There is not enough discipline among your disciples.'" In his *mea culpa,* the

President admitted to only "mixed success" in keeping the promises of his 1976 campaign. Then, in a final section of the speech, he outlined the specifics of a "new" energy policy—new goals of energy independence for the United States, import quotas on foreign oil, development of alternative sources, the creation of an agency to finance that effort, pressure on utilities to move away from oil to coal, an "energy mobilization board," a conservation program.

But the heart of his message was, in essence, an attempt to shift blame from himself to the people. There was, he said, a "fundamental threat to American democracy" in what he called "a crisis of confidence . . . that strikes at the very heart and soul and spirit of our national will." Nor did the political system and Washington, that old devil from his 1976 campaign, escape untouched. The people had looked to Washington, he said, "and found it isolated from the mainstream of our nation's life." Looking for honest answers, they were given "easy answers"; seeking leadership, they were given "false claims and evasiveness and politics as usual." The "special interests" were prospering while the country was afflicted with "paralysis, stagnation, and drift." What was lacking—and could not realistically have been expected—was a genuine recognition of his own failures of competence and leadership.

It became known, instantly, as Carter's "malaise speech," although that word was never used, and Caddell insists he hadn't used it, either. ("This is an example of what the press can do by latching onto a term," he complained later.) The following day Carter flew to Kansas City, to detail his energy program before the National Association of Counties, and then to Detroit, to address the Communications Workers of America, one of the unions most reliable in its political support for him. The CWA speech, although brief, was significant because it had been written largely by Caddell and lifted from the Sunday night speech. Thus, it summed up the President's purpose and intentions and reached back to reclaim his political link to the voters. "In the months ahead," Carter told the union audience, "I will come to you throughout America with fresh proposals. Some will involve the traditional government, some will not. Above all, I will defend our common national purpose against those narrow special interests who often forget the overriding needs of America. I will persuade, I will speak against, I will fight any selfish interest that undermines our national purpose, and I will demand that the government reflect those commitments which I make to you today."

In Washington, the whole exercise was received with predictable skepticism. What Carter had done, so far as anyone could see, was simply to spend ten days at Camp David and then produce some largely predictable energy plans and a new scapegoat for his own failures. Some believers, however, in both the press and political community, thought Carter had been transformed: he was described, for example, as tougher and less preoccupied with detail. *Newsweek* reported on a moment with the President confronted by his staff with some "marginal" issue: "The Old Jimmy would have noted it all on his yellow pad and engineered a decision. The New Jimmy waved them away. 'Y'all take care of that,' he said. 'If I don't need to know about it, y'all just do it.'" Attorney General Griffin Bell declared: "I've never seen the President act tougher. He was a transformed man." And across the country, where the voices of the skeptics had not yet reached, the response to his Sunday night speech seemed supportive. Carter's "approval rating" shot up 11 percentage points in the Gallup Poll, and Caddell's own surveys found gains of 20 to 30 points on the President's handling of some issues. The "support levels" for particulars of the administration's energy program ran 75 to 80 percent. The crowds at Kansas City and Detroit had been large and responsive. The mail, overwhelmingly favorable, came into the White House at a greater rate than at any time since Gerald Ford had pardoned Richard Nixon.

Mondale, who had left Washington for a five-day trip preaching the merits of the strategic arms limitation treaty, found "ebullience" outside the capital. "The speech itself was upbeat and the response was upbeat," he said. And indeed, it became an article of faith among the Carter loyalists that the President "could have turned it around" right there. But that assumes that Carter could have followed the rhetoric with a level of performance quite different from what he had shown in his first thirty months in office—a long leap of faith.

As it developed, the euphoria lasted only two or three days, in large measure because neither Carter nor his advisers were confident that the speech was enough to accomplish anything. After all, he had given many speeches in those thirty months, and the experience had been consistently disappointing. If the new Carter image was to be projected with any force, something more was needed. "Because nobody really believed that the speech was going to have the impact that it had," one Carter adviser said, "there was a desperate feeling ... that if the President didn't do something to change people, the people wouldn't think he was serious."

The possibility of seeking "mass" resignations from the Cabinet and White House staff had been discussed at Camp David, but Carter himself had never given any clear signal that was his intention. At one meeting, Mondale's chief of staff, Richard Moe, had objected that it would be "Nixonian" and as such politically counter-productive, but he enlisted no allies among the President's men. After all, neither Carter nor any of those closest to him had been in Washington when Nixon employed just that device to suggest a new start after the 1972 election. Nor had any of them been there during the Watergate crisis of 1973 and 1974 when Nixon forced other resignations in an attempt to save himself.

In any event, on July 17 resignations were solicited from sixteen Cabinet and Cabinet-level officials and eighteen members of the senior staff at the White House. There was no substantive reason it needed to be done that way. It was clear the intention was simply to give the impression of a fresh start under fresh leadership. Carter never intended to replace more than a handful of the thirty-four. And, of course, it was the ultimate excess. As Rafshoon, the image expert, would himself observe: "You don't need high drama when you've got high drama."

Among the thirty-four there were two obvious targets—Secretary of Health, Education and Welfare Joseph Califano and Secretary of the Treasury Michael Blumenthal. Califano was a particular irritant to the White House staff and had been from the beginning of the administration. Because of his own experience in the White House a decade earlier, he knew how to ignore or circumvent those who worked at 1600 Pennsylvania

Avenue. He had made no secret of his opposition to the Department of Education that Carter had proposed, or of his lack of enthusiasm for Carter's policy on national health insurance. "Joe always had his own agenda," a friend said. Moreover, he failed to observe the niceties. (At one point, for example, he chose a chairman for an advisory commission on mental health without consulting Rosalynn Carter, who had taken a special interest in that issue even before she arrived at the White House. "The paint was peeling all over the place," an insider said of the heat it caused. "You know, there are certain things you do. I think he lost some substantial blood in that encounter.") The situation was particularly pointed in July, moreover, because Califano had been out of the country and planning his own brief stopover in Hawaii, while the administration's hospital cost-containment program was being abused in Congress. Only ten days earlier, learning about that, Carter had told Mondale to have Califano "get his ass back here."

Blumenthal was a somewhat different case. From the outset he had never seemed to fit, but Carter had been impressed by his intelligence and, perhaps, by his background as chairman of the Bendix Corporation. The White House staff complained that Blumenthal took too much credit for himself on economic issues, and they suspected that Joseph Laitin, a veteran and highly respected bureaucrat who served Blumenthal as his public information officer, had been planting stories about the making of economic policy that reflected badly on the White House. And, finally, some of the Georgians had never forgiven Blumenthal for the fact that Bert Lance's downfall in 1977 was caused largely by agencies under Blumenthal's control.

The third direct victim was Secretary of Transportation Brock Adams. He had been told he could stay if he replaced some of those who worked directly for him, and to no one's surprise, he had found that a price he could not pay.

The true nature of this process as essentially public relations was made evident, however, by Carter's decision to choose this occasion to accept the resignation of both Secretary of Energy James Schlesinger and Attorney General Griffin Bell. The last was especially callous since Bell had announced several months before that he planned to leave anyway, although he had earned a reputation in and out of the White House as one of the ablest members of the Cabinet. Moreover, the FBI checks already had been completed on Benjamin Civiletti, who was to be Bell's successor, which meant that Carter might have made that change separately. Instead, Bell became just another scalp—and another example of Carter's willingness to do whatever was necessary to save himself.

It was also clear that Carter, despite his visits with the plain folk of Carnegie and Martinsburg, did not understand, or would not accept, the popular opinion on two other members of his administration who had been the targets of criticism at Camp David—Andrew Young and Hamilton Jordan.

Young, who had been Carter's most valuable credential with blacks during the 1976 campaign, had become a liability as ambassador to the United Nations. He had seemed determined to voice his own foreign policy, often to the embarrassment of both Secretary of State Cyrus Vance and Carter himself. Britain, Young suggested, was "racist." Americans, he said, were "paranoid" about a few Communists in Africa. Arab hatred of Israel was compared to the attitude of the Ku Klux Klan toward blacks. There were "hundreds and perhaps even thousands" of political prisoners in the United States. The Cubans were providing "stability" in Angola. During the July 17 Cabinet meeting that culminated in the letters of resignation, Carter berated Young for many of these statements, but there was never any thought of accepting his resignation. On the contrary, Jordan was assuring reporters that Andy Young was the one Cabinet member, other than Vance and Secretary of Defense Harold Brown, whose position was unassailable.

Jordan himself was another blind spot for Carter, as the President made clear when he chose this same moment to appoint him as White House chief of staff.

The young Georgian was a precocious political operator who had shown considerable skill in organizing such things as the campaign to win ratification of the Panama Canal treaties. But he also had shown a genius for getting himself involved in "incidents" on the social ramble—to the point that many voters viewed him as immature and irresponsible. And this very week newspapers across the country were carrying a picture of his car locked into place by a "Denver boot" because of unpaid parking tickets, a picture that reinforced that image. The President, however, was stubbornly resistant to permitting the possibility of some political damage to deter him from giving Jordan broad new authority.

That was not surprising, however, because Carter seemed to have endless patience in dealing with those who were close to him. Once, after a dinner at the White House, we asked the President how he felt about his "closest friends" always doing things to embarrass him. Carter shook his head ruefully, and replied, "Yeah, isn't it awful?" Then he ticked off several of the cases in which just that had happened.

"Don't you ever just get mad as hell, Mr. President, and tell them to cut it out?"

Carter shrugged and smiled. "No," he said, "that wouldn't do any good."

In part because he had this reputation, the purge of the Cabinet caused what politicians are quick to call a "firestorm" of criticism. With a single stroke the President had destroyed whatever goodwill he had created for himself. In Washington the reaction ranged from suggestions that he was emotionally unbalanced to predictable gallows humor. "If you see the President coming and he's got a pin in his hand," the story went, "run like hell, because he's got a grenade in his mouth."

At first Jody Powell argued that this reaction was typical of the insular federal city. But out on the road Fritz Mondale was finding that all the benefits of the July 15 speech had been lost by the unsettling turmoil in the government. "There was a feeling we'd done it, for a few days," the Vice President reflected later. "I think the press felt something was happening. The people did, I know that based on my travels. Then, suddenly, bang, we were right back down in the ditch again." The change was rapid and complete, and the questions from reporters became overwhelmingly negative. "There was a sense of almost joy in the country for two days—joy, expectation, we're on our way again," he said. "But by the time I got to Philadelphia I had to cut the news conference off."

Mondale's findings could be duplicated almost anywhere. We

went to Des Moines a week later, for example, and found politicians there laughing at what Senator John Culver had said at a party meeting over the weekend: "No greater love hath any man than to lay down his friends to save his life." A leading political operative for the United Auto Workers, Charles Gifford, put it this way: "A lot of people thought the speech was pretty Class A stuff coming from Carter. What really spun them around were the Cabinet resignations." And at a suburban shopping center outside Des Moines, a woman buying a shirt for her grandson told us: "I don't understand what's happening back East, but it seems like Mr. Carter doesn't know which way to go."

Carter was both dismayed and angered by these reactions, but he was characteristically tenacious in trying to turn public opinion in his direction. On Friday, July 20, he marched into the White House press room, read a five-paragraph statement for the cameras, then walked out, ignoring the questions called out to him from the mob of reporters who crowded the room. "I need the full support of the American people in the future," he read. "I am well pleased with all the changes that have been made—every single change. It has been a positive change." The appearance was all over in less than ninety seconds, but it left a vivid memory of a President who was obviously both angry and upset. Inevitably, it reminded some of another late afternoon when Richard Nixon had walked into the same press room to make a similarly angry statement about the Senate's resistance to his nomination of G. Harrold Carswell to the Supreme Court.

The following day, Saturday, the President persisted. At mid-morning members of Powell's staff began telephoning reporters who regularly covered the White House, summoning them to a "backgrounder" with the President. By 12:45 p.m. about thirty had been rounded up and brought into the State Dining Room for hamburgers and beer and one more try to "get the story across." Carter was, as he always seemed to be in meeting with small groups, forceful and articulate. Asked if he had taken into account how unsettling all of the changes would be, he replied: "I did. I thought that the best thing to do was to follow a thirty-month period with no changes in the Cabinet with a complete reassessment, which has been ongoing for several weeks, some-

times several months, to make the changes in as quick and inci-
sive and thorough way as possible and to have replacements
designated for every departing member of the Cabinet at the
time the departure was announced.

"This was done in every case except with Brock Adams. I was
inclined to keep Brock if he would make a couple of changes
that I felt were imperative. He decided not to. He is gone. Already his replacement is at work this morning. And in every instance I believe that no president could have acted more quickly
and incisively and gotten the thing over with.

"I recognized, as was inevitable, that the cancellation of my
energy speech would create some doubt and some consterna-
tion, some temporary semblance of disarray or uncertainty. But
I don't believe that in retrospect anybody can say that a substantial change in the Cabinet, which I consider to be necessary,
was prolonged. It was rapid and as thorough as I could possibly
make it."

The President described what he called "the quiet periods of
consultation" in those ten days at Camp David. But the description of his experience focused less on his own failures than on
what the press was calling, justifiably or not, his finding of a malaise in the land. "I became convinced and my thoughts co-
alesced—obviously thought processes go on for months, weeks,
sometimes a lifetime—but I became thoroughly convinced that
we had a basic problem in our country, that the attitude of the
country was negative, the people had lost confidence in themselves, that they had lost confidence to a great degree in our government. In some cases there was an antagonism that was
evolving rapidly, even more than in the past, against government, and I felt that I should do as best I could do to alleviate
these problems by a frank description of them, first of all."

As Carter talked the resentments he harbored came into
sharper relief. Yes, he said, he was abandoning his commitment
to press conferences twice a month in Washington; there were
other ways to reach the public that did not "rely so heavily just
on the White House press corps." The problem, he suggested at
one point, was that the press corps was too inextricably involved
with the permanent life of the capital. He said:

"One problem that I have faced, and I think it is time for you all, if you don't mind my being blunt, to look at the substance of what I have done rather than having as a preeminent consideration how much it has shaken the so-called Washington establishment.

"You know, I admit it has shaken the Washington establishment for two days. So be it. You take a dynamic, aggressive independent secretary" [obviously Califano] "who is extremely intelligent, who can forge a problem and cannot work with me and cannot work with his fellow Cabinet members, who cannot work with my staff and cannot work with OMB, and assess how much of that brilliant product gets through the Congress, and you will find that in most cases none of it gets through the Congress.

"You take another Cabinet member" [apparently Schlesinger] "equally brilliant, who hammers out along with me and my staff and OMB and other Cabinet members a very difficult decision, for instance in energy, and then works as a team player, you see how much legislation gets through."

The reporters, said the President, should "take a look at the substantive questions that I have to face as President and quit dealing almost exclusively with personalities and whose feelings got hurt and whether an administration employee who is a contact of yours thinks he might lose his job because he has to have a fitness report."

But the fact was that the press, the Washington establishment, and, more to the point, the public were indeed focusing on the "substantive questions," and did indeed recognize that this had been a contrived crisis. There had been no demand for broad social change, as had been the case during the struggle over civil rights fifteen years earlier. There had been no national reaction against an important government policy, as had been the case in the national debate over the Vietnam war a decade earlier. There had been no corruption of the system that needed to be eliminated, as had been the case with Watergate five or six years earlier. All that had happened—and it was plain to everyone— was that a president in the most extreme political peril had "rolled the dice" in an attempt to change the public perception of his presidency. And in doing so, he had, to use a favorite political cliché, shot himself in the foot. Nothing really had changed. "Rapidly things returned somewhat to normal," said one of those inside the White House.

The tightest of the tight little circles around the President had been defined during those days at Camp David, and it remained essentially the same as the campaign approached—Rosalynn Carter, Hamilton Jordan, Jody Powell, Patrick Caddell, Gerald Rafshoon, and Charles Kirbo. The President himself continued to be defensive and resentful. At a press conference in late July he called the way the decision to appoint Hamilton Jordan chief of staff had been received by the press and political community "one of the most grossly distorted of my career in politics." At a "town meeting" in Bardstown, Kentucky, a few days later, he once again complained about the "insulation and isolation" of Washington.

On July 30 Carter held a luncheon for his consultants at Camp David to thank them for their "constructive and helpful" criticism, but only 85 of the almost 150 turned up at the White House. The "malaise summit" was not something with which the politicians were eager to be identified.

There was, too, a return to public relations at the expense of serious political leadership that might have persuaded people that things had changed at the White House. On August 17 the President began a "working vacation" on the riverboat *Delta Queen*, for a week's steaming down the Mississippi from St. Paul to St. Louis. It was just two days after Andy Young finally had gone so far that even he had to be fired: he had met privately with officials of the Palestine Liberation Organization in direct contradiction to administration policy. Throughout the "working vacation" the country had a picture of their President bantering with voters along the river while a searing public dispute developed between Jews and blacks over United States policy toward the PLO.

All through July, August, and early September, Carter's troubles seemed to grow, just as they had before he went to Camp David. George McGovern endorsed an increasingly restless Edward Kennedy for the Democratic presidential nomination, and Henry M. Jackson predicted Kennedy would win it. Jerry Brown, the brash young governor of California, was emboldened to establish a campaign committee. And on the Republican side, as many as a dozen men were lining up for the chance to take Carter on, with Ronald Reagan in the forefront. (In addition to Reagan, Republicans either declared as candidates or expressing interest included Senators Howard Baker of Tennessee, Bob Dole of Kansas, Larry Pressler of South Dakota, and Lowell Weicker of Connecticut; former CIA director George Bush; former Governor John B. Connally of Texas; Representatives Phil Crane and John B. Anderson of Illinois and Jack Kemp of New York; former Secretary of the Treasury William Simon; General Alexander Haig of NATO; and a Los Angeles businessman, Benjamin Fernandez.)

Griffin Bell suggested that Carter had suffered because he tried "to act like he wasn't President" when the country wanted just the opposite. Indeed, Carter personally seemed plagued by error, both trivial and consequential. Late in August the story got out that he had been attacked by an angry rabbit on a pond at Plains. In mid-September the gasping President was forced to drop out of a ten-kilometer run. On September 7 the President issued a statement declaring that the presence of Soviet troops in Cuba was "not acceptable" to the United States—only to back off later. An Associated Press–NBC poll found that his job rating had reached a new low.

Much later, on a cold afternoon a month after Carter's defeat in 1980, Jody Powell was asked if the fiasco of Camp David had been a "turning point" in the President's political decline. "No," he said, "it could have been a turning point for the better, and it turned out not to be." Then he added after a moment: "I'm not sure the potential was there to pick up on that theme."

That, of course, was the basic failure. Except for Mondale no one at Camp David—in an official capacity, at least—had raised the question whether it was realistic to expect any president to be able to change the national mood or himself with mere words. The most that could be said about Camp David was that the President and Pat Caddell had identified a national condition. But defining and quantifying a problem is only a precondition to solving it, not a solution in itself.

Jimmy Carter wasn't trying to solve anything, anyway, other than the political problem quantified in those terrible figures from the public-opinion polls. He and his band of political technicians couldn't alter the record of his performance, so they tried to alter the public perception of where the blame should be placed. "It was," one of the participants in those meetings said later, "all blue smoke and mirrors. What was needed was fundamental change." It didn't come, and the voters knew it. And, significantly, so did Edward Kennedy.

3.
"Why Do You Want to Be President?"

While President Carter was capturing the attention of the nation with his soul-searching at Camp David, another prominent Democrat was deeply involved in some summer soul-searching of his own. Senator Edward Kennedy, after nearly three years of saying he expected that Jimmy Carter would be renominated and reelected and of vowing his intention to support him, was reassessing.

The last three years had been for Kennedy a period of disenchantment with a presidency that from the start had been alien to his own political ideology, objectives, and style. He had played the good Democrat, backing Carter on Capitol Hill on most issues for most of that time, but his heart was never in it. All through 1979 the pressure built to challenge Carter, and he doggedly resisted it, but his rationale for staying on the sidelines was now rapidly eroding.

A challenge, indeed, seemed inevitable. On both ideological and personal grounds, the two men had no use for each other. In 1976, when Kennedy criticized Carter for waffling on a statement to the Democratic convention platform committee, Carter cracked that "I don't have to kiss his ass" to get elected. Kennedy laughed it off, but he came from a family with long memories. And they differed often enough in their approaches to major political issues. In 1977, when George McGovern accused Carter of trying to balance the federal budget at the expense of the poor, Carter slapped him down as a solitary carping voice, but Kennedy rushed in to say he agreed with the liberal from South Dakota. He pushed for sweeping national health insurance and accused Carter of "a failure of leadership" on the issue.

Some close to the President, such as Gerald Rafshoon, had contempt for Kennedy and thought it good politically to have Carter openly break with him as a way of demonstrating Carter's toughness. If Kennedy decided to challenge him in 1980, Carter told some editors and broadcasters, that was fine with him; he had been "perfectly willing, even eager" to run against him in 1976. That was true enough. Indeed, in his first days in national politics, he used to tell his young advisers that one of his goals was to free the Democratic Party from the grip of George C. Wallace—and the Kennedy family.

Kennedy, however, continued to turn away all queries with what aides came to call his "E, E, and I" answer—that he *expected* Carter would be renominated, he *expected* he'd be reelected, and he *intended* to support him. But Kennedy's lead over Carter in the polls continued to grow—40 percent to 21 among Democrats and independents in the ABC News–Harris survey in September 1978. And he continued to send teasing hints.

In December the Kennedy-Carter breach had widened when Kennedy used the Democratic Party's mini-convention in Memphis to deliver an arm-waving, podium-pounding harangue on the need for national health insurance and an end to social-welfare budget cuts. Jody Powell labeled the speech "demagoguery," and Carter worsened matters by seeming to attribute Kennedy's appeal only to his family identity. "There is a special aura of appreciation to him that is personified because of the position of his family in our nation and in our party," Carter told a press conference, adding, "I recognize it and I have no objection to that."

By 1979 Kennedy seemed to be taking pokes at Carter every chance he had: when the administration cut funds for biomedical research and local law-enforcement agencies, when Bella Abzug was dismissed as Carter's adviser on women's issues, when Carter enunciated his policy on Taiwan. And Carter for his part seemed to be striking back. When Vice Premier Deng Xiao-ping of China visited Washington in late January, not long after Kennedy had visited China, Kennedy was not invited to the lavish White House dinner in Deng's honor until the last minute. After a television correspondent raised the issue, it was found that "an American businessman" couldn't make the dinner, and there was a place for Kennedy after all. Still, whenever asked, Kennedy reiterated the "E, E, and I" answer.

Yet as early as February 1979 key advisers gathered at his home in McLean, Virginia, for what one of them called "state of the art meetings" on the political outlook. These early meetings were a closely held secret. The conferees included Kennedy's sister Jean and her husband, Steven Smith, later his campaign manager; Joseph Kennedy, son of the late Robert F. Kennedy; the senator's former aides Paul Kirk, a lawyer, and David Burke, now an ABC vice president; his current aides Carey Parker, Rick Burke, and Dr. Larry Horowitz; and old Kennedy hands John Douglas, a Washington lawyer, the historian Arthur Schlesinger, Jr., John Siegenthaler, publisher of the *Nashville Tennessean,* Theodore Sorensen, John F. Kennedy's speechwriter and a lawyer who also had been chief draftsman of the senator's televised explanation of the events at Chappaquiddick, and others.

The prognosis was always bleak for Carter's chances for reelection, but Kennedy was reluctant to take him on. Significant in terms of what happened later, one close aide said, was that the meetings' "greatest focus was not on *how* one would do it if one decided to do it, but *whether* one should do it." Kennedy did ask Sorensen to write a discussion paper, but that, too, focused on a rationale for running against an incumbent, not on the strategy to be followed when one did so.

One who refused to accept the "E, E, and I" answer was the fiery, profane, Carter-hating head of the International Association of Machinists, William "Wimpy" Winpisinger. He was determined that the Democratic Party should draft Kennedy, and in late March members of his union and others in Iowa formed a draft committee. A group of congressmen led by Rick Nolan of Minnesota did likewise; so did some liberal activists in New Hampshire, and the Cuyahoga County (Ohio) Democratic Committee was soon to become the first party unit to sign on. The Kennedy-Carter feud grew hotter. When in April the President proposed a modest windfall profits tax on oil, Kennedy called it "a transparent fig leaf over the vast new profits the industry will reap." Carter's pithy response: "That's a lot of baloney."

On May 31, a major meeting was held in Steve and Jean Smith's New York apartment, but the insiders' strong consensus was still against running. "Everybody with the exception of John Douglas felt pretty strongly it would be a lot of trouble," one participant recalled, "and he and Joan would be most of it." The reference, of course, was to the fact that Kennedy's wife, Joan, was under treatment for alcoholism and living apart from him, in Boston, amid continuing rumors of his past involvement with other women. "It was said generally," this insider said, " 'Look, she cannot get through this campaign without causing trouble for you.' A recent article saying Joan Kennedy had stopped drinking scared everybody because she hadn't. She didn't get a grip on it until just about when he announced. It was really a bad situation as far as she was concerned."

Also, of course, there was Chappaquiddick. Its tenth anniversary was approaching and all present agreed the episode was certain to be remembered and reexamined. But, Paul Kirk recalled, there was no in-depth discussion of how to cope with the problem because Kennedy "felt anything he had to say about it had been said, and there wasn't anything he could do to redress or correct or alter the situation."

Kennedy listened intently as each adviser spoke, but he didn't seem to want to be put off by any considerations they raised. "Listen," one recalled him saying, "let's assume I know the depths of these problems and I assume personal and security problems are such that I can handle [them]. What will Carter do? What should I do? Should I continue to show availability?" It became apparent, this adviser said, "that he was really moving in the other direction [toward running]. I think he thought a wall had been built [against that decision] before he got in there." In any event, nothing was settled.

In mid-June, Carter finally came out with his own national health insurance plan. In Kennedy's view it was so deficient that he had to face the reality now that their differences were irreconcilable. And that, indeed, was the message Carter intended to convey. Some policy people in the White House believed, one political aide said, "that if we gave Kennedy what he wanted on health care he wouldn't run," but the political people felt "he would run if he thought he could win. If Carter had caved in he would have looked foolish, so it would be a plus for him to draw the line and say who he was and who Kennedy was." And Jody Powell said: "All that crap we got, like 'Just make him feel more at home, love him up a little bit,' was just crap. He wanted a relatively sure shot before he got in."

These views appealed to Carter, who was confident as always that he could beat Kennedy. In fact, conscious of the personal problems Kennedy carried, one key Carter aide said at the time: "There are two hundred million people in this country who can beat Jimmy Carter and one who can't, and that's Kennedy."

Perhaps to convey to Kennedy the peril in challenging an incumbent, Carter pointedly told a group of Democratic congressmen at a White House dinner in June that if Kennedy ran against him, "I'll whip his ass." When one of them asked Carter if he had meant to say that, he assured him he had. And when an aide later asked the same question, the President said: "Yes. I don't see anything wrong with that." In fact, the White House subsequently informed some of the congressmen that nobody would be angry if the observation was leaked to the press. More Mr. Tough Guy.

It was in this hostile climate that Kennedy observed (but was never invited to) Carter's national psychoanalysis sessions at Camp David in the summer of 1979—an episode that no doubt unwittingly served to overshadow the Chappaquiddick anniversary. "It was buried by the President's summer spectacular," one Kennedy aide said later. But that, he went on, "gave us an inappropriate gauge" of how important the issue would be in the campaign. More immediately important was how Kennedy reacted to Carter's "malaise" speech. "I thought his assessment of the country," he said in an interview later, "its spirit, its direction, its ability to cope with the problems of our time, whether it was the economy or energy or foreign policy, just ran so contrary to everything I believe in and that I was brought up to believe in, that it added impetus to the thinking I was giving [to running for president] at that time."

Kennedy went off on the August congressional recess, with Kirk and a very few other insiders aware that he intended to use the time to make a final decision. Some senators up for reelection, Carey Parker said, were telling Kennedy, "This is going to be a disaster in 1980. What are we going to do? You're the only one who can save us." It was not senatorial pressure, however, but Kennedy's own assessment that would decide, and all that held him up now were family considerations. Mindful of what had happened to his two brothers, at one point he spoke to his sister Eunice Shriver about his concerns for the future of his youngest son, Patrick, then 12, and to his mother, wife, and two older children, Kara and Teddy, Jr., who had had reservations about his safety.

One Kennedy insider gives this account of a meeting the senator had with his wife and children: "It was pretty traumatic. There was some concern on the part of the children for his safety and for his relationship with [Joan]. As a family they had had some finger-pointing. The kids were very protective of her and they worried about him running, about what it would do to his safety and what it would do to her. He told them he wanted to hear from them. And in the final analysis Joan really wanted him to do it. She didn't want the monkey on her back. She didn't want it said that she stood in the way. She told him if he did run, she'd be there, he could count on her."

Kennedy himself said later that he had never actually gone to his mother, his wife, and his children and sought their acquiescence about running, but he did have "conversations with them about my decision, and it was clear from those conversations that they were going to support whatever ultimate decision I made." Another aide said, however, that had Joan Kennedy's health not permitted her to participate, or would have been damaged by his candidacy, he never would have run. "He made it absolutely clear that unless there was a medical green light for Joan, he'd have no part of it," this aide said.

In mid-August the President dispatched Tim Kraft, then his campaign manager, to notify Senator Kennedy, through his old political friend and associate Gerard Doherty of Boston, that Carter intended to stay in the race to the bitter end. It was a clear warning that Kennedy could not count on a bloodless political coup of the sort that deposed Lyndon Johnson in 1968. The warning reflected the prevailing White House view that Kennedy would run only if he thought he would have an easy time of it.

Publicly Kennedy was still saying nothing. But around Labor Day, at a cookout at his summer home in Hyannis Port, he took Kirk aside and told him he was going to run. "If the thing doesn't work out," Kirk remembers Kennedy saying, "I think I'll just be able to live with myself better for having taken up the cause that's drifting away." No more was said, and the next thing Kirk knew was that he was reading in the newspapers that Rose and Joan Kennedy had said that Teddy's running was all right with them. "I thought that was a rather strange way to launch a balloon," he recalled, laughing.

Now everywhere Kennedy went he was besieged by reporters. It was time for political hardball at the White House. Carter told some newspaper editors that he wasn't worried about slipping in the polls, because voters would be looking at "your character assessment, the reputation that you have for being steady in an emergency." And in a speech in New York, he said: "I've never been afraid since I've been in office to tackle a difficult issue. I don't think I panicked in a crisis." There was a public furor over this remark, and Carter sent a handwritten note to Kennedy assuring him he wasn't referring to the senator's behavior at Chappaquiddick. Yet the unwritten message was clear—if Kennedy got into the race there would be political blood on the floor before it was over. (Nevertheless, about the same time Dr. Larry Horowitz of Kennedy's staff approached Dr. William Lukash, the official White House physician, for advice on security arrangements, and Lukash volunteered to ask Carter to authorize Secret Service protection for Kennedy. Carter agreed without hesitation, and it was provided—weeks before Kennedy's formal declaration of his candidacy.)

In Florida at this time, some free-lance Kennedy backers were challenging Carter in a party straw vote. The White House threw heavy resources into this fight, coming away with a two-to-one victory in delegates elected to a state convention. And in the almost daily Kennedy-Carter sparring now, the President on one occasion went directly to Kennedy's home base and returned untarnished, or better. As the main speaker at the dedication of the John F. Kennedy Library in Boston in mid-October, the President spoke graciously at an occasion that was obviously strongly pro-Kennedy. He kidded the senator and, while praising the late President, observed pointedly, "The world of 1980 is as different from that of 1960 as the world of 1960 was from that of 1940. Our efforts to improve that world must be different as well."

With the library dedication behind him, Kennedy finally abandoned all pretense of deference toward Carter. In Philadelphia, he shouted: "We want action, not excuses . . . leadership that inspires the people, not leadership that . . . blames the people for malaise." And he started preparing politically, dispatching Steve Smith and Doherty to Chicago to enlist the showcase endorsement of Mayor Jane Byrne, who until then had hinted broadly that she was on the brink of endorsing Carter. The Illinois primary in mid-March promised to be critical, and this was a bold and eye-catching raid. Here was the vaunted "well-oiled Kennedy machine" of old shifting into gear, or so it seemed. In a few more days Smith announced the formation of a Kennedy-for-President committee authorized to raise campaign funds. By November 1 Carter's general approval rating in the Gallup Poll had nosedived to 29 percent among all voters, his lowest ever, and he trailed Kennedy by two to one among Democrats as a presidential choice.

Now all that remained was Kennedy's formal announcement of his candidacy, set for Boston on Wednesday, November 7. On the Sunday night before, however, there took place one of those events beyond the control of the campaign strategists and managers on either side that affected the entire course of the ensuing campaign for the Democratic nomination. It was an event that shook a nation's conception of one of its most prominent, seemingly best-known public figures and forced him into a defensive posture that undermined his claim to be an aggressive, tenacious challenger.

On that night, CBS News broadcast a one-hour television documentary written by and featuring one of its star reporters, Roger Mudd, that included segments of two lengthy interviews with Kennedy. They touched on all of the major controversial elements of his political career, from Chappaquiddick to his relationship with his wife and the rumors of other women.

Kennedy's performance was, in a word, a disaster. He was halting and seemed uncertain in his answers to tough but low-keyed questions posed by a benign but firm Mudd, questions not only about Chappaquiddick and about his marital situation but also about the basic matter of why he wanted to be president. Kennedy hemmed and hawed and talked in vague generalities about the mood of the country. Later, some of his aides said the reason for Kennedy's uncertainties was that Mudd had done the first interview in August, before he had definitely decided to run, but that was not true: Mudd conducted that interview on September 29—nearly a month after Kennedy had told Kirk and others he intended to make the race. Besides, the question about why he wanted to be president came in the second interview, which had been taped in Kennedy's Senate office in Washington on October 12.

Probably never before had a pair of television interviews had such an effect on a presidential campaign. For that reason it may be constructive to examine how they came about and in what context they were conducted.

The idea for a documentary on Kennedy originated not with Mudd but with Robert Chandler, vice president for public affairs of CBS News, in charge of documentaries. Sometime in June, he told Mudd that Bill Leonard, president of the news division, thought they ought to do an hour-long show on Kennedy, because whatever he did in the approaching year would be politically important. Would Mudd do it?

Mudd did not immediately say yes. "I wanted to sort out in my own mind," he recalled later, "whether my publicly identified friendship with some Kennedys would prove difficult, and whether I could in my own mind approach the interview professionally and wouldn't have any problem asking any questions that ought to be asked." Mudd and his wife, E. J., were good friends of Ethel Kennedy, Robert's widow, and often went to parties and casual evenings at her home. Mudd also participated in the annual benefit pro-celebrity tennis tournament that she helped to organize. But the Mudds were not particularly close to Ted Kennedy. Actually they had been to his home perhaps three times on social occasions and had seen him from time to time at Hickory Hill, Ethel's house. Mudd had about the same social relationship with him that many Washington reporters have with many members of Congress they have covered over the years.

After a few days Mudd told Chandler he'd take on the assignment. Shortly thereafter, Mudd explained to Tom Southwick, Kennedy's press secretary, in a general way what CBS had in mind, and arranged for some time with the senator for himself, Howard Stringer, the executive producer of *CBS Reports,* and Andrew Lack, the producer of the show. He told Kennedy, Mudd recalled, that it was to be a serious broadcast for which CBS was making a serious commitment. Mudd came away with the sense that Kennedy had already decided to cooperate. Southwick, on the other hand, had the impression that Kennedy at first was not inclined to agree to do the show, which would require frequent access to him at work and with his family, but Southwick urged him to. "He likes to use the fact that people are interested in who he is and what he is," Southwick said, "to advance the kinds of issues that he's interested in. For instance, he's usually much happier giving an interview on national health insurance than he is on how it feels to be the head of the Kennedy family. But my feeling was, based on talking to them, that it would be a chance to have a picture of him in a broad sense of what he was doing in the Senate as well as the family kinds of things, and show people that he does have a record as a senator; that he does do a lot of things, that these eighteen-hour days are not just for nothing, that this was something worth doing."

Mudd thought Kennedy "was receptive to it because he knew we were going to do it anyway. I sort of said to him, 'Whether you cooperate or not will not deter us. We'll go ahead and do it. It'll just be a lot better, fuller, more informative broadcast if we in fact have your cooperation.' " Mudd also told Kennedy at this meeting that CBS wanted two interviews of at least an hour each, one at his Cape Cod home and one at his office or his home in Washington, and wanted access to him on Capitol Hill and with his family. "That was all fine," Mudd recalled.

With Walter Cronkite on summer vacation, Mudd as usual was substituting as anchorman on the CBS evening news. So he returned to New York and Lack remained in Washington with a crew to shoot film on Kennedy. In August Lack and the crew went to Hyannis and accompanied Kennedy on his annual camping trip to western Massachusetts with a host of Kennedy children. Meanwhile Mudd spent considerable time in the CBS documentary section in New York going over research on Kennedy in preparation for the interview. In the course of this work, Mudd discovered a surprising thing: Kennedy, for all his years of public service and celebrity, apparently had never sat down for a long television interview, aside from occasional panel shows devoted to discussion of specific issues.

"Generally speaking," Mudd said, "most Americans' impression of him had been formed from minute-and-a-half clips on the evening news in which he was seen throwing a football or excoriating some corporate biggie in the [Senate] hearings. It was a very glamorous television image he had, but there had never been a sustained interview about him and his life and what he believed in. And we were determined that while we knew we would have to make it complete, while we knew the hour would have to contain pictures of his family and an accounting of his glamorous life, we were determined that the bulk of the hour would be this interview."

Also, Mudd said, "I knew that he probably would not be an easy interview." The Kennedy brothers, he knew, seldom "let go very much unless they wanted to let go of it. They didn't generally let things slip unless they were sure of what they were doing. It was very difficult to pry anything out of them. Occasionally a little light would shine, but not often. Normally they wanted to be very sure of the ground up ahead before they let anything go." One of the most celebrated television interviews of any Kennedy, in fact, had been one Mudd conducted with Robert Kennedy on the night of the California primary in 1968, only a short time before the senator was shot. Mudd kept asking him why he thought people regarded him as "ruthless." That interview had a wistful, even comical tone to it, as Kennedy, determinedly benign, avoided the slightest trace of "ruthlessness" in answering—or, rather, avoiding an answer.

Through the rest of August and into September, as Lack and the film crew followed Ted Kennedy around gathering the visual part of this comprehensive report of the senator at work and play, Mudd continued to prepare for the interviews by reading "anything and everything I could get my hands on" in the CBS research department in New York.

When the story broke just after Labor Day in which Kennedy said his mother's and his wife's objections to his running had been overcome, Mudd, as Cronkite's substitute, argued for and won using the news as the lead item on the CBS evening news. No other network gave the story comparable weight, but Mudd recognized correctly that it was the most important signal yet that Kennedy was clearing the decks for 1980.

The development was a break for the CBS documentary team. Interest in the senator and the activity around him intensified greatly when he got back to Washington, enriching the film Lack and his crew were accumulating. "The thing sort of fell into our laps," Mudd recalled. "Everywhere he went there was an absolute elephant herd of reporters and cameras, and he just couldn't move. So the pictures were much more intense than they usually are of a candidate, because it seemed like the whole world was following him from one [Senate] hearing room to another." The CBS team was anxious now to do the interviews for a very practical reason. It was abundantly clear that Kennedy was going to challenge Carter, and the network had to be sure it could complete this costly, complicated show and get it on the air before his formal announcement of candidacy. Failure to do so would leave CBS subject to the equal-time provisions of federal communications law—the requirement that stations provide all declared candidates equal time if one is given air time. The practical effect, everyone connected with the project knew, would be to kill it.

Around the middle of September Mudd had lunch in New York with Steve Smith and brought him up to date on the project. "I said, 'I really need some off-the-record guidance. . . . If you're planning to announce early I've got to know that because the broadcast will die if we can't get it together until after you announce.' So all during this period Steve would say, 'It looks like early December.'" There was never any question raised that Kennedy would run. "Steve kept saying, 'My only problem is trying to hold down the candidate,'" Mudd recalled. So the program was tentatively set for November 14, and later moved up a week, to November 7. "That looked safe," Mudd said. "It would be a couple of weeks before Kennedy announced, it would be in the height of the political season, and that would be a good time."

On September 28 Mudd, Lack and Stringer accompanied Kennedy to Boston, where he made a rousing anti-Carter speech before the Massachusetts State Labor Council at the Park Plaza Hotel. Women wearing bright yellow "Kennedy in '80" T-shirts yelled "We want Ted," as 750 union members approved a resolution urging the national AFL-CIO to endorse him for president.* And they went wild when Kennedy told them: "You'll be hearing about my response to that resolution in the not too many days and weeks to come—and I don't think you'll be disappointed." Yet as late as the end of 1980, some Kennedy insiders were still offering the defense that Mudd's questions had been posed to the senator in August, during the congressional recess when he was still trying to decide whether or not to run. One of them, Carey Parker, said that Kennedy had decided "around Labor Day" to run, and it was his understanding the first interview had been done at a time when "the decision hadn't been made to run at all . . . I think it was the last week in August."

At any rate, Mudd, Stringer and Lack, with two film crews, drove down to the Cape from Boston Friday and went over to Kennedy's place by prearrangement Saturday morning. The senator was off at a local dedication ceremony at the time and returned wearing a business suit and tie. Mudd was dressed casually, in a sports jacket and blue jeans, and Kennedy went in-

---

*The AFL-CIO remained neutral, but some individual unions, like the Machinists, did endorse Kennedy, and some, like the Communications Workers of America, endorsed Carter.

side the house and changed to a double-breasted blue blazer and slacks and a dark shirt open at the neck, with no tie. Then at Kennedy's suggestion he and Mudd took lawn chairs on the grass behind the gray shingled house on a cliff overlooking the ocean and, with the two crews rolling their film, began the interview.

The mood according to Mudd was friendly and casual at the start. But, as Mudd had anticipated, it was like pulling teeth to get anything substantive out of Kennedy. They talked first, Mudd said, "about what Camelot meant, how he defined it, whether it was applicable to 1980, how he accounted for his political popularity and his political position in America, what the political benefits were of being a Kennedy and a brother of, and a sole surviving male of the family. We talked about physical danger to him, about his religion." Through all this, Mudd said later, Kennedy seemed relaxed, "not terribly articulate," couching his answers in generalities about his sense of commitment. "It was not any kind of rolling oratory," Mudd said, but for him as for other reporters who long had covered Kennedy up close, the pauses and incomplete sentences were what he had come to expect.

At one point, during a break to permit the changing of film magazines on the cameras, Kennedy went inside and Mudd walked down to the cliff overlooking the water with Stringer and Lack. "The three of us said, 'Boy, this is tough.' We were just not getting any good, vigorous, graphic kinds of words from him," Mudd recalled. Stringer and Lack, who had not been exposed to Kennedy in this fashion before, seemed to Mudd "more alarmed than I did at his lack of vivid responses."

Mudd, continuing on the personal thread when the interview resumed, discussed with Kennedy his role as a father. Mudd asked Kennedy whether he thought the press had been fair to him and his family, and he said yes. Kennedy recalled that when his son Teddy had cancer and faced amputation of his leg, reporters who knew about the situation agreed to hold off reporting it until the senator could break the news himself to the boy. And when Mudd asked "what sort of separatism" the press ought to maintain "between your public life and your private life, or any public official's," Kennedy acknowledged "a natural inquisitiveness of people about all aspects of [public] people's lives" and added: "I sort of understand that."*

Up to this point Kennedy's demeanor seemed guarded but not unfriendly. Then came the first abrupt stiffening. Mudd, following the same line of questioning, asked: "What's the present state of your marriage, Senator?"

Mudd described the reaction later: "There was this sudden groping for words. I didn't know at the time whether it was that he didn't expect a question like that or whether he never thought he was going to have to answer a question like that. But it was obviously painful for him to answer. But it was not a prosecutorial question; it was not asked that way. It was asked in a way that indicated I was seeking information, and [a question] I thought anybody who was running for the presidency had to answer."

Kennedy, Mudd recalled, was "very awkward" through this sequence, "and trying to answer but not wanting to and not quite knowing what to say." But he did not complain or try to put the conversation off the record, which Mudd thought was to Kennedy's credit. The burden of the answer was, with much halting, that he and his wife had had "some difficult times" but had "been able to make some very good progress" and (according to the CBS transcript) "it's—I would say that it's—it's—it's—I'm delighted that we're able to—to share the time and the relationship that we—that we do share."

Mudd: "Are—are you separated, or are you just—what—how do you describe the—the situation?"

Kennedy: "Well, I don't know whether there's a single word that should—have a description for it. Joan's involved in a continuing program to deal with the problems of—of alcoholism, and—and she's doing magnificently well, and I'm immensely proud of the fact that she's faced up to it and made the progress that she's made. And I'm—but that—that process continues, and that—it's the type of disease that one has to continue to—to work on, and she continues to work on, and the program that's been devised is—is in Boston."

Mudd: "Is there a prospect that she will soon resume her life with you in—in Washington?"

Kennedy: "Well, we'll have a—the—the most important is for her full and complete recovery, and she's made enormous strides and doing exceedingly well, and I think she's taking—and we're taking it sort of day by day or week by week."

Now Mudd for the first time broached the subject of Chappaquiddick, but only tangentially, recalling that Kennedy in his television talk after the accident had mentioned thinking "there was some awful curse that was hanging over the Kennedy family." Did he still think about that? Kennedy said no; in the last ten years his life had been more normal, and he had been able to get a better perspective on life.

(It was at this juncture in the actual telecast that CBS cameras sought to recapture the scene on Chappaquiddick Island that night of July 18, 1969. The most effective segment, with voice-over by Mudd, retraced the drive Kennedy took with Mary Jo Kopechne. After the interviews, Mudd, Stringer, Lack, and the film crew had gone to the island for that purpose. Mudd himself drove a car repeatedly over the route, both day and night, to familiarize himself with it and with the actual driving sensations. Finally a camera was attached to the side of the car's left front fender with only the car's headlights to show the way. The route then was filmed starting at the same time as the actual incident, about forty-five minutes before midnight. The technique was eerily effective. In Mudd's words later: "What you saw was, going down the road on the smooth road, and then they took the right-hand turn. And then you saw this wheel just jumping up and down on the washboard road [the camera being jounced]. You stayed with that and suddenly up ahead through the headlights you saw the bridge in that candid angle that the bridge is attached to the road." The film, coupled with Mudd's narration, was devastating. Southwick later questioned whether it had been fair not to specify that the film was taken of the road ten years after the incident.)

Now that the subject of Chappaquiddick had been opened up, Mudd pursued it. It had been his intent, he said later, not to rehash the detailed questions raised in the inquest of Mary Jo Kopechne's death, but rather to put the whole episode, and its political implications, in the new context of Edward Kennedy as a prospective candidate. He tried to give Kennedy, he said, an opportunity to say something to satisfy public doubts, now that he was about to ask voters to consider him as a candidate—in Mudd's words later, "an open-ended question, an invitation for him to make some comment, not specifics about right and left turns, about who was drinking and wasn't drinking—a political question." Mudd asked him: "Don't you think, because of your rapidly changing position as a national leader rather than as a senator from Massachusetts, that you on your own ought to say something more to illuminate in people's minds what indeed went on that night, other than saying it's all in the record?"

Kennedy, however, was having none of it. "Well," he said, "I expect I'll be asked about the incident during the course of the campaign, and I'd be prepared to respond to any of the questions, as I have been over the period of the time that I've been in public life. I mean, I'd respond to any particular questions that you'd have."

Mudd pressed him. "Well," he asked, "what happens, Senator, if some heckler stands up at a rally, a Kennedy rally, and says, you know, in the loud voice, red-faced, he's angry at you, and he says, 'Kennedy, you know, you were drinking, you lied, and you covered up!' What are you going to tell him in a situation like that?. . . I mean, that's the way those questions will come at you, I would think."

Kennedy: "Sure. I, as I say, I'll answer any of the, any of the questions that do come up during the course of a campaign, whether if it's a particular heckler on X, Y, Z issue. But I will answer the questions, and if you have questions right now, you ask them to me, because I'll answer them. I've answered them in the past. I've answered them completely, honestly, and to the best of my ability. And I'm glad to answer any question that you have right now on any of the aspects of it."

It was, for Mudd, the moment of truth. "In the course of the next two minutes," he recalled, "he [Kennedy] became really sort of defiant. I went and read the transcript the other night and nine times once the subject was brought up he challenged me to ask him questions. One challenge after another—'If you have any questions, I'll answer them. If you have them right now

I'll answer them. Any question you want to ask me, ask me, because I'll answer it, as I have in the past.' Nine times. I think he was trying to make me back down." Also, as Mudd said later, "I was a guest in his home. When you sit and interview him he's an imposing person physically, so you're really at a disadvantage— his furniture, his yard, his home, and his turf—which made those nine challenges to me to ask him any questions so much more formidable.

"That was a very sweaty moment for me, because it was all right there. I had a choice. I could back down and destroy myself professionally, and not be true to my calling, or I could just go on through the wall. I did not rise to the bait, as it were, but asked another couple of questions just generally about that evening and about its political implications, and reasked the first question, to give him one more chance to say it in his own way, so that I would not have to enter into this district attorney role, which I was prepared to do.

"One of my feelings beforehand was that I didn't want to make it another Chappaquiddick show, because everybody had gone over the ground. I knew he had given those anniversary interviews and they weren't very satisfactory, because the reporters they had sent to do them always were a little nervous about asking the pertinent questions. But I also knew, having reread all that material and done some strong, heavy research into it, that there was no way we could do an hour on him without coming to grips with that issue. I no longer regarded the issue as a personal one. I regarded it as important as any of his votes in the Senate. It was a question of whether he told the truth or didn't tell the truth, and I thought that was basic to anybody's public candidacy."

Now, however, it seemed clear to Mudd that Kennedy not only wasn't going to accept his invitation to offer more on his own, but, by repeatedly challenging him to ask questions, was attempting to bully him verbally. "After being challenged and trying to come at it a little obliquely," Mudd recalled thinking, "finally then in my own mind I said, 'Okay, Rog, go ahead. There it is. You've got thirty seconds to decide which road you're going to take.' "

The road Mudd took, of course, was the one Kennedy had

driven on that fateful night. Mudd proceeded to ask the question that had plagued everyone: "How was it that you took that right-hand turn? When all signs led you to the left, the surface of the road led you to the left, how was it that you could possibly have turned right?"

The fat was in the fire. Mudd asked why the bumpy, unpaved road had not alerted Kennedy; why he had later referred to a clock in the car that had taken him back to the scene of the accident when there was no clock in it; whether he thought "anybody really will ever fully believe your explanation"; what guarantee there was that "you would not again act, as you said, irresponsibly or inexplicably when your own career came in conflict with the public's right to know."

Kennedy offered nothing new. On the matter of the wrong turn, he argued that "it isn't described as all the signs led to a different way." There was, indeed, only one specific sign there showing that the paved road veered to the left, but Mudd had said "signs" not "the signs"—meaning various indications, including the jarring bumps encountered as soon as a car got off the paved road, so graphically demonstrated in the film taken two weeks later for the show.

From this point on Kennedy demonstrated marked discomfort but still did not complain about any of the questions. Once, near the end, when magazines on the cameras were being changed again, he asked Mudd whether the interview could be wrapped up soon but, Mudd recalled, "there were no critical comments." Yet when Mudd asked about the possibility of an interview with Joan Kennedy, there were no promises. Mudd said she originally had been scheduled to be there but had to be with the senator's mother, then hospitalized. As soon as the interview was over Kennedy went into the house, changed clothes again, and went off on his boat with his son Patrick and some other Kennedy children, with Mudd's crew filming them from an accompanying boat. If Kennedy was displeased, he did not make any attempt to terminate the CBS access to him.

The interview had been "a major, major disappointment" for Mudd. "My view of him changed radically that day," he said later. "For me it was almost a process of original discovery. It was as if I had been in a room that nobody else had ever been in. I knew that he tended to be inarticulate, but when it was all over and particularly then with the second interview [two weeks later], it came to me that indeed we had a very revealing interview, and that professionally, for television anyhow, it was an original piece."

Steve Smith and Southwick both claimed later that this first Mudd interview with Kennedy at Cape Cod had been sprung on the senator unawares. Mudd was "less than forthcoming" by indicating the interview would merely concern "what the Cape had meant to the Kennedys," Smith said Kennedy himself had told him later. If the senator had expected the interview to be more substantive, he said, "you would have sat down and given it more thought. He gave it none." After accompanying Kennedy to Boston, Southwick said, "they [Mudd and Lack] wanted to go down to Hyannis the next day. . . . It was our sense that this would be just sort of footage of him walking on the beach at the Cape and that kind of thing," he said. "That was the impression we got, because the senator was very tired, and he said, 'I just don't want them down there for very long. I'd like to have some time to myself and the family. If this is going to be a long, involved thing, I'd prefer to do it some other time.' It was our sense that they were going to maybe ask a few questions about the family, do some footage of him walking along the beach and in the compound, and we set a time for an interview that was to be held in Washington a week or so later. And none of the staff members went down with the senator to Hyannis. I was not there for the interview, which was a bad mistake on my part, for sure."

What probably convinced Southwick of that was a phone call he got from Kennedy immediately after the interview. "He basically said, 'This thing was a disaster.' He said Roger came in and started asking him . . . 'Your nephew David is a drug addict. Do you feel that because you've taken so much time to work in politics that you somehow contributed to that problem?' And asked him about his daughter Kara and whether she smoked marijuana or slept with people, and how he felt about that. I think he felt that this person, Mudd, had been invited down to come to his house and to sit in his living room, and that basically he had a lot of nerve sitting there and asking questions like that. 'Do you love your wife?' and those kinds of things."

At the same time, Southwick conceded, Kennedy did not regard the visit merely as one from a friend. "He and Roger have—had before this—a very amicable but nevertheless adversarial relationship," he said. "They'd kid each other a lot. They were like two fighters kind of circling each other a little bit."

Mudd denies that he ever asked Kennedy about any of his children specifically, and said he thought Southwick was speaking a "deliberate falsehood" in suggesting that he had. Mudd quoted from a portion of the interview transcript not used in the broadcast in which he did inquire whether the Kennedy children were church-going Catholics and whether the senator as a parent had had to "go through a drug crisis" with his children as so many other Americans had. The transcript also showed that Mudd asked Kennedy a general question referring to the present-generation phenomenon of young people "living together without marriage" and inquiring how Kennedy "would handle it" in his own family if it came up, but he specifically noted that he was not suggesting there was such a situation in Kennedy's family. The senator replied that the matter really hadn't come up and he did not "see it on the horizon yet."

At any rate, in the Kennedy camp the feeling was now very strong, as Southwick said, "that we wanted to have another interview to give him a chance to do a little bit better." On Monday he phoned Lack in New York and told him so. (In fact, another hour had been agreed to from the start. The first interview, Lack and Mudd said later, was to be on personal and family matters, and the second on his official side as a senator.) And although Kennedy clearly felt the first interview had gone badly for him, there was no request either to scrap it or to reopen the previous area of personal questioning. Mudd and Lack, however, anticipated that Kennedy might want to backtrack and decided to give him a chance to do so.

The second interview took place on October 12 in Kennedy's Senate office. This time, in addition to Kennedy, Mudd, Stringer, Lack, the crew, and the Secret Service agents, Southwick and

Horowitz were present. It was crowded and more formal because of the setting, but Mudd sensed no particular hostility or contentiousness. Mudd started off by saying he had been derelict in not having asked some follow-up questions about Chappaquiddick and did so. But again Kennedy referred him to the inquest record. It was clear once again that no new ground would be broken. If Kennedy had wanted to improve on his answers of the first interview, here was his opportunity, but he did not take it. Finally, frustrated by Kennedy's repeated referrals to the inquest record, Mudd pointed out to him that the judge had concluded that Kennedy had been guilty of criminal conduct. Kennedy replied that it was the judge's conclusion, not his own. Back to square one.

There was no use pursuing the matter any further, Mudd realized. There was a pause, and then Mudd, feeling stymied, simply asked: "Why do you want to be president?" It was not a question that Mudd had written down or planned on before going into Kennedy's office. To Mudd's astonishment—and that of millions of viewers when the show finally was put on the air— Kennedy seemed to have only the broadest and most rambling generalities to offer as his reason:

"Well, I'm—were I to—to make the announcement and—to run, the reasons that I would run is because I have a great belief in this country, that it is—has more natural resources than any nation in the world, has the greatest educated population in the world, the greatest technology of any country in the world, the greatest capacity for innovation in the world, and the greatest political system in the world. And yet, I see at the current time that most of the industrial nations of the world are exceeding us in terms of productivity, are doing better than us in terms of meeting the problems of inflation, that they're dealing with their problems of energy and their problems of unemployment. And it just seems to me that this nation can cope and deal with its problems in a way that it has in the past.

"We're facing complex issues and problems in this nation at this time, but we have faced similar challenges at other times. And the energies and the resourcefulness of this nation, I think, should be focused on these problems in a way that brings a sense of restoration in this country by its people to—in dealing with the problems that we face—primarily the issues on the economy, the problems of inflation, and the problems of energy. And I would basically feel that—that it's imperative for this country to either move forward, that it can't stand still, or otherwise it moves back."

Mudd recalled his reaction to the answer: "So there this thing was. I sort of privately blinked. It was like 'I want to be president because the sea is so deep and the sky is so blue.' You know, you're always a little professionally embarrassed to ask a question like that because you can read the stitches on a pitch like that. It comes across the plate about nine miles an hour. But the more I thought about it after, the more I think it's a very valid question. It gives a politician the opportunity to eliminate in his answer those things that are not important and makes him stand up and say, 'These are my reasons.' It may sound silly asking the question, but the answer is always revealing no matter how far the guy knocks the ball out, because if he's a demagogue, I think it'll probably come out in the answer. If he's never asked the question of himself, if his priorities are screwed up, it'll come out in the answer. Because he's really on his own there."

As for the suggestions made thereafter by Kennedy's staff to various news agencies around Washington that the senator hadn't decided whether he would run, Mudd said: "This is October 12th. You had to be a certifiable idiot to believe he hadn't made up his mind at that point." But Kennedy, he went on, "was trying to maintain that fiction, and my feeling at the time he said it," Mudd recalled, "was, 'Oh my God, he hasn't thought about it before.' Maybe he had. And maybe he'd not thought about it before or asked himself before because there'd been no occasion to ask himself the question. His candidacy was so preordained that maybe the question never came up." Southwick, however, clung to the explanation that Kennedy "wasn't flat-out sure that he was going to go for it, and one of the things he was trying to decide was what it is you say to yourself when you decide to run for president. It isn't something you just wake up one day and decide to do." Kennedy, of course, had been confronted with the prospect of running for president for at least eleven years—way back to the Democratic convention of 1968, when supporters of his slain brother Robert began an effort to draft him that he had had to short-circuit.

When this second interview was over Kennedy and Mudd joked a bit as was often their custom, Mudd remarking—after taking more than two hours of the senator's valuable time—that he didn't know "whether we can use any of this or not." Kennedy, Mudd said later, "understood immediately what I was saying and sort of rolled his eyes, as much as to indicate that it probably didn't come out the way he had hoped. But there wasn't anything embittered or any feeling that he was stricken by panic. It was not difficult at all."

After the election, we asked Senator Kennedy about the circumstances of the Mudd interviews, and the complaint of some of his aides that the CBS team had somehow misled them and him into thinking there would be only filming and some casual questioning at Hyannis Port. He declined to comment on the matter other than to say: "I've known Roger Mudd over a number of years as a news commentator and interviewer, and I'd just as soon not get on into the background of the interview itself, although I'm quite prepared to comment about my assessment of it and its impact on the candidacy. . . . It wasn't helpful, but I think there were other start-up problems we were facing during . . . that period that also complicated our ability to get our message across and marshal the kind of support I would like to have seen."

What about why he was unable to give a more effective answer in the second interview to Mudd's question about why he wanted to be president? "First of all I wish I had been," Kennedy said. "But secondly, I was really caught in a dichotomy, where on the one hand I'd made up my mind and on the other hand I had not made the announcement. I was reluctant to make the kind of statement talking about running for the presidency that would be a statement of candidacy. On the other hand I knew in my own mind that I was going to be a candidate. This created a kind of dichotomy in my own mind, but clearly I could have and should have been able to weave my way through that dichotomy in a more effective way. I'd been hopeful that I would have been able to remain here in the Senate during the remainder of the session participating in the windfall profits tax [fight]. This was something I was very much interested in, and really [preferred that I] had not gotten into an announcement until the end of the year. But I felt the pressures, the internal pressures as well as the external pressures of being asked about my intentions, to make an earlier announcement. . . . I was really caught up in that kind of internal tension."

Kennedy never sought to employ the excuse that one or both of the interviews took place before he had made up his mind about running. He did, however, offer another possible explanation—that nearly all the internal discussion until then had been about whether he should run, not why or how. "I spent a good deal of time thinking about running," Kennedy said. "I wasn't interested in dividing the party but I was very much concerned about the direction of the party and of the country, and I was very much concerned about what I thought would be the results if we didn't have an alternative or change. I spent time thinking of that and probably not as much time as I should have about how I'd spend the early days of the campaign, and developing and fashioning the kind of themes that I think probably would have aroused the most positive response."

Kennedy's aides were distressed that Mudd had not focused more on Kennedy's record on the issues he had worked on during seventeen years in the Senate, but Lack argued that Kennedy was asked and his answers couldn't be used "because they weren't coherent. . . . In fact, he led us into other areas *because* we couldn't get solid answers on issues we could present to the public." The CBS team, he said, wanted all along for the message to come "from his lips . . . not from ours."

Another thing of which Southwick made an issue was that Lack had insisted on accompanying Kennedy on his August camping trip with his children and then in the telecast seemed to make it sound like a publicity gimmick. (Mudd's voiceover in fact did say: "But no Kennedy camping trip can ever be just a family camping trip—not with a driver and an advance man, not when the route and the stops are made public, not when the senator and the children are on almost constant display.")

"The senator," Southwick said later, "would just as soon not have any goddamned press around during that camping trip." Yet the CBS team, he said, had insisted on knowing what the route and the stops were. But Lack claimed that he and his crew had gotten no special access and left when they were asked to after the first day.

Still another complaint was that the documentary showed Kennedy in his office being handed a phone by his personal aide Rick Burke, while being reminded that the first name of the caller, Congressman Markey of his own Massachusetts delegation, was Ed. But all these gripes did not touch on the revealing elements that made the show what Kennedy himself called "a disaster."

After the second interview, the technical work began of piecing the film together, "laying down the track" or the voiceover, which Mudd wrote and recorded, and cutting. When all the duplication, out-of-focus shots, undue pauses, and so on were cut away from the more than two hours of interview, about an hour and twenty minutes was left, and it had to be reduced to fifty-three minutes. Mudd was in a room in the Wyndham Hotel in New York writing when, on the night of October 24, Steve Smith phoned. They joked for a while, and Smith asked how the show was going. Mudd cracked that they were taking the questions he had asked Kennedy and using answers Smith had given to Mudd in another interview, because they were the same as Kennedy's. As they talked Smith asked when Mudd thought CBS was going to put the show on, and Mudd told him in two weeks, on November 7. That date, it had been decided, would definitely assure airing before Kennedy's announcement and would beat the equal-time problem. Lack had been checking from time to time with Southwick on the announcement date to make sure, and, the CBS producer said, he too was operating on the basis that Kennedy was going to declare in early December.

Four days later, when Mudd was back in Washington, Smith called an early afternoon press conference at an old Cadillac showroom where the Kennedy forces later set up their campaign headquarters. The CBS Washington bureau was only a few blocks away, and Mudd walked over. Smith, Mudd recalled, "got out of a car and was going into the building, and I was cutting through one of those back alleys. I said, 'Hey, Steve, wait,' and I ran over and we shook hands. I said, 'Are you still announcing in early December?' And he said, 'No, no, we're announcing an exploratory committee today, and he's announcing up in Faneuil Hall in Boston next Wednesday.' I said, 'You're kidding.' He said, 'No.' I said, 'What time?' He said, 'Ten in the morning,' or whatever it was. I said, 'God Almighty, Steve, that's the night we're scheduled to go on the air.' And Steve said, 'I guess I should have called you,'" and he walked into the building.

Mudd, with visions of the months of work and the interviews going up in smoke, ignored the press conference and ran back to the CBS bureau. He phoned New York. Bill Leonard, the president of CBS News, was out to lunch. Mudd got the number of the Slate Restaurant, where CBS executives often lunched, got Leonard on the phone, and broke the news. "You could see the broadcast going down the drain," Mudd said, because if it went on that Wednesday night as already set in network promotions, it would be subject to the equal-time provision. Lack said later he didn't believe, however, that the Kennedy camp had timed the announcement in the hope of scuttling the CBS documentary. "I don't think they had any way of measuring what the performance was," he said, meaning how damaging to Kennedy it would prove to be.

Leonard by this time had seen the documentary and was just as enthusiastic about it as were Mudd and the team that put it together. He had ordered the full promotion treatment. "Oh boy, this is just great," Mudd remembers Leonard saying. "Just stay right there. I'll be back in touch with you."

Suddenly the whole documentary was in jeopardy because of the timing of Kennedy's announcement. There was talk of cutting up the interview and putting parts of it on *60 Minutes* on the Sunday night before, and some CBS lawyers were said to be arguing that the whole show should be scrapped. But Leonard— "to his everlasting credit," Mudd said—insisted that it be neither chopped up nor shelved.

The next problem was finding a time to broadcast the show before the Wednesday morning announcement. The matter went to Gene Jankowski, president of CBS. Leonard first rejected an hour on Saturday night as inadequate for a documentary of such importance. Mudd became so concerned about its fate that at one point he told Stringer, " 'If this program doesn't remain intact, I'll have serious problems.' I didn't say it in so many words, but I was prepared to resign if it was scrapped or cut up. But Leonard was just terrific the whole time. It was finally set for ten o'clock Sunday night."

The show was up against the first television showing of the movie *Jaws* on ABC and *MacArthur* on NBC, but the CBS team was happy. (Later Senator Bob Dole, never at a loss for a wisecrack, observed that "seventy-five percent of the country watched *Jaws*, twenty-five percent watched Roger Mudd, and half of them couldn't tell the difference.")

By midweek transcripts and tapes of the show were in Washington for embargoed release to the press, but copies inevitably were leaked. Kennedy aides later suggested the White House had obtained a copy, duplicated it, and circulated the transcripts. Carter's political strategists did in fact obtain a copy but they denied doing anything with it. Their political judgment was that no comment on it was necessary; Kennedy was hanging himself without any help from the opposition.

The CBS bureau previewed the show for reporters, and even before it was broadcast, newspaper stories were describing, often with a sense of the same "original discovery" of which Mudd spoke, Kennedy's abysmal performance. Martin F. Nolan of *The Boston Globe* wrote the first story, observing that Kennedy appeared "inarticulate and flustered for much of the interview" and predicting—correctly—that the documentary would prove to be "a major political event." Also, two days before the broadcast, we interviewed Kennedy in his Senate office for a lengthy article in *The Washington Star* covering some of the more troublesome questions raised by the night on Chappaquiddick. In that interview, too, he was extremely awkward and ill at ease, and while again he said he was willing to answer all questions, he relied once more on the basic defense that he had already told all there was to tell.

The same was true concerning an interview with Kennedy shown on ABC's *20/20* on the Thursday night before Mudd's documentary was broadcast. It was taped that same afternoon, and ABC News correspondent Tom Jarriel was much less diplomatic with Kennedy, firing an extremely tough, barbed question right at the start. "Senator Kennedy," Jarriel said, "you cheated in college, you panicked at Chappaquiddick. Do you have what it takes to be president of the United States?" Kennedy replied benignly: "Well, that will be a question that will be decided by the people all over this country, during the course of the primaries and the caucuses, and hopefully it will be decided after that, were I to gain the nomination of the Democratic Party." Jarriel, in recalling the interview later, volunteered that his opening inquiry was "a good shock question, but we were going for box office"—knowing by now that Mudd's show, to be broadcast three nights later, would also delve into Chappaquiddick.

Other pointed questions from Jarriel about Chappaquiddick and Kennedy's marital situation elicited defensive answers, though they were somewhat more coherent than those Kennedy had given to Mudd, perhaps because the Jarriel interview took place nearly three weeks after the second session with Mudd. Jarriel said later that Kennedy was "incensed" at his stiff questioning but shook hands when the interview was over. Jarriel said he had no sense that Kennedy at that time felt he had done poorly in the Mudd interviews or that he was doing the ABC interview to "redeem" himself. Jarriel for one was surprised at the effect of Mudd's documentary, which he felt was much easier on Kennedy than he had been. "I couldn't believe how soft it was," he said later. He said, too, that his interview with the senator had more than twice the share of the national television audience—but clearly nowhere near the political ramifications of Mudd's.

On Sunday night Steve Smith and Southwick watched Mudd's show from the basement of Ted Kennedy's home. Kennedy was elsewhere in the house but, Southwick said, "I have a feeling he didn't watch it." Why not? "He knew what it was," his old press secretary said. "Our feeling was there was nothing we could do about it and we just had to go on from there and do the best we could." Jody Powell, who had never seen *Jaws* but by this time had read the transcript of the Mudd-Kennedy show, spent the hour at home twisting the dial of his television set, picking up the documentary during commercials of the movie. He said later he didn't know whether President Carter had watched either.

By Monday morning Roger Mudd's interview had the American political community buzzing. Polls indicated that the CBS documentary, in competition with *Jaws* on ABC, had been watched by only 15 percent of the nationwide television audience, but among Americans interested in politics, especially politicians and opinion-makers in the news media, the percentage was surely higher. Just why Mudd's documentary created a greater furor than Jarriel's interview three nights earlier may have been the result of several factors. First, the CBS show was a carefully crafted examination of a full hour's duration. Second, Mudd's rather benign style of interrogation may have highlighted Kennedy's rambling more effectively than did Jarriel's "box office" aggressiveness. Third, Mudd had the reputation, however mistakenly, of being a Kennedy insider, so his hard questions, no matter how benignly posed, may have carried more weight with viewers. And, finally, there was that question of Mudd's that had nothing to do with Chappaquiddick but the answer to which was so disappointing: "Why do you want to be president?"

In any event, it was soon commonly accepted that Kennedy's performance had been awful. Until now, favorable polls and a long-standing conviction among politicians and opinion-makers that Kennedy had only to enter the race and he would sweep the beleaguered Carter aside had made it seem inevitable that Ted Kennedy would one day occupy the White House. But now maybe the invincible Ted Kennedy, the man the nation was clamoring for, wasn't invincible after all.

Against this background, Edward Moore Kennedy, after eleven years of personal and political soul-searching, finally took the first step on the road back to Camelot at Faneuil Hall in Boston three days later. Among those in the audience was Roger Mudd. Before Kennedy took the microphone, one of his nieces, Maria Shriver, came by to say hello to Mudd and his wife. And when the new candidate's sister Eunice Shriver came in, she waggled her finger at Mudd and jokingly said something to him about getting even when they got him up to Hyannis Port the next summer. It all seemed like letting bygones be bygones. (But it was not what it seemed. From that time, a great freeze descended on Mudd—not only from Ted Kennedy and his immediate family and staff, but also from the Mudds' good friend and frequent hostess Ethel Kennedy.)

In his speech declaring his presidential candidacy, Kennedy said he would work to "release the native energy of the people" to do all the things Jimmy Carter had failed to do for lack of leadership and vision. "The only thing that paralyzes us today is the myth that we cannot move," he said. "If Americans are pessimistic, it is because they are also realistic. They have made a fair judgment on how government is doing—and they are demanding something better.... We must restore the faith of citizens that the system can be made to work, if they will make government work for them."

Now all the guesswork and the reading of Kennedy tea leaves was over. Ted Kennedy at last was a declared candidate for president of the United States. Now the political professionals, the pollsters, and all the other technicians would move in to embellish the beneficial truths and to blur the politically harmful truths about him, to try to shape and augment the positive perceptions and neutralize the negatives. But in all they would attempt to do, both positive and negative, they now had to deal with "the Mudd interview."

Later, Tom Southwick would say that Mudd's interview was probably "the most important" ingredient in Kennedy's ultimate failure to wrest the Democratic nomination from Carter—with one exception. That exception was another event that had occurred half a world away on the very same day that Mudd's documentary was broadcast, an event that in time dwarfed the interview in political significance. In Iran's capital city of Tehran, the American embassy was stormed by a mob, and sixty-six American citizens were taken hostage. Almost at once the entire political landscape was changed, as the presidential campaign of 1980 was barely beginning.

4.
A Campaign Held Hostage

On Saturday night, November 3, 1979, as President Carter was spending the weekend at Camp David with his family, his supporters were out in force at the annual Democratic Party Jefferson-Jackson Day dinner in Ames, Iowa. At the same dinner four years earlier, the fledgling campaign organization of little-known Jimmy Carter had packed the house and delivered a first-place finish for him in a straw poll of the diners. Although he won only 23 percent of the 1094 ballots cast, it was enough to propel him into national attention by a press that had waited impatiently for four years for some reason to pin the front-runner label on somebody.

This time a Carter victory in the Iowa straw poll was a foregone conclusion. He was the incumbent, and this was one of his special states. He had worked it personally and relentlessly in 1975 and 1976, and Iowa took particular pride in its importance in nominating him. There was, however, one factor that attracted national reporters to Ames—the impending candidacy of Ted Kennedy. In four more days he would be a declared candidate, and in the process of downplaying the earlier Florida straw vote, Kennedy had declared—unwisely, some of his aides thought—that the first real test between Carter and himself would come in the Iowa party caucuses in January.

And although Iowa clearly was regarded as Carter turf, there were some factors that nourished optimism among supporters of Kennedy, long recognized as one of his party's leading liberals

by virtue of his record as sponsor and faithful advocate of a host
of social-welfare programs. First of all, Democrats considered
Iowa one of the most progressive states in the Midwest, with an
active, liberal state party machinery that took pride in its encouragement of grass-roots participation. Second, there was the
early draft-Kennedy effort, spearheaded by the Machinists'
Union and joined by important local members of the United
Auto Workers. Third, the polls—in Iowa and nationwide—
showed Kennedy comfortably ahead of Carter. Finally, there
was that intangible though untested Kennedy mystique, the
thought of Camelot Returned. (Among those present at the
Ames dinner that night were Ethel Kennedy, making a rare political appearance, and her eldest son, Joe. They received standing applause on arrival.) But when the straw votes were
tabulated Carter had 70.6 percent to only 26 percent for Kennedy and 0.82 percent for the only other Democrat on the ballot, Jerry Brown.

That straw vote proved, eleven weeks later, to be a roughly accurate prophecy of the relative strengths of Carter and Kennedy
in the Iowa precinct caucuses that initiated the actual delegate-
selection process for the 1980 Democratic convention. In an important sense, however, nothing that was said or done that night
in Ames, or anywhere in Iowa in the ensuing eleven weeks,
made the difference. What really mattered was what was happening in Iran.

As Iowa Democrats were dining that night, a mob of militant
young Iranians was stirring in the streets of Tehran, spurred by
a radio speech three days earlier from their spiritual leader, the
Ayatollah Ruhollah Khomeini. In it, he had urged them to mark
the first anniversary of an earlier, violent street demonstration
by expanding "with all their might their attacks against the United States and Israel, so they may force the United States to return the deposed and cruel Shah." That demand came as a result
of a decision by President Carter one week before, in spite of
warnings of consequences from American diplomats in Iran, to
admit the ailing Shah of Iran, then in exile in Mexico, to the United States for emergency treatment of cancer and gallstones. Predictably, that action had enraged Iranians and dovetailed

perfectly with Khomeini's strategy of painting the United States as "the great Satan" at whose doorstep all of Iran's considerable domestic ills could be laid.

On November 4 the mob aroused by Khomeini laid siege to the American embassy in Tehran. The assault had not been totally unexpected. Nearly nine months earlier, the same embassy had been seized by armed men who killed one Iranian and held 101 persons hostage, including American Ambassador William Sullivan and nineteen marine guards. Government forces freed them three and a half hours later, and subsequently the United States had installed additional steel doors and increased the marine guard. But there never were enough to hold off a mob indefinitely. The expectation always had been that Iranian police or soldiers would step in to assure the diplomatic integrity of the embassy under international law. Still, it seemed incredible in retrospect that given this history greater precautions had not been taken to protect the Americans in the embassy—or to evacuate them if their safety could not be guaranteed. Indeed, Carter was reported later to have asked at one staff meeting on whether to admit the Shah, months in advance of the assault: "When the Iranians take our people in Tehran hostage, what will you advise me then?"

But pressures on him from such of the Shah's American friends as New York banker David Rockefeller and former Secretary of State Henry Kissinger persuaded Carter to grant the Shah an entry visa, in spite of all the warnings about what might happen.

President Carter was asleep at Camp David that early Sunday morning when word came of the seizure of the embassy. The marine guards had held out for about three hours before they were overrun and the hostages taken. The State Department reported that the Iranian government had "given assurances that our people being held are safe and well" and that "it will do its best to resolve the matter satisfactorily." To which the State Department replied, "We appreciate the efforts of the Iranian government." Indeed, according to Hodding Carter, then the State Department spokesman, high Iranian officials who had served or been educated in the United States told him in effect: "Look, think of this as a takeover of an ROTC building in the sixties or early seventies by youthful protesters in your own country. We will soon have this under control."

But within two days that government, headed by the moderate Prime Minister Mehdi Bazargan, had collapsed and been replaced by a Revolutionary Council answerable to Khomeini. In short order the air was thick with charges and threats—charges that many of the Americans held hostage were members of the Central Intelligence Agency and were spies, and threats that they would be killed or placed on trial if the United States did not return the Shah to Iran. Carter, now back in Washington, plunged into a round of meetings with his foreign policy advisers but without a clear picture of what was going on or, more critically, with whom he could deal in Iran to achieve a speedy resolution of the crisis. But one thing was established from the start—the Shah would not be surrendered to such intimidation. "We are not going to turn him over," said Hodding Carter at the State Department. "We expect the government of Iran to secure the release of the Americans and to return the embassy compound to our control." Jody Powell was asked whether the use of military force to free them had been ruled out. "Yes," he said.

As every day passed, the rhetoric and the resolve of the captors and Khomeini to hold the Americans escalated. Although plans were going forward for Carter's formal declaration of candidacy in early December, the focus at the White House was now almost exclusively on Iran—on extricating the hostages safely. On November 9 the President canceled a two-day visit to Canada and a weekend at Camp David so that he could concentrate solely on the Iranian crisis. In the next days he asked the United Nations Security Council to condemn the takeover of the American embassy and to call for the hostages' release; he reviewed the status of Iranian students in this country with an eye to possible deportation; he halted all oil imports from Iran, calling off a trip to Pennsylvania so he could continue to monitor the situation from the White House; he froze all Iranian assets in the United States; he canceled a political trip to Florida and a Thanksgiving vacation in Georgia.

At that point, Vice President Mondale noted later, there was very little alternative to Carter's devoting full time to the crisis, and hence little thought given to the political ramifications, or the political advantages, of staying off the campaign trail. "When it first happened, I think that was what the public wanted," recalled Mondale in an interview after the election. "We all thought the hostage situation could be resolved, and at the outset there was good and sufficient reason for the President to do little else. We had so many diplomatic problems, so many problems of trying to learn what the situation was. We were intensely studying the possibilities of a rescue mission with all the incredible complexities that that involved, questions of how you seized assets and froze them, who would retaliate, what the impact would be. No one realizes, when you do these unprecedented things, the amount of study and care [required]. There was a fantastic range of exceedingly complex, technical problems coupled with serious policy problems that all had to be done as quickly as possible, and much of it requiring the President's personal attention."

Also, as Powell recalled later, in the first highly charged weeks there was a real threat that the hostages might be physically harmed. "We really were concerned about keeping them alive from one day to the next," he said. "Information was very scarce. . . . During that period they were shooting people there right and left. There were pictures in the papers of bodies of generals and ministers from previous governments. Well up into December you had very real concern about whether anybody over there had any control over what might happen, and whether you could get a phone call in the middle of the night that says five of them are dead or somebody's been shot, reportedly trying to escape. Or an announcement that a decision had been made to convene trials, and no real knowledge of what trials would mean, and a strong concern that there was nobody in Iran who could say with any certainty what trials would mean. Things over there during that period tended to have sort of a life of their own."

Through all this Carter remained resolute. The seizure of the American embassy and hostages was a crime in international law and the President made it clear there would be no "deal" on the Shah. "It is unthinkable," he told an AFL-CIO convention in

Washington, "that any responsible government in today's modern world could regard the seizure of the diplomatic officials of another nation as a realistic means to advance any cause whatever. Terrorism is not an acceptable means to resolve disputes between individuals or nations. The actions of Iranian leaders and the radicals who invaded our embassy were completely unjustified. They and all others must know that the United States of America will not yield to international terrorism or blackmail. . . . Only after the hostages are released will we be willing to address Iran's concerns."

Two weeks after the seizure Khomeini ordered the release of thirteen blacks and women not accused of being spies. But it was patently clear by now that the United States, and Carter, might be in for a long ordeal. Although the President hoped that some breakthrough could be achieved soon, he and his chief aides realized that the matter could drag on, perhaps for weeks or even months. Powell and others went back to State Department files and read summaries of what had happened, and how the American government had responded when the American intelligence ship *Pueblo* was seized by the North Koreans in 1968 and its crew of eighty-three held for eleven months. Then as now, restraint and patience were the prudent courses, in order not to jeopardize the lives of the captive Americans.

As December approached Carter's inner circle took on the obvious question: Could he, should he, campaign while the hostages were still being held in Tehran? The practical need that he give his undivided attention to the crisis had already been amply demonstrated, and the political benefit of doing so was also already becoming apparent. As in most occasions of trouble abroad, Americans rallied to their President; with the lives of other Americans in peril, a surge of patriotism welled up and overflowed in support of Jimmy Carter. It was therefore clear that the best way for him to campaign for renomination was to be the President on the job. No one expected then, of course, that the hostage situation would drag on for months. Indeed, when two weeks after the Americans were taken we asked Hamilton Jordan what would happen politically if the captivity were to stretch out so long that it became an accepted condition, he replied: "We just can't let that happen."

"There were days in there," Powell recounted later, "and maybe several days at a stretch when [he] could have gone out, but you couldn't predict when those were going to be." In the midst of secret negotiations, any sudden breakoff in campaigning would have been taken as a signal, Powell said, and might have had a negative effect on the negotiations. It was simpler just to stay in Washington, and it was politically advantageous as well. In the face of the tremendous public outpouring of support for the President, his Republican and Democratic challengers alike found themselves immobilized as foreign-policy critics. Taking isssue with the Commander-in-Chief in the prevailing patriotic climate was simply too risky politically. So Ronald Reagan and a bumper crop of other Republican hopefuls, and Carter's prime Democratic opponent, Ted Kennedy, all held their tongues on the Iranian crisis—for the time being, anyway.

Not having to campaign was particularly fortunate for Carter because Kennedy could not seem to get his own campaign going. A relatively junior group of news reporters assigned to him seized on every fluff—and there were quite a few, as there always are with a new campaign, but especially one begun with so little thought about *how* and *why*. And because this was Ted Kennedy campaigning for the presidency, after more than a decade of great expectations, the mistakes were magnified and examined in a fairly negative light, given public reaction both to Mudd's interview and to Kennedy's continuing personal problems. At one point David Garth, the New York media advertising expert and campaign consultant, was recruited to help get Kennedy on track. A better answer to the Chappaquiddick questions was composed in advance of an appearance on NBC's *Meet the Press,* and at the first opportunity, Kennedy invoked it. There was "no new information" to be uncovered, he said categorically, and if there was "there would be absolutely no reason" for his "remaining in public life, let alone run for the presidency of the United States. Absolutely none." Kennedy reminded his questioner of the "series of tragedies" in his life—the loss of his brothers "under the most trying and tragic circumstance" and a son victimized by cancer—and observed: "I have responded to those challenges by one, acting responsibly, and two, by the continuing commitment that I have to public service." He would not run for the presidency, he concluded, "unless I was completely satisfied that I could deal with any of the pressures that would come to that particular position."

Three weeks after his declaration of candidacy, however, Kennedy was still struggling to formulate a rationale for running, beyond his conviction that he could do a better job than Carter. "You can give the same plays to Cedar Rapids High School and the Dallas Cowboys," he told us, "and get entirely different results." The Republican candidates, of course, also contended they could be more effective than the incumbent Democratic President. But with the heavy competition for their own party's nomination, the task for each one was to separate himself from the pack, to demonstrate why he should be the one to take on Carter—or Kennedy or Brown—in the fall.

Meanwhile the atmosphere of crisis intensified in Washington. The American embassy in Islamabad, capital of Pakistan, was attacked by a Moslem mob; surgery on the Shah was completed and soon he would be able to leave New York; the Mexican government announced it would not permit him to return to his exile home in Cuernavaca; and threats increased from Iran to place the American hostages on trial if the Shah was not returned to Iran. A White House statement warned ominously that peaceful resolution of the crisis was "far preferable to the other remedies available to the United States." And each of these developments produced another surge of patriotic support for the President. An Associated Press–NBC News poll indicated more than seven of ten Americans surveyed believed he was doing all he could to free the hostages. About two-thirds said they would not extradite the Shah and would approve use of military force to get the hostages back if they were put on trial. Ronald Reagan and Henry Kissinger, among others, urged that the Shah, an American ally for thirty years, be permitted to remain in the United States.

The President certainly was not being hurt politically by giving all his attention to the crisis. In fact, an ABC News–Lou Harris poll taken in late November showed Carter pulling ahead of Kennedy for the first time, 48 to 46 percent, among Democrats and independents. And if that point needed any further emphasis, Kennedy provided it. In an interview on television station

KRON in San Francisco, he was asked about Reagan's and Kissinger's calls for political asylum for the Shah. Kennedy asked in return: "Because the Shah had the reins of power, and ran one of the most violent regimes in the history of mankind, in the form of terrorism, and of the basic and fundamental violations of human rights under the most cruel circumstances to his own people? How do we justify that in the United States?" How, he asked, could the United States admit "that individual because he would like to come here and stay here with his umpteen billion dollars that he'd stolen from Iran, and at the same time say to Hispanics who are here legally that they have to wait nine years to bring their wife and their children to this country? Or someone who comes across the border from Mexico whose only desire is to work and provide for their family, that we may even put them in jail?" In his view, Kennedy said, the Shah had over the last thirty years been "looking out after one person—himself," and that "to tie American fortunes . . . on one man rather than a whole nation and a people is a policy that's bankrupt."

The White House, Carter's supporters on Capitol Hill, and Republicans everywhere immediately jumped on Kennedy for discussing the Iranian situation so openly and critically within the context of a partisan political campaign. Carter himself remained properly aloof, leaving it to Powell to say "the President made it clear he did not think it appropriate to be drawn into a political debate on this matter while our people are being held in Tehran." Robert Strauss, Carter's campaign chairman, said Kennedy's remarks were "ill-advised" and would be damaging to his candidacy. John White, the party's national chairman, who never let his supposedly neutral position get in the way of his fealty to Carter, said that Kennedy's statement would divide Americans and confuse Iranian authorities about American resolve. And, obviously at the White House's urging, Secretary of State Vance through a spokesman called Kennedy's observations "unfortunate and not helpful."

Kennedy tried to draw a line between his criticism of the Shah and the general situation concerning the hostages, but, he went on, "Few things could more seriously undermine our efforts to secure the release of the hostages than for the United States to condone the repressive dictatorship of the Shah. . . . Support for the hostages does not mean support for the Shah." And, he added later, the question of whether giving permanent asylum to the Shah might affect treatment of the hostages should have been debated openly.

But by any yardstick Kennedy's comments were a political blunder. It was not that his evaluation of the Shah was off base, for he was only saying what many Americans believed—that the Shah was a self-serving despot. Kennedy's mistake was his seeming to ignore the sensitivity of the situation at a time the nation needed to speak with one voice—the President's—in dealing with a tough foe. He appeared to be undermining Carter for political reasons—and his remarks had the opposite effect, of making the President an object of greater public sympathy.

To the political community, it looked simply like a very dumb move when Kennedy could least afford more criticism. The Mudd interview was still in people's minds and the campaign was getting off to a rocky start, what with the candidate's uncertainty and uneven stump performance and the high expectations raised by the very fact he was a Kennedy. One Kennedy insider said later: "We asked ourselves why did Kennedy's statement become so much an issue and Reagan's wasn't?" The answer, of course, was that Kennedy, not Reagan, was challenging Carter for the Democratic nomination. Republicans are expected to attack Democrats, and vice versa; besides, Reagan was urging asylum and hence did not appear to be siding with the hostages' captors, who were demanding the Shah's return; Kennedy had laid himself open to just such an allegation. In the end, it was not a very difficult decision for the President to decide not to campaign. But the decision obviously left Carter's strategists with having to run a campaign without a candidate who could travel to the early caucus and primary states. The President's speechwriters moved deftly to make maximum capital of the circumstance. In keeping with the somber mood of the country, they fashioned Carter's announcement of his candidacy as a sober, get-on-with-it statement, and on December 4 he went on nationwide television and wrapped the flag around himself.

"At the height of the Civil War," he said, "Abraham Lincoln said, 'I have but one task and that is to save the Union.'" Carter added modestly, "Now I must devote my considered efforts to resolving the Iranian crisis." He would curtail as long as necessary his own campaign activities and remain close to the White House, Carter said, "to define and lead our response to the ever-changing situation of the greatest sensitivity and importance." Accordingly, he canceled a scheduled appearance at a $500-a-plate dinner for his own campaign that very night in Washington.

Nobody was yet calling it a "Rose Garden strategy," but whatever the name, the strategy was working. In a Gallup Poll among Democratic voters completed a few days after he formally entered the race, Carter surged to an 8 percent lead over Kennedy.

The Iranian crisis continued to hold the nation's attention. In mid-December, the Shah was suddenly spirited out of the United States aboard an American military plane and taken to a small island off the coast of Panama, where sanctuary had been arranged for him by the American government in secret negotiations conducted by Hamilton Jordan. In Iran, the reaction was a renewed threat that the hostages would be put on trial as spies. Carter called on the United Nations to impose economic sanctions against Iran—and continued to climb in the polls. A Yankelovich, Skelly, and White survey now had him 20 percentage points ahead of Kennedy. In an interview with the *Des Moines Register and Tribune,* conducted, of course, in Washington, the President attributed his rising political fortunes to the fact that Kennedy as an active candidate had moved from what he derisively called "a vision of perfection" to "a real flesh-and-blood candidate." But that was only part of it.

The Christmas holiday was marked by another event that almost at once had a direct, critical bearing on the presidential campaign of 1980. Once again, this one occurred half a world away, in Afghanistan. A massive airlift of Russian troops and armaments descended on that country—shortly to be recognized for what it was, an invasion of this once independent state that had fallen increasingly under Soviet influence.

Suddenly Carter was confronted with yet another crisis, and again it provided a rationale for staying off the campaign trail. Four days after the Russian invasion of Afghanistan, he sent a telegram to the *Des Moines Register and Tribune,* which was sponsoring a scheduled debate among the Democratic candidates Carter, Kennedy, and Brown, withdrawing on the grounds that the crisis required that he stay in Washington. Iran, he suggested, might deliberately "precipitate a crisis or an incident" during any absence. Moreover, Powell said, the crisis made it inappropriate for the President to debate by way of a television hookup from the Oval Office. On the same grounds Carter rejected a proposal that he debate Kennedy and Brown on domestic issues alone, with Iran off-limits by agreement.* Rosalynn Carter and the President's old friend Charles Kirbo were said to share his position against debating.

At a lunch with reporters, Carter expanded on these matters. It would not be wise for him, he said, to do anything of a personal, political nature that could jeopardize national unity. He said he hoped to be able to start campaigning soon, but he had no intention of doing so until either the hostages were freed or there was a good prospect that they were about to be. Both Kennedy and Brown complained loudly, and so did the *Des Moines Register,* but to no avail.

The President's decision to pull out of the Iowa debate had in fact been reached only after serious disagreements were voiced among his political advisers, with Carter himself directly involved. Most of his aides argued that he ought to go ahead with the debate, as an opportunity to bury Kennedy before his campaign could get off the ground. Mondale said much later: "I've always thought that if the President had been able to debate Kennedy in Iowa, it would have been over right there." Others believed he should do so because otherwise Kennedy had an excuse for staying in the campaign until he could redeem himself somewhere else. But Carter was mindful of the need to preserve his presidential posture. "If I debate," one insider recalled him saying at one meeting, "I'll go out to Iowa a president and come

*For a time, the newspaper threatened to exclude Brown from the Democratic debate on grounds he really wasn't running in Iowa. But Brown set up a campaign headquarters across from the *Register and Tribune* building, began appearing in the state, and complained persistently enough so that the paper finally yielded.

back a candidate." And that, he said, wouldn't help his efforts either to free the hostages or to be renominated. And besides, there was still the general expectation that the crisis would be resolved in a few weeks or months at most.

To justify the President's decision not to debate, Powell leaked a fascinating document to one of Carter's favorite, and favorably disposed, reporters. It was a memo Powell had written to Carter summing up all the reasons the President's political advisers had mustered as to why he *should* debate in Iowa, among them: "A debate in this format places you in the strongest position and EMK [Kennedy] in the weakest. He has shown signs of late that he is perfecting his stump speech but there is no reason to believe that he is able to handle a tough give-and-take. Since there is little chance that you will be able to campaign personally in Iowa, the debate is your own chance to have a personal impact before the first round of caucuses. EMK is practically living in the state and his continued presence will help him." The memo also argued that once Carter decided to forgo the Iowa debate and stay off the campaign trail, it would be very difficult to resume until the hostage crisis was over, and "that could be longer than any of us would like to think." The memo acknowledged the political strategists knew of arguments against debating advanced by Vance, Brzezinski, and other foreign-policy advisers, and that there might be factors concerning Afghanistan they could not assess, "but we thought you should at least have the benefit of our view from the political trenches."

But the most important thing about the memo was a notation written on it in Carter's hand: "Jody—I can't disagree with any of this but I cannot break away from my duties here which are extraordinary now and ones which only I can fulfill. We will just have to take the adverse political consequences and make the best of it. Right now both Iran and Afghanistan look bad and will need my constant attention."

Bud Abbott had never served up a better straight line to Lou Costello than Powell to Carter, and the memo was quickly characterized as such in the press. Carter's notation was so self-serving that the immediate and widespread suspicion was that the whole thing had been a put-up job. One Carter insider, while professing not to know whether that was the case, described the language used as "Nixonian"—stilted and laden with self-righteousness. Carter aides, insisting the memo itself was legitimate, acknowledged sheepishly that Carter's handwritten comments may have been less than spontaneous.

Long afterward, Kennedy acknowledged that Carter's decision to duck the debate in Iowa hurt his own campaign and "complicated it enormously. . . . The economic policies were ripe for the kind of dialogue, discussion and debate which I think we could have had," he said. That kind of debate, he went on, would have attracted enormous attention and had a major effect on the outcome of the campaign. As for Carter, had he looked down the road, he might have seen trouble ahead in not debating, but he did not.

Going into the Iowa precinct caucuses, all the presidential candidates of both parties except one—Jimmy Carter—were now in the field, campaigning aggressively and turning their professionals, their masters of the new political technology, loose on the voters. But because of what was happening in Iran and Afghanistan, the presidential campaign of 1980 was getting under way with all of the principals themselves reduced to captives of circumstance.

5.
"The Functional Equivalent of a Primary"

John P. Sears, Ronald Reagan's campaign manager, seemed uncharacteristically defensive when he arrived in Des Moines on January 19, 1980. It was just two days before the precinct caucuses at which Republicans were to begin the process of choosing delegates, who in turn would choose their presidential nominee. At dinner at the Fort Des Moines Hotel, we badgered him about Ronald Reagan behaving as the Imperial Candidate and devoting so little attention to the Iowa campaign. And Sears could reply only that the organization was in place to produce the required vote. Wait and see. Everything was under control; no further explanation was required.

On the face of it, Ronald Wilson Reagan had reason enough to behave as an Imperial Candidate, and John Sears at least some excuse for complacency. Almost from the moment of Gerald Ford's defeat at the hands of Jimmy Carter in 1976, the conservative former governor of California had been accepted throughout the party as its leading candidate for the 1980 nomination.

Ford himself continued to rank with Reagan in surveys of the presidential preference of Republicans. But few who knew Ford believed he would be willing to subject himself to another campaign, and the fact that he had lost the White House as an incumbent minimized the demand for him to do so. Moreover, Reagan seemed ideally positioned to lead a party turning ever more to the right.

Reagan's primacy did not mean, however, that he had the field to himself. The obvious vulnerability of Jimmy Carter had given added value to the Republican nomination; if he could be president, several long-odds candidates reasoned, what the hell, anyone could be president.

Reagan's age—if elected in 1980, he would be seventy years old seventeen days after taking office—also made the situation more fluid than it might otherwise have been. The primary voters had never been confronted with a candidate with that much mileage on him, and no one knew how they might react. Moreover, there was always the unspoken thought that Reagan could be eliminated overnight if he fell victim to an illness of even minimal severity. One result of this uncertainty was the presence in the field of other conservatives who were willing, at least privately, to concede they were running on the chance the Reagan candidacy might collapse, for one reason or another, and an heir on the right would be needed. One of these was Senator Bob Dole, the acerbic Kansan who had been Ford's running mate in 1976. Another was Philip Crane, an Illinois congressman of ten years' experience whose collar-ad good looks and ability to articulate conservative theory had built a small but dedicated following for him, especially among rightists concerned about Reagan's age.

Others were drawn into the campaign by still another reality of the Republican condition. Although Reagan was clearly ascendant, there was a substantial enough bloc of nonbelievers in the party to encourage visions of a coalition somewhere down the road behind "a moderate alternative."

By the time Sears arrived in Des Moines there had been nothing to suggest any such weakness on Reagan's part or any hint of a coalition against him. But there was good cause for some uneasiness in the Reagan campaign, nonetheless, in the signs that this first genuine test of 1980 might not be following the form charts. The morning after dinner at the Fort Des Moines Hotel Sears began to feel it himself. "I got very concerned," he said later. "I went to church on Sunday and the priest was up there telling people in a nonpartisan way how they could go about voting in the caucuses. I said, 'Jesus, if that's happening in places like this, we're in trouble.' "

Ronald Reagan's strategy for Iowa, devised by Sears, had been dictated by the history of Republican Party caucuses in Iowa. Only a handful of people would actually participate, so the main thing was to build a machine of workers who would see to it that your candidate's supporters reached the caucuses at the appointed hour. Sears had just such a "program," as he liked to call it, in place. It would produce 30,000 votes for Reagan on the night of January 21, enough to be certain of winning in a multicandidate field even if the turnout reached 50,000 or 60,000—more than twice the 22,000 who had taken part in the competition between Gerald Ford and Ronald Reagan four years earlier. Everything was under control.

But the world had turned since 1976. When the results started coming in from the 2531 precincts in Iowa, it was quickly clear that Sears and his chief lieutenant in the Reagan campaign, political director Charles Black, had miscalculated. "I remember the night of the thing," Sears said long after the fact. "We got down there and we had quotas in each of the precincts, you know, [based on] past experience and our program. Well, the program worked and we got our thirty thousand, a little more."

But what was obvious from the returns in the sample precincts, however, was that Iowa Republicans were not conforming to the "program." "We were getting the first few precincts in," Sears said, "and we knew where they were coming from, what each precinct was, what we ought to get to make our thirty. So we started to look at that and, hell, we were right on point. But the numbers . . . didn't look right. I said to Charlie, 'This isn't right.' Everybody was wildly happy, because the numbers we were looking for were all there. Except, when you looked at everybody else's numbers, I said, 'Jesus, let's add up these things and find out what the turnout is going to be.' "

So Sears and Black made some quick new calculations and projected a turnout across Iowa of 120,000 Republicans, more than five times what it had been in 1976, an all-time high. And these last-minute projections, unlike the strategy, proved correct. More than 110,000 Republicans had voted.* What Ronald Rea-

*The precise number will never be known. On caucus night there was a computer malfunction at the state party tabulation center in Des Moines, and a few precincts never bothered to report.

gan and his managers discovered that night was that the rules had changed. The Iowa caucuses had been transformed by a series of factors into what one of Reagan's competitors, Senator Howard H. Baker of Tennessee, had been saying for weeks was the "functional equivalent of a primary." Indeed, it was. That turnout of something approaching 120,000 represented more than 20 percent of Iowa's enrolled Republicans, and there were several states whose primary vote never reached those proportions.

This meant, of course, that the "program" for Ronald Reagan was inadequate. He did get his 30,000 votes—31,348 in fact—for just under 30 percent of the total. But George Bush, the former ambassador, congressman, and CIA director, had 33,530, or almost 33 percent. No one else was close. Baker received 16 percent, John B. Connally, Jr., just under 10 percent. Representatives Crane and John B. Anderson and Senator Dole, none of whom had made an intensive effort to campaign in Iowa, trailed far behind.

Sears was not the only political operative who had miscalculated in Iowa, not by any means. But he *was* the only one managing the campaign of a front-running candidate who suffered from the miscalculations because he failed to fulfill the expectations he had raised in the press and political community.

The managers of George Bush were just as mistaken, if more successful. A few days before the voting Rich Bond, the young New Yorker running Bush's operation, had identified about 8000 likely supporters to be brought to the caucuses one way or the other. It was enough for a base that would give Bush at least a reasonable chance to win if the turnout was, as Bond expected, about 40,000.

Rich Bond's operation was extraordinarily thorough. Because he feared that some supporters new to politics might be hesitant about attending the caucuses, he arranged to send to each of those identified as pro-Bush a mailing telling him when and where his caucus would be held, and listing the names of neighbors who also were supporting Bush and would be there. There were also broader efforts. One mailing of 400,000 pieces was sent to every Republican household in the state. Others were targeted to, for example, farmers in Republican areas. Bush commercials had run on local television as early as Labor Day of 1979. At the local level the Bush campaign was similarly intense. For example, at Mason City, the community of 33,000 that was Meredith Willson's model for "River City" in *The Music Man,* local coordinator Diane Ruebling had established a bank of twenty telephones on which 2000 calls to Republican voters were completed eight days before the caucuses.

But the assumption in Bush's camp, as in Reagan's, was that this was a controlled situation. The difference was that Bush had given the state months of personal campaigning to reinforce that organizational effort, so that it was possible to get what politicians call a multiplier effect. The votes didn't have to come from organization alone. They might walk in off the street.

Iowa politicians also had underestimated the interest in this first test of the 1980 campaign. Steve Roberts, the Republican state chairman at the time, was talking in terms of 50,000 to 60,000 votes, although others cautioned that might be a little high. They couldn't imagine that many people coming out on a cold Monday night in January, and that is the only kind of night you have in Iowa at that time of year. The only exception seemed to be Richard Redman, a perceptive semiprofessional from Des Moines who had been brought in to try to salvage Howard Baker's campaign. What he was hearing, he said at lunch one day, suggested very big numbers—perhaps even as many as 100,000.

The night of the voting it was clear Redman was right. In precinct after precinct, the turnout set new standards. In Precinct 1, in a largely Democratic neighborhood on Des Moines' east side, for example, there had been forty people crowded into Mike Hartley's basement four years earlier. This time, meeting at the Adams Elementary School, there were three times that many Democrats, and down the corridor fifty-one Republicans met in a small auditorium; in 1976 there had been only four.

On the face of it, there seemed to be far more reason to expect a substantial turnout among Democrats. Their caucuses had become something of a tradition. Although most of the national press ignored them, George McGovern and Edmund S. Muskie had competed there in 1972, and some union leaders had conducted a campaign for "uncommitted" votes with the idea of throwing them to Hubert H. Humphrey later in the delegate-selection process. And 1976, of course, was the year in which the caucuses established an unknown politician from Georgia as a serious factor in the Democratic presidential equation. The turnout then was 38,500 Democrats, so now—with an incumbent president being challenged by a Kennedy—there was reason to expect growth. No one seriously disputed the prediction of Democratic State Chairman Ed Campbell that the figure would reach 75,000 and perhaps higher. As it turned out the Democratic vote also went over 100,000.

What was less obvious was the effect of the currents running in the Republican competition that would make it inevitably the "functional equivalent of a primary." For one thing, the campaign in Iowa itself and elsewhere had been under way for a year or more. Politicians always fight the last war, and the lesson of Jimmy Carter's unprecedented success in 1976 had been that the way to succeed was to start early and build a following brick by brick. Phil Crane, for example, had announced his candidacy even before the midterm elections, on August 2, 1978. Bush had been enlisting local backers in Iowa since the spring of 1979, long before there was any serious competition for their services or commitment.

But Reagan also had moved quickly after Ford's defeat in 1976 by establishing in February 1977 a valuable campaign resource for conservative Republican office-seekers. He took a million dollars left from his presidential campaign and set up Citizens for the Republic with himself as chairman. The new group, with old Reagan hand Lyn Nofziger as the staff director, would give financial and other support to selected conservative Republicans and, in Nofziger's words, "try to help broaden the conservative Republican base." The organization was immediately seen for what it was—a vehicle for encouraging (some said buying) support within the party for a 1980 Reagan rerun.

Shortly afterward, Reagan was in Washington to throw cold water on talk among conservatives about a third, national conservative party. "It makes more sense to build on that [existing] grouping than to break it up and start over," he told the annual Conservative Political Action Conference. "Rather than a third party we can have a new first party made up of people who share our principles." And the next day Reagan was on Capitol Hill paying courtesy calls on Republican senators and congressmen. Was he going to run in 1980? "I've no way of knowing," he said, with that patented naïveté of his. But he added: "I've learned not to close my mind."

All through 1977 and well into 1978, Reagan continued to play it coy while positioning himself for another campaign. Citizens for the Republic quickly became the money well into which only conservative Republicans could dip. At the Republican National Committee, one of Reagan's chief 1976 political hands, Charles Black, was installed as political director. And Reagan himself continued to be a spokesman of Republican opposition to the Panama Canal treaties as negotiated by Carter—in 1977 the litmus test of true conservatism. His charge of 1976 that Ford wanted to "give away" the Canal was now a standard part of the conservative Republican catechism, and much more readily voiced against a Democratic President.

In early June 1978 a development in Reagan's own California seemed to many at the time to give Reagan a lock on the 1980 nomination. The state's voters, after a highly emotional campaign, overwhelmingly approved Proposition 13, an initiative imposing a lid on property taxes. The initiative had been placed on the California ballot through the efforts of two longtime critics of state tax policy, Howard Jarvis and Paul Gann. But the forerunner of Proposition 13 was a similar tax-limiting proposal, called Proposition 1 in 1973, pushed unsuccessfully by Reagan while he was governor. Suddenly "Prop 13" became a household word all over the country, triggering a "taxpayers' revolt" that threatened to make all of Reagan's dreams about "cutting government down to size" come true. Overnight he was an economic prophet, and he reveled in it.

On the night of June 6, 1978, when the dimensions of what the California electorate had done were becoming clear, Reagan was in Denver speaking at a dinner for Colorado Republican legislative candidates. He brought them to their feet with all the old taxpayers' revolt lines: "Herbert Hoover was the first President to give his entire salary to the federal government. And now we're all doing it.... We're robbing Peter to pay Paul. They don't know we're all named Paul. Peter died a long time ago.... Proposition 13 was opposed by the same people who have their snouts in the trough. It's the Boston Tea Party without the tea." It was all, as it always was with Reagan, very simple. It was like coping with a free-spending son. "You can tell him to be less extravagant," Reagan said, "or you can cut his allowance. Well, it's time to cut the government's allowance." The audience loved it.

One of the dinner hosts that night was the ultraconservative beer magnate Joseph Coors. He introduced Reagan as the "father" of the taxpayers' revolt and "the man who should be in the White House, and will be after 1980." Reagan smiled benignly. He clearly did not disagree. On the hotel elevator on the way up to his room later, we informed him of the early returns from California, and he broke into a broad grin. "I hope it's really big," he said. In his suite he talked proudly of his refunds of budget surpluses in California and of Proposition 1, thus readily acknowledging paternity of Prop 13. It would not be long, he said, before there would be a Constitutional amendment clamping a lid on federal spending. And in our conversation he edged even closer to a 1980 candidacy. "I haven't closed any doors," he said, "and I don't have the same restrictions I had [in 1976]." He meant, of course, that this time the incumbent was a Democrat, not a Republican.

Reagan's remarks to the state legislative candidates in Denver that night can be seen in retrospect as the slogans of the sweeping social revolution he would eventually embark upon once he was elected president. They were slogans and catch-phrases that had marked his oratory ever since he first embarked on the speaking circuit as a spokesman/booster for General Electric in 1954 and eventually, in 1964, as a campaigner for Republican presidential candidate Barry Goldwater. A month seldom went by in the intervening sixteen years when he did not voice them with a maddening repetition, but as the country gradually grew more conservative, they found an ever wider and more responsive audience. They were the chief components of the ideological engine that drove his ambitions. And so, if there had been any doubt before that Reagan would try for the presidency again in 1980, the phenomenon of Prop 13 and the taxpayers' revolt ended it. In state after state, groups sprang up to sponsor legislation or initiatives to put a clamp on state taxing or spending, or both. Also, as Reagan had noted, a move for a Constitutional amendment to limit taxes was rolling through state legislatures. A proposal to call a Constitutional convention to write such an amendment had quietly been winning approval in the legislatures. The taxpayers' revolt seemed to be sweeping the country, and it was not far-fetched then to see it sweeping Ronald Reagan into the White House as well. In late October, State Representative Fred Eckert of New York reported that Reagan, campaigning for him in Rochester, had confided: "Fred, we're going."

By that time, it was like announcing that the sun was rising. A few months later John Sears, who had masterminded Reagan's 1976 campaign, began putting the organization together again.

What was clear to all the other prospective candidates was that although Reagan might be vulnerable because of his age, he was certain to be the front-runner—and one with enough of a following so that if anyone were to compete with him effectively, or even be there to pick up the pieces, he would have to make early and intensive efforts. The press also seemed eager for anything that might reveal the pecking order in the Republican Party. As far back as March 1979, for example, political reporters had gathered at a Midwest Republican Leadership Conference in Indianapolis at which several prospective candidates—but not Ronald Reagan—spoke. This was the first of a series of events that became known as "the cattle shows"—Republican dinners or "candidate forums" to which the candidates were bidden to show themselves, while the local Republicans enjoyed the press attention and, not incidentally, often used them shamelessly to raise money for their own purposes. In many cases, someone would distribute straw ballots. At Indianapolis, for example, it was CBS News, and Connally won easily after giving a characteristically forceful speech.

There was a conspicuous lack of subtlety in some of these af-

fairs. A state fund-raising dinner at the New Hampshire High-
way Hotel in Concord in the spring of 1979 lured Connally,
Bush, Anderson, Crane, Dole, and the ubiquitous Harold Stassen.
As a preliminary to the dinner speeches (where the judges of the
press declared Connally the "winner" again) the candidates
were lined up on a podium for a picture-taking session. Then
each was assigned to a small area of the room in which to stand
to be interviewed by anyone who happened to be interested.
Connally was the star of the show and attracted a small crowd.
Some of the others were saved from awkward moments only by
friends in the national press who found the whole thing a little
embarrassing themselves and stopped by to ask a question or
two.

By the fall of 1979 some of these events were becoming more
sophisticated and, by the estimates of both politicians and press,
more important in gauging the relative positions of the candidates. Reagan, following Sears's strategy of remaining above the
mob, snubbed most of these events. His lead in the national opinion polls, due largely to his wider recognition among the voters,
already had given him a position as king of the hill that was not
worth risking by mixing with the rabble. The only Republican
close to him in those surveys was the man who had defeated him
for the nomination four years earlier, Gerald R. Ford, and few
Republicans who knew the former President believed he would
be willing to run again.

But two events, in one of which Reagan was forced to participate, did have some bearing on the way the candidates were
seen long before attention turned to Iowa. The first was a "presidential forum" held by Maine Republicans in Portland on November 3, 1979, a year and a day before the election. It dealt a
blow to Howard Baker from which he never really recovered.

From the outset Baker had been a special figure in the politics of this presidential campaign—what might be called the
Washington candidate. He was more highly respected by politicians and the press than any of the others because he was so intelligent, knowledgeable, and personable. Inside the White
House both President Carter and Vice President Mondale made
it clear they considered Baker the most formidable of their po-

tential adversaries, and reporters and political operatives alike shared that view. It was recognized, of course, that he had problems with the Far Right of the Republican Party, in large measure because he had supported ratification of the Panama Canal treaties. But he was seen as so demonstrably the "class" of the Republican field that it seemed only a matter of time before he would put that handicap behind him by winning in the primaries.

The press and the political professionals, however, had been wrong about such candidates in the past—Ed Muskie in 1972 is a classic example—and they were wrong about Howard Baker, although it was by no means apparent as the campaign grew more intense during the fall of 1979.

Despite the special place he held, there were always some nagging questions about Baker. Did he want the presidency enough to do the things required to win it? Or was he, like so many others, too accustomed to the cosseted life of a congressional power to survive a national campaign? Baker was aware of these doubts about whether he had the requisite "fire in the belly," and so was his principal political adviser, consultant Douglas Bailey. So what Bailey proposed, and Baker seriously considered, was that he simply resign from the Senate to demonstrate his commitment.

"I thought about resigning," Baker said later, "and Doug Bailey urged, wrote memoranda, discussed, wheedled, and pled with me to resign from the Senate in order to run for president. Looking back on it, that would have been a remarkable public relations gesture because it would have said all sorts of things." In addition to demonstrating his "absolute commitment" to the race, Baker reasoned, a resignation would have given him "absolute freedom of time and movement" away from the demands of the Senate and his position as minority leader.

The arguments over this decision were often heated. At one point Baker's wife Joy (the daughter of another minority leader, Everett McKinley Dirksen) burst into tears as her husband was pressed to put it all aside and get on the road. "It was an attractive thing to do," Baker said. But he recognized that it "sounded too slick" and, more to the point, would put him in an untenable

position with the voters of Tennessee, who had just reelected
him in 1978. "I kept thinking, 'How in hell am I going to explain
to all those folks that, you know, they elected me to the Senate
and then I resigned?'" There was, of course, no answer. "It
made the Senate race in '78 and my service here and my reelection as leader . . . so clearly and unambiguously connected to the
presidential campaign that finally I decided [against it]."

So early in 1979 he took a less dramatic course, set up an "exploratory" campaign operation, and began making Lincoln Day
speeches to Republican groups in such remote places as Gales-
burg, Illinois, to demonstrate his zeal. But throughout the spring
and summer, while agents for George Bush won commitments
from leading Republican moderates in Iowa, the Baker campaign was largely invisible. The candidate himself stayed on the
job as minority leader of the Senate. The decision on the new
Strategic Arms Limitation Treaty was supposed to be coming to
the floor, and Baker and his lieutenants were convinced it would
be the center of a major national debate over foreign policy in
which he wanted to participate. And if he was on those nightly
network news programs leading the opposition to SALT II, so
much the better for his campaign.

That "great debate" never materialized. Finally, it was decided that Baker would make his announcement November 1 and
then embark on what the press always calls a "whirlwind" campaign trip that would take him through Boston, Providence, Burlington, Vermont, and Concord, New Hampshire, before
arriving at Portland, Maine, for that presidential forum. A victory there would give his campaign a running start, and a planeload of national reporters—Baker's stature assured that kind of
coverage—would be along to see that the message reached Republicans across the country. Two weeks before the event, Baker
strategists were confiding that they were sure of winning the
Maine forum.

There was, of course, reason for optimism. Hattie Bickmore,
the Maine Republican state chairman, was counted as a Baker
supporter, and, more important, Senator Bill Cohen, the most
popular politician in the state, had endorsed him. Maine Republicans are predominately moderate, anyway, so it seemed nothing could go wrong, even considering that George Bush had a

summer home in the state. Reagan had a professional named Cynthia Adams running an operation in Portland, but it was not fertile ground for the conservative from California. And John Connally's campaign was scarcely visible.

On the eve of the forum, Baker arrived as scheduled with his planeload of reporters. Like the others, he opened a hospitality suite for the delegates at the big Holiday Inn downtown. But he left for bed before many of the delegates had a chance to meet him, and there were some sotto voce complaints, helped along by the drinks being poured in every suite, about being taken for granted. The following morning, at the convention center itself, groups of delegates came out of meetings with Senator Cohen making the same complaint somewhat more openly. And when it came time for Baker, normally an accomplished stump speaker, to address the delegates, he gave a dreadful performance to an audience that earlier had cheered both Connally and Bush with great enthusiasm. Watching from the bleachers along the side of the hall, a Baker worker from Boston, Carolyn Stewart, confessed that she was getting uneasy.

She had reason to be. When the ballots were finally counted, George Bush had defeated Baker 466 to 446. The planeload of reporters had a much better story than they had anticipated—a "stunning upset," to use the favored cliché, rather than a predictable victory. On the flight back to Washington late that night Baker's longtime assistant, Ron McMahan, drank six miniatures of Jack Daniels in quick succession and tried out various alibis to explain what had happened, including the suggestion that the Reagan managers had sandbagged them by diverting Reagan votes to Bush to put him over the top. Baker himself was aware of how serious a loss he had suffered. Later that night he told his wife, McMahan, and another close adviser, James Cannon, "It may not be possible to recover from this."

It was, of course, an intrinsically trivial event. But, like so many things in American politics, it was given disproportionate significance at the time because of the way it affected perceptions of the candidates. Baker's loss seemed to confirm the whispers about the ineptitude of his campaign operation. More to the point, the struggling Bush had earned another credential in his effort to be "taken seriously" as a valid contender for moderate

Republican support. The discovery several weeks later that Josie Martin, a twenty-two-year-old state legislator from New Hampshire, had been in Portland quietly working the state for Bush for several weeks before the forum did nothing to take the gloss off his success. Spontaneous or not, it was a victory.

Baker's blunder in allowing his prospects in Maine to be overstated paled in comparison, however, to a similar gaffe made by another candidate trying to establish himself as the prime alternative to Reagan—John B. Connally, Jr. It happened only two weeks later in Orlando, Florida.

Florida Republicans, too, had been following the early attention the press was giving the 1980 campaign and the success other organizations had been having with their straw votes. Bill Taylor, the state party chairman, saw an opportunity to capture some of that attention and, simultaneously, build the lists of activist Republicans and potential contributors in a state in which Democrats had always held an overwhelming advantage.

The result was a complex scheme under which each county caucus would choose delegates to a state convention in Orlando at which there would be a vote on presidential preference. The interest of the press would force the candidates to spend both time and money trying to enlist their backers at the lowest levels. And unlike Maine, Florida was a state of sufficient political importance—its primary in March had been established since 1972 as the most significant of the Southern contests—that even Ronald Reagan could not refuse to participate.

Connally saw this as an opportunity to cut Reagan quickly down to size. A defeat for the conservative leader here, where he would be presumed to be at his best, could change the whole shape of the campaign. Throughout the summer and early fall Connally went to Florida repeatedly to seek support at the county meetings. He installed a professional operation, enlisted some respected local supporters, and even began testing television advertising spots in the Tampa-St. Petersburg market. His spending in the state would reach something over $300,000.

As the time for the convention drew closer, Connally appeared to be doing well. Reagan was winning most of the official delegates, particularly from the smaller counties, but in those

areas in which the results seemed to turn on organizational effort, Connally was at least holding his own. There were indications of trouble backstage in the Reagan campaign in Florida,
and the Connally managers became infected with optimism. By
the time of the convention at Orlando Reagan was still the clear
favorite to win the vote, but it seemed Connally might make a
close race of it, enough to win one of those triumphs over expectations that often keep politicians afloat. Then the Connally
camp blundered. Connally himself and Eddie Mahe, the veteran
professional running his political operation, suggested incau-
tiously to reporters that they expected to come within an ace of
Reagan at a minimum, and might very well defeat him.

Connally, however, had been a flawed candidate from the beginning. The power of his personality, coupled with his obvious
ability, had made him a favorite of those businessmen who suspected Reagan lacked the capacity to be president. But Connally
evoked such a strong negative reaction among voters that
months before, Democratic pollster Pat Caddell, studying his
own data, had been willing to bet the farm Connally would never be nominated. In South Carolina a skilled young professional
named Lee Atwater, later to serve in Reagan's White House, had
been pressed by Senator Strom Thurmond to run Connally's
campaign there, but had refused for just that reason. On the basis of a study of eighty polls involving various candidates,
Atwater had formulated a rule that no one could succeed if he
had "negatives" of 35 percent or higher, unless his "positives"
were at least 15 percentage points better. And thirteen polls on
Connally, taken in a variety of states, had shown "negatives" of
37 percent, "positives" of only 26.

This, of course, was not clear to everyone in politics by any
means. Sears, for example, believed Connally would be Reagan's
most formidable opponent. And Bush, who detested his fellow
Houstonian, was apprehensive about him. One of the products of
that force of personality was Connally's extraordinary ability to
raise money, and at this stage everyone was thinking in terms of
a more conventional campaign, based on organizational effort
and television advertising, than the one that finally developed.

That they were overestimating Connally became clear when

the votes were counted that warm afternoon in Orlando. Reagan had won with 36 percent and Connally had just under 27. George Bush, largely on the strength of an eleventh-hour effort, had finished a respectable third with 21 percent. There were 267 representatives of the news media there to cover the whole thing—and to alter, once again, the perceptions of the candidates.

As had been the case in Maine, the event in a conventional sense was not meaningful; no delegates were elected to the nominating convention, still eight months away. But the news media could describe Reagan's candidacy as reinforced, just as Bush's had been in Maine earlier in the month, and strengthen the public's doubts about Connally's viability. He had spent $300,000 and much of his personal effort in Florida and failed to deliver. His protestation that it was now obviously a two-man contest was less convincing.

None of these events passed unnoticed in Iowa. The *Des Moines Register and Tribune*, newspapers with an extraordinary commitment to national politics considering their distance from Washington, followed the progress of the candidates in detail, interspersing reports on Florida and Maine with their own detailed coverage of the evolving campaign in Iowa. Indeed, by the time the horde of national reporters arrived right after January 1 to cover the caucus campaign, the *Register* had prepared sets of clippings from its library to anticipate the requests for background that poured in to political writer James Flansburg. A set comprised more than one hundred articles.

The arrival of the national press became still another pressure on Iowans to participate. Now it was not just the *Des Moines Register* and local television talking about the caucuses, but all three national networks as well. So what if only a fraction of the voters would come to the caucuses? What would it matter that Iowa Democrats were choosing only 50 of their party's 3331 national delegates and the Republicans only 37 of their 1994? Who cared if the precinct caucuses were only the first step in a process that would lead through conventions at county, congressional district, and state levels before the final delegations were chosen? It was the first state in which real live voters were to make a substantive decision, and there was no escape from the media. Straw votes in Maine and Florida might be dismissed as artificial; this was the genuine article. The campaign had truly begun.

This media riot was a new experience for Iowa. Although the caucuses of 1976 had attracted intensive coverage, it had been heavily weighted by those news organizations that regularly devote a great deal of talent and money to covering national politics. This time there was a quantum leap. Nearly every newspaper or broadcasting outlet of even modest pretension had its own reporter on the scene. All three television networks had camera crews roaming all over the state, covering the candidates, seeking out feature stories, interviewing local politicians and voters, spending untold millions of dollars.

NBC was set up at the Hotel Fort Des Moines, known locally as "the Republican hotel," and not only John Chancellor and the nightly news program but also Tom Brokaw and the *Today* show originated from there. CBS had not only Walter Cronkite to broadcast from the downtown Civic Center, but enough reporters, technicians, and publicists—more than two hundred at one point—so that the telephone company assigned the network its own prefix for the extra lines being installed. The same was true for ABC, based at the "Democratic hotel," the Savery.

Correspondents and cameras had arrived from Swedish, French, and German networks, and, the *Register* reported at one point, there were two separate crews from Japanese television. The city was awash in reporters, and so was much of the state. A reporter who pulled into a truck stop along Interstate 35 to sample that special Iowa delicacy, the pork loin sandwich, could see a wire-service reporter from Washington driving out and a few moments later another from the New York *Daily News* arriving to join him at the counter. The parking lot of the Savery was crammed with rental cars, and the Chamber of Commerce estimated the caucuses would bring in 1200 outsiders who would spend $500,000 locally, an estimate that probably did not gauge properly either their hunger or their thirst. It was the kind of attention that could not avoid stimulating interest in the caucuses. If there were that many people paying that much attention, there must be something important going on.

But the interest in the caucuses among Republicans could not be attributed solely to the intensity of the news media. What quickly became apparent, even before all the network stars arrived, is that Republican voters were unusually interested this year, particularly at the prospect of new faces. Less than six years after Watergate and the resignation of Richard Nixon, they were willing to become involved in the political system again.

The most obvious evidence was their willingness to turn up at meetings at which the candidates were to appear. This was no surprise, of course, when the candidate was a genuine celebrity—meaning a president or vice president, a Ted Kennedy or Ronald Reagan. But even those who were relatively unknown, such as George Bush or Howard Baker, could find an audience of several hundred waiting on a chilly, dark night in Iowa City. They were attentive listeners, too. Many of them were undecided on their choice but determined to take part for the first time and at least have a voice. The issues—concern over inflation at home, uncertainty over the meaning of the hostage crisis in Iran—were compelling enough to dictate just such participation. A teacher in Knoxville, a small town less than an hour southeast of Des Moines, told us one icy Saturday morning: "Everyone always says this is an important election this time. They say it every four years, and you know it's just so much Bull Durham. But I think people really feel that way this year. Things are in a hell of a mess."

Dick Redman, belatedly trying to rescue Senator Baker's campaign, understood this reaction. And so, to a degree at least, did those running Bush's campaign at both the national and state levels. But John Sears and the other Reagan strategists were not "on the ground" and were hearing nothing of the kind. Some of the local Reagan leaders had been sending early warnings. And Kenny Kling, a field man, had sent Black a memo in May 1979 saying the caucuses were going to be just like a primary this time. But at headquarters in Washington and Los Angeles it was easy to brush aside such memos as the myopia of those too close to a situation to understand its place in the great scheme of things. And when local leaders complained during the fall of "slippage" in Reagan's position, it was easy to dismiss that as the kind of thing "national" always hears from field men who want to get more of the candidate's personal time and attention. After all, although Bush had made some modest gains, the Iowa Poll published by the *Register and Tribune* continued to show Reagan holding a commanding lead. In the survey taken November 28–December 1, 1979, he had 50 percent of the Republicans to only 14 for Bush, 12 for Connally, 11 for Baker. (Baker had been running second in August but lost ground after the fiasco in Maine.)

Morcover, Reagan was a familiar figure in Iowa. He had been making speeches there since 1967 and had built a strong core of support in 1976. Dutch Reagan was practically a local boy. He had started out as a sports broadcaster in Davenport and Des Moines. Would Iowans turn on him now? For George Bush?

The confidence, or complacency, among the Reagan strategists led to several decisions. There would be no polling of their own because it could not accurately measure anything, when so few voters actually would take part in the end. There would be no general mailings or television advertising. Reagan would make enough personal appearances to satisfy local leaders, at least one in each media market, but no more. And most important, he would not agree to debate in Iowa.

The Iowa debate was something new. The idea originated with James Gannon, a former *Wall Street Journal* reporter who was now executive editor of the *Register and Tribune.* The newspapers planned to sponsor two of them: one for the Republicans on January 5, and the other for the Democrats on January 7, two weeks before the caucuses. They would solicit television coverage, and all the candidates who were actively competing in the state would be invited to participate.

At Sears's urging, Reagan quickly rejected the invitation, arguing that a debate among Republican candidates would be "divisive." This was a strange concern, coming from someone who had challenged an incumbent president of his own party four years earlier. But Reagan had always been publicly devoted to the so-called eleventh commandment of the Republican Party: "Thou shalt not speak ill of another Republican," written during his 1966 campaign in California by the Republican state chairman at that time, Gaylord Parkinson. And now he feared a debate would "contribute to polarizing" the Republicans. "I was very sincere in that," he told us in the Oval Office after his inauguration. "I wasn't ducking it because I thought I was above the fray or anything. I just felt it was the wrong thing to do."

The real reason for Sears, however, had nothing to do with divisiveness. He had never been as confident as some of the Californians of Reagan's ability to handle himself well in such circumstances. Reagan was inclined to make outlandish—and politically damaging—statements at times, and this might be one of those occasions. The memory of Gerald Ford's gaffe on Poland in the 1976 presidential debates was fresh in Sears's memory. Why take the chance when his candidate was so clearly far ahead of the pack? "When you are the front-runner," he said later, "you're in a position where you want to cut back on your risks, naturally. You're the guy who gets the most attention wherever the hell you go ... so it's not necessarily to your advantage to have everyone discussing whether you did well or didn't."

But the basic judgment Sears had made about the likely turnout at the caucuses also influenced this decision. He was aware there would be pressure to debate in New Hampshire, before the primary there, and he was prepared to accept that. In Iowa, however, the program was to win with organization by turning out those 30,000 votes, and it didn't make sense, he said, to "raise the relevance" of the caucuses by joining the debate. "Any extra attention that we gave to the whole thing might not be good because we might get more people out to vote than we wanted to," he said.

There was no serious quarrel with Sears's decision within the Reagan campaign. The candidate himself yielded to Sears on such things, and so did Senator Paul Laxalt, the Nevada Republican who served as campaign chairman and was one of those closest to Reagan. "We had a lot of trouble," Laxalt said later. "Our own people thought Iowa was being ignored or neglected and Bush was moving in effectively. But it was decided that due to the fact the governor was best-known nationally and strongest, with Iowa roots, he should remain above the fray. . . . So going into Iowa, there was a great reluctance on John's role, but we were all deferring to the fact that he was a good strategist." Or, as Charlie Black put it, "John had been right about everything up to that time."

What Sears did not reckon with, of course, was the growing interest in the debate that was generated not only by the *Register* but by the voters' interest in the candidates. The "relevance" of the debate as an event became well established, and Reagan was the odd man out.

The debate itself was not memorable, although all of the Republicans who did participate—Anderson, Baker, Bush, Connally, Crane, and Dole—managed to avoid making any gaffes. If there was a winner, it was probably Anderson, who alone chose to defend the President's decision to impose an embargo on grain shipments to the Soviet Union. But Reagan, watching it on television at his home in California, began to feel uneasy about his decision not to take part. "I have to say that, having seen it, I got the first feeling that I had been wrong," he said later, "that seeing it . . . there didn't seem to be that kind of polarization."

Reagan's refusal to debate was made more pointed by his limited campaign schedule. In the end he made only eight stops in Iowa, and his opponents delighted in pointing out that he had spent fewer hours in the state than Bush had spent days. This decision also had been made by Sears, and, again, it was essentially a defensive one. His candidate had only one speech, a catalogue of "horror stories" about government's failures, and Sears feared that with too much exposure, the repetition would not wear well.

There was, however, a moment when, considering the closeness of the vote January 21, the result might have been altered. Reagan had a rally scheduled just outside Des Moines for the final Saturday night of the campaign, and half an hour of television time on a statewide network had been purchased. Sears proposed that Reagan forget his cue cards and use that time for a new speech criticizing President Carter's handling of the hostage situation. It would capture the headlines Sunday and Monday, the day of caucuses.

There was some risk, of course, in the notion of using the Iran issue in the campaign. A few weeks earlier Ted Kennedy had been sharply criticized for raising questions about United States policy toward the Shah. But Reagan was playing to a Republican constituency, and support for Carter's handling of the crisis among Republicans had never been as conspicuous as it seemed to be in the electorate as a whole.

Moreover, Sears was convinced that the President had become vulnerable by that time. "Carter had sort of topped out, I think, on the issue," he said. "He had gotten everything that was of value to him out of it. As you're going up the hill, if you hit a guy, then he lays back on you. The minute he's over the top of the hump, you can criticize him and everybody joins in and says, 'Yeah, that's right.' Well, I thought at that particular time he had just crossed over the hump, and it was right to take him on and to challenge him on why he hadn't done specifically more about [Iran] than what he was doing about it."

There was other evidence that the voters were more ready to hear something about Iran than the candidates seemed willing to say. When Howard Baker seemed to cross the line with a five-minute television commercial, which professionals considered the best in the early campaign, it lifted him out of the pack of anonymous also-rans in the Republican field. (It was built around a piece of film Douglas Bailey made during a speech Baker gave before students at Iowa State University. In it he proposed that an elite force should be created to deal with future crises involving terrorists, a group of 50,000 to be known as "America's First Brigade" that could be dispatched in just such emergencies as the one that had developed in Tehran. During the question period after the speech, an angry Iranian student rose and asked Baker why he was so concerned about international law being violated in the case of the hostages, but had not been similarly concerned during the reign of the Shah. Baker, obviously hot, pointed a finger at the student and replied: "Because, my friend, I'm interested in fifty Americans, that's why," and the crowd erupted into cheers.)

Reagan, however, rejected Sears's proposal, less because he had any qualms about attacking Carter than because he felt more comfortable with the familiar material. His lead among Republicans in the Iowa Poll had dropped—it was now Reagan 26 percent, Baker 18 percent, Bush 17 percent—but the survey had been made right after the debate, so it was easy to brush those figures aside as a temporary aberration. So Reagan used his half-hour of television for a carefully staged rally that would have done credit to Richard Nixon but earned no headlines.

The morning after the votes were counted, waiting for Sears to finish an appearance on the *Today* show, Charlie Black turned to Steve Roberts, the Republican state chairman, and shook his head. "Hell," he said, "I didn't know it was going to be a *primary.*"

That, however, is just what the Iowa caucuses had proven to be. They had done the job that in the past had belonged to the New Hampshire primary—clearing the underbrush of candidates with little future, and establishing a definite pecking order among those who remained.

Reagan had lost by only 2182 votes, but he was tarnished by his failure to meet the expectations he had raised (just as he had been, in the same way, when he lost the New Hampshire primary to Gerald Ford by only 1317 votes four years earlier).

The contest for the Republican nomination was indeed down to two men, as John Connally had been predicting all along. But the two were Ronald Reagan and George Bush. And if Reagan was not prepared to lose in Iowa, it was soon apparent that George Bush had not been prepared to win.

6.
Ambush at
Nashua

On December 21, 1979, just a month before the precinct caucuses were to be held in Iowa, Richard Wirthlin wrote a summary of the opinion surveys his firm, Decision Making Information, had just completed for Ronald Reagan. Reagan's lead over George Bush nationally was 57 percent to 13 percent, and he was ahead in every state in which a poll had been taken. Bush was still so little known that more than 40 percent of the Republicans who were questioned professed not to know enough about him even to rank him among the contenders for the 1980 presidential nomination. "While this is a liability," Wirthlin wrote, "it does indicate, however, that should he grab the early headlines by a win in Iowa, he could fast become, through favorable and massive media exposure, a rather and perhaps the only formidable opponent."

What this suggested was that George Bush enjoyed what the politicians call a "clean slate" nationally, just as he had statewide in Iowa when he began campaigning there ten months earlier. Voters had few negative preconceptions about him, such as those that plagued John Connally. So, what was critical for Bush, once he had won in Iowa, was what he wrote on that slate.

From the outset, the public perception of Bush had been distorted. As a former congressman from Texas, ambassador to the United Nations and to Peking, director of the Central Intelligence Agency, and chairman of the Republican National Committee, he was well known to activists in his party and the political establishment. Among Republicans, he was given particular credit for his service as party chairman during the difficult period of the Watergate investigations. Indeed, it had become an article of faith among Republican regulars that Bush had "kept Watergate away from the party" during those awkward times, despite the contradictory evidence of the 1974 congressional elections.

But except among those closest to him, George Bush was believed to be an essentially "moderate" Republican who was competing with Howard Baker for support from the centrist elements of his party who were not prepared to accept the conservatism of Ronald Reagan, John Connally, or Philip Crane. He was a Yalie who still wore the striped ties and half-glasses that were hallmarks of the Eastern liberal establishment, and his father, Prescott Bush, had been a senator from Connecticut and a moderate. Although George Bush had built a career in Texas, he still had a summer home in Maine and sounded like it. Yet the fact was that Bush was every bit as conservative as Reagan on virtually every issue that Republicans use as measuring sticks. (One incident makes the point. After that "cattle show" in Concord, New Hampshire, Roger Stone, a young professional working for Reagan, tore the identifying headings off the texts of speeches the different candidates had given, and then showed them to Senator Orrin Hatch of Utah, a devoted conservative backer of Reagan. Hatch mistook Bush's speech for that of Phil Crane, by all odds the conservative purist in the field.) Bush's reputation as a moderate was founded largely on stylistic criteria rather than on any close analysis of his positions on economic or national security issues.

That reputation was reinforced during those early months of organizational work in Iowa. Many of the people who joined his campaign there in the early stages were known to be political allies of Governor Robert D. Ray, a moderate by any measure. Other prominent Republicans in the state and elsewhere agonized semipublicly about "choosing between" Baker and Bush. And as Baker's campaign seemed to flounder, more and more of them turned to Bush as the one hope for denying the nomination to Ronald Reagan. In short, George Bush was able to build an identification that was based far more on his associations than on his views. That was enough to carry him through the Iowa caucuses, in large measure because of his organizational strength, but it was not enough to satisfy the larger universe of voters now focusing their attention on him. "We had solved the George Who problem in Iowa," Bush's campaign manager, James Baker, said long after the fact. "We did not answer the question of George Why." Or, as the pollster Robert Teeter saw it, Bush had built an organizational base but now needed a substantive one. So Baker, Teeter, and the campaign's political director, David Keene, argued vehemently to Bush that it was now essential for him to construct a foundation under his new celebrity, with specific positions on important issues that would give voters in New Hampshire a "hook"—a rationale beyond the knowledge of his success in Iowa to vote for him.

There were, in this case, other reasons to do so. Even as Bush had been becoming the "moderate alternative" to Reagan, doubts about him were growing within his party. Professionals viewed his impressive résumé as a public official as "a mile long and an inch deep." Sotto voce suggestions were made that Bush was "too light" on the issues, particularly in comparison with Senator Baker.* For these reasons, moderate Republican governors, to whom Reagan had always been anathema, were proving reluctant to get behind Bush. No one questioned his energy or tenacity—his mother once disclosed that as a child he had been known as "Willing Feet" because of those same qualities. But there were questions about whether he had the force of personality to withstand the new pressures he would feel as the principal opposition, and perhaps the only opposition, to Ronald Reagan.

There were doubts, too, about Bush's ability as a campaigner. His organization was universally applauded but he had not shown that he could make a vivid impression on voters. He was

*Indeed, one of the leading strategists in Bush's campaign had been among those in 1973 who, after the resignation of Spiro Agnew, petitioned Ford to choose Nelson Rockefeller rather than Bush for Vice President on the ground that Bush was too light.

one of those candidates who is like a sheet of plate glass, undeniably there, but not always visible to the naked eye. Though before he ever announced his candidacy on May 1, 1979, he had campaigned for months, visiting forty-two states, his presence never caused even a blip in the public-opinion polls.* His style was so boyishly enthusiastic it had already given rise to private derision that became public later when Garry Trudeau made him the subject of a sequence in his political cartoon strip "Doonesbury." He was too much a preppy, the kinder critics said. He was a wimp, said the less kind ones.

But in politics there is no vindication to compare with winning, and Bush's victory in Iowa sent him into new transports of enthusiasm. Now, he announced, he had "the Big Mo" —that mysterious quality labeled momentum, which politicians prize so highly. His managers winced when he declared for the television cameras that if he could win New Hampshire, too, "there'll be absolutely no stopping me."

Warmed by all this new attention—suddenly there were forty more reporters vying for places on his campaign plane—Bush was in no humor to listen to Teeter, Keene, or even his old friend Jim Baker. He became a victim of the classic self-deception of a political candidate. He began to believe his own press notices and to be beguiled because people were now pressing forward to shake his hand in circumstances under which he would have been totally ignored only a few weeks earlier. "You're not out there," he told his strategists. "You haven't seen what it's like." Moreover, he argued, it was essential that he keep "firing up the troops" by stressing the new momentum the campaign had achieved. Besides, he was talking about issues, too, even if the press wasn't paying attention.

Moreover, Bush said long after the campaign, he was misled by the success he had enjoyed in Iowa. "There was a feeling, well, now you've got to be more substantive," he recalled, "and

---

*This phenomenon moved us to write a column on May 1, 1979, that began with these ill-starred words: "After several months of stumping the country, George Bush has declared his candidacy for the Republican presidential nomination at a time when many professionals in his party suspect his campaign already has peaked." Bush was not amused.

I would argue with them: I think I am being substantive, I'm answering questions every day. . . . I just didn't see it. I'll readily concede at this point I might have been wrong. But I didn't feel any great need to do something different." In short, if it worked in Iowa, why not in New Hampshire?

The first opinion surveys in New Hampshire and across the country seemed to support his argument. Wirthlin's polls, for example, found that just prior to Iowa Reagan had been leading Bush by 19 percentage points among Republicans in New Hampshire, but five days after the caucuses Reagan was six points behind. Nor was that the worst of it for Reagan. A few days later, after having been caught telling an ethnic joke to reporters on a bus,* Reagan fell 13 percentage points behind in New Hampshire. In other states where Reagan had not been so active, both Wirthlin and Teeter found Bush's gain even more substantial. He was even leading for a time in Florida, where an important primary was in the offing. In Massachusetts, where the primary would follow the one in New Hampshire by a week, Bush was 40 percentage points ahead. In Illinois, where the first test would be made in a major industrial state, he led by 11 points. In the primary in Puerto Rico in mid-February, he buried Howard Baker, 60 to 37 percent.

Ronald Reagan was no longer the complacent Imperial Candidate. On January 23, two days after the shock in Iowa, he met with Sears and other campaign advisers in Chicago and insisted on a new campaign style. They settled on a strategy of intensive campaigning in New Hampshire and a daily effort to "make news," with statements on the issues. He had always had a strong base in New Hampshire (where he lost the primary to Gerald Ford by only 1317 votes in 1976), and he had an organization there built by Gerald Carmen, a former Republican state chairman, and overseen by Jim Lake, one of the most respected professionals on his national staff. Now that Bush was isolated as the principal alternative, Sears argued, voters would be taking a

---

*The joke goes: How do you tell the Polish guy at a cockfight? He brings a duck. How do you tell the Italian guy? He bets on the duck. How do you know the Mafia is there? The duck wins.

more serious look at the candidates than they might have. New Hampshire was no longer a place to make the first cut. It might even be the finals.

The other Republicans competing in New Hampshire, it was soon apparent, were becoming victims of their own strategic miscalculations. Phil Crane had been working the state since the summer of 1978, hoping to use the primary to establish himself as a realistic possibility for the nomination, but his failure in Iowa (6.7 percent) now branded him as a mere also-ran. John Connally had been following what he called a "national strategy," the strange premise of which seemed to be that the first important verdicts would be those handed down in the South and particularly in the South Carolina primary, ten days after New Hampshire. John B. Anderson had a core of support in the "Concord crowd" of liberal-to-moderate Republicans, but Bush's success had drained many of them away.

Anderson was a somewhat different case, in any event. Although his following in New Hampshire was clearly limited, he had used the primary campaign there—and the attention turned on him by the media—to lay the foundation of a national reputation as a "different" political personality. He was not only the only thing approaching a "liberal" in the Republican field but also the candidate who was most successful in projecting an image of independence. In most respects that reputation squared with the one he had earned in Washington in twenty years as a congressman from Illinois.

Perhaps the most obvious victim of the new realities in New Hampshire, however, was Howard Baker, although it was hard to see this at the start. His organizational problems had been solved, or at least ameliorated, by his decision to retain Douglas Bailey and John Deardourff of Washington, two leading consultants. And such perceptive veterans of New Hampshire campaigns as Stewart Lamprey, a longtime guru of Republican politics there, were persuaded that Baker was the kind of candidate who would, as Lamprey put it, "wear well" with the voters in a primary campaign that would run a full month.

This was the first New Hampshire presidential primary in which television advertising would be a major element. Because

there are only two stations within the state, each with a small audience, most voters watch television originating in Boston, and
it had always been considered wasteful to buy time there solely
to reach the New Hampshire part of the audience. Two years
earlier, however, a Democrat named Hugh Gallen invested
$35,000 in Boston television commercials and won a surprising
victory over the incumbent Republican governor, Meldrim
Thomson. So now the premium would be on the work of the media experts, and Howard Baker had two of the best in Bailey and
Deardourff.

It didn't turn out that way. For one thing, all the candidates
were spending money so heavily on television ads—Bush commercials had run as far back as early October—that they can-
celled each other out and none was able to stand out from the
pack. More to the point, the television commercials seemed irrelevant to the real news of the campaign, George Bush's advance in Iowa and the spreading feeling that this contest had
already become a two-candidate one. It was no longer possible
to use the New Hampshire primary as the early cornerstone for
a long campaign.

The press was not quick to see this change, or to accept it, perhaps because so many reporters enjoy covering the New Hampshire primary. It is a familiar and manageable campaign for
them. They live at the Sheraton Wayfarer in Bedford, just outside Manchester, and most of the voters and campaign events
are less than an hour away. It is necessary to run up to Hanover
or over to Durham and Portsmouth once or twice, but they are
only ninety minutes away. And the obligatory trip all the way up
to Berlin, a largely Democratic papermaking center in the isolated north, has to be made only once. It is possible most days to
make it back to the Wayfarer and then run over to Daffodil's for
a lobster with some of the local politicians, many of whom reporters have known through three or four campaigns. Some of
the reporters remembered Hugh Gregg, Bush's chairman, from
as far back as Nelson Rockefeller's campaign in 1964. And the
two women who were leading Edward Kennedy's campaign in
1980 had been involved in one liberal Democratic campaign
after another—Joanne Symons had worked for both George Mc-

Govern in 1972 and Morris Udall in 1976, and Dudley W. Dudley for both of them plus Eugene McCarthy in 1968. Even the buildings used for campaign headquarters had histories. The Concord storefront in which Baker was based, for example, had been used by Gerald Ford in 1976—and by organizers for Henry Cabot Lodge in 1964. New Hampshire may not be representative—no state that gives publishing room to William Loeb and his outlandish *Manchester Union Leader* could be—but it is familiar and comfortable, so the press of 1980 gave New Hampshire the same kind of attention it had always received, although its role was considerably altered.

Reagan took advantage of this fact in making his new beginning, and a few days into February he began to gain ground as the glow of Iowa faded. Day by day, campaigning with a vigor that belied his sixty-nine years, he closed the gap on Bush until, a week before the primary, he was essentially even with him. That night, February 20, all seven Republican candidates—Bush, Reagan, Baker, Connally, Crane, Dole, and Anderson—appeared in a televised debate in Manchester sponsored by the League of Women Voters.

It was at this point that George Bush's "Big Mo" became a liability rather than an asset. He had raised great expectations with his victory in Iowa. He was now the star of network news broadcasts, weekly newsmagazines, and *The Boston Globe*. But in the debate he appeared—and acted like—just another candidate, perhaps even less than that because he seemed nervous and defensive, just as he had in Iowa. Bush always approached these debates, his advisers said, with more concern about the damage he could do himself with a mistake than confidence that they presented him with an opportunity to make a positive impression on the voters. In the politics of 1980 the Republicans were looking for someone who did more than avoid error. And they found it that night in Ronald Reagan rather than George Bush. Reagan made a strong closing statement about his "vision of America," and he won the sympathy of the audience when he was questioned about his ethnic joke and responded with just the right combination of anger and self-deprecating humor.

A member of the audience had reminded him about the joke

and said Reagan had issued "some kind of abject apology and explanation." Then he asked if "ethnic humor of this kind has any place in the campaign for the highest office of this land?"

"I'm glad you asked that question," Reagan said with some show of asperity, "because I don't think my apology was abject. It was sincere. I had told the story the way it was reported by the reporter who reported it. I do not go around telling ethnic jokes. I have been on the opposite side of that question, on the right side, long before there was anything called civil rights. And very frankly, I was the victim of—in the slang expression of the press—I was stiffed. And I did not do it in the manner in which it was said. I did not tell the story to the press for that purpose.

"And all I can do is say to those people who might have thought that there was an insult intended, they have my apology. But I plead that I was the victim of something that was done. The discussion happened to deal with humor and jokes and to a few people of my own surrounding, not knowing anyone was overhearing, I said that here was one that had come along that was a new twist in the so-called ethnic joke. But you can rest assured I don't tell them, I don't like them. And from now on, I'm going to look over both shoulders and then I'm only going to tell stories about Irishmen, because I'm Irish."

As an explanation, this was obviously lame, but Reagan's demeanor and tone implied enough candor that the defense was successful.

The public-opinion polls after the debate in Manchester all showed the same thing. By defying those low expectations formed after Iowa, Reagan had been a clear winner. In Wirthlin's data, for example, it was found that 37 percent of the state's Republicans had watched the debate and that 86 percent of those had identified a winner. And Reagan had twice as many supporters as anyone else, with 33 percent to 17 percent for Bush, 14 for Anderson, 12 for Baker. He scored highest on "strength of leadership" and "competency."

It was a sharp setback for Bush. As Jim Baker said later, "The real story of Iowa wasn't that Bush won, but that Reagan came as close without campaigning. It set us up beautifully for New Hampshire." And now Reagan moved steadily upward, widening his lead in the polls over Bush. "When I saw this dramatic change," said Wirthlin, "I said, 'We got him.'"

There was, however, another card to play. Even before the debate in Manchester, Reagan's managers had begun angling to arrange a two-man debate with Bush alone, and the *Nashua Telegraph* had come forward to sponsor it. Each candidate had his own reason to favor such a confrontation. John Sears, no admirer of Bush, believed it would drive home to the voters the realization that this was the choice for 1980 and that they had better begin to give it some serious thought. Bush's managers, Keene and Baker, welcomed the chance for their candidate to be depicted as the only realistic alternative, because they thought it might attract voters who had been toying with voting for Howard Baker or John Anderson. "We thought it was the best thing since sliced bread," Jim Baker recalled. The other candidates would squawk about being excluded, of course, but the *Nashua Telegraph* would be the target.

It didn't prove to be so simple, however. After Bob Dole complained, the Federal Elections Commission ruled that the newspaper's sponsorship of the debate would amount to an illegal corporate contribution to Reagan's and Bush's campaigns. So the Reagan people suggested that the two campaigns split the $3,500 cost, and, when Bush balked at that, because he felt Reagan was trying to manipulate him, Reagan agreed to pay for the whole thing.

Meanwhile, however, Sears began to have second thoughts, after seeing Wirthlin's figures on the results of the seven-man debate in Manchester. If Reagan could do that well in a field of seven candidates, answering only every seventh question, why take the chance of obliging him to answer every second question and increase the odds that he might make a mistake? Moreover, now that they were paying the bill, why risk the antagonism? As Lake put it, "We didn't need those other candidates out there bad-mouthing us the last three days."

So the Reagan people began to plan to include the five other candidates. The motivation was largely defensive, but Sears was also beguiled by the notion of stirring the pot a little. He considered Bush both arrogant and personally uncertain, and he relished the idea of putting added pressure on him by changing the rules. Moreover, Bush's New Hampshire campaign director, Hugh Gregg, a flinty former governor of the state, was someone Sears knew well because he had run *Reagan*'s 1976 campaign in New Hampshire. Gregg was a stubborn man, and the publisher of the *Nashua Telegraph,* J. Herman Pouliot, and its editor, Jon Breen, were his friends. He would not take kindly to Reagan playing the hero at his friends' expense.

The Bush people, of course, knew for several days that an attempt might be made to change the format. Jim Lake had been sounding out Breen and talking to the other candidates as well. And Bush had met with the Nashua editor and his own advisers to decide on a strategy. It was agreed that if Reagan made such a grandstand play, Breen would recount the events that had led up to the debate, thus squarely assigning the blame, and Bush then would say he was determined to keep his original commitment to the *Nashua Telegraph* for a two-man debate.

The following morning Sears and Lake began to telephone the other candidates, inviting them to come to Nashua High School and join the debate. Breen refused to agree to the change in plans, but Lake argued that Reagan was the sponsor of the event once he agreed to pay its costs and could make the decision. At the Wayfarer, the word began to spread among reporters late in the afternoon that something was in the works. John Sears was trying to pull another fast one, and the rental cars began to converge on the high school.

Reagan himself had always been "uncomfortable," he said later, with the two-man debate because he was uneasy about excluding the other candidates. So when Lake told him of the change, as they drove toward Nashua less than an hour before the debate was scheduled to begin, Reagan quickly agreed.

At the high school itself the gymnasium was packed with 2400 people—Bush, Reagan, and the *Telegraph* each had controlled one-third of the tickets—buzzing with reports that they were going to see the whole Republican field. Dozens of reporters and camera crews crowded into a press area of the main hall, while other dozens patrolled the corridors trying to find out what was happening. The word spread through the school that Howard

Baker, Bob Dole, John Anderson, and Phil Crane had arrived and were meeting with Reagan. (Only John Connally, campaigning in South Carolina, had failed to make it back to Nashua.) At the other end of a long hall Bush and his advisers—Baker, Keene, Gregg, press secretary Peter Teeley—were waiting in another room. A delegation of Republican congressmen supporting Bush, led by Barber Conable of New York, arrived in the press room but could throw no real light on what was happening.

A few minutes before the debate was to begin, Sears sent word through an advance man that he would like to see Bush, but he didn't specify why. Dave Keene replied with some heat that "it doesn't work that way," meaning in terms of protocol, and Jim Baker, Sears's opposite number, was dispatched to the Reagan holding area.

Sears told Baker, "The governor wants to open [up] the debate." Baker replied that it was a matter for the *Nashua Telegraph* to decide. "John," he said, "we're not the people to talk to." Then, as he was leaving, a door to an adjoining room opened and Baker saw not only Reagan but the other four candidates, inevitably "the Nashua Four."

"That was the first time we knew the other candidates were there," Baker said. "We realized the meeting would not have been a one-on-one with Reagan, but it would be an ambush."

When Bush refused to meet with the other candidates, the Reagan camp sent another ambassador, Senator Gordon Humphrey of New Hampshire, who encountered Bush in the corridor on the way to the gymnasium.

"If you don't come right now," he told Bush, "you're doing a disservice to party unity."

Bush was snappish. "Don't tell me about unifying the Republican Party!" he shot back. "I've done more for this party than you'll ever do!" And he added angrily: "I've worked too hard for this and they're not going to take it away from me."

Back in the Reagan bivouac the rejected candidates were angry too, but time was running out. Charlie Black, Reagan's political director, burst into the room. "Governor," he said, "they're going to start in about thirty seconds, whether you're there or not."

But Reagan was going to hang tough. If the other four were barred, he said, starting for the door, then he would walk out with them. But Sears, Lake, Jerry Carmen, and Humphrey all argued that he couldn't be seen to be running away. "If you do that," Humphrey declared, "you'll lose New Hampshire. This will be written that you ratted on George Bush."

Reagan shrugged, apparently resigned, and the whole group started down the hall. "Let's go," Dole said. "I've been thrown out of better places than this."

As Reagan marched down the corridor with Humphrey on one side and Lake on the other, it was still not absolutely clear what he intended to do. "When he got up there," Lake said later, "he had sort of a mad look on his face, and I wasn't sure what was going to happen." So Lake quickly scribbled a note on his yellow pad and passed it up to the podium: "Governor, everybody's with you here. Give him hell." Reagan, still apparently fuming, unfolded it, read it, and then looked out at Lake and winked broadly. He was clearly in control.

The audience, meanwhile, had become less restrained. They cheered boisterously when the four candidates mounted the stage with Reagan and lined up across the back. Publisher Pouliot told the crowd: "This is getting to sound more like a boxing match. In the rear are four other candidates who have not been invited by the *Nashua Telegraph*." The crowd booed him. And there was another round of cheers when a woman shouted: "Get them chairs."

Editor Breen, the moderator, was silent, and Bush sat in his place, staring straight ahead and refusing to acknowledge even the presence of his four opponents. Then, as Reagan tried to make his case for opening up the debate and bringing in more chairs, Breen gave the veteran performer one of the classic straight lines of American politics.

Looking toward the sound technician, Breen said: "Turn Mr. Reagan's microphone off."

Reagan flushed, leaned forward, and replied: "I'm paying for this microphone, Mr. Green."

When the audience erupted in cheers, it was clear that although Reagan had mistaken the name of the moderator, he had not missed the political opportunity he had been presented.

Finally, when it became apparent that neither the *Telegraph* nor Bush would yield, the four candidates began to file off the stage. Dole leaned over toward Bush, who was still staring out at the audience, and told him: "There'll be another day, George."

Now there were many things Bush might have done, even in the absence of a statement from Breen, to avoid disaster. His refusal to meet with the other four, all of them Republican office-holders of some prominence, was an unnecessary insult. If he had met them, Senator Baker said later, "he would have gotten away with it. We would have disbanded. What held that gang together was its rage." Or, even once the others were on stage, Bush might have saved the situation by making some good-humored fun of Reagan's stratagem and explaining the virtues of keeping his commitments to the *Nashua Telegraph*. He might even have gotten away with kidding Reagan about being afraid to meet him alone. Instead he simply froze, and no one mistook it. "What can I say?" an adviser shrugged. "He choked up."

Reagan and Bush proceeded to debate *á deux,* and Reagan was a clear winner here, too, according to those who saw the debate. (A staff member later told Bush, "The good news is that nobody paid any attention to the debate. The bad news is that you lost that, too.") The martyred candidates gathered in a music room to provide the press and television cameras with evidence of their outrage. Anderson called it "a travesty on the whole democratic process," and Howard Baker declared that in fifteen years in politics "this is the most flagrant attempt to return to the closed door I've ever seen." Dole, characteristically, joked that he might even announce his candidacy again and start all over. Only Phil Crane suggested, and then by indirection, that Ronald Reagan might have been using them.

Although there had been no live television coverage of the mayhem at the high school, stories about it spread through the electorate almost instantly. Film of Reagan grabbing the microphone while Bush sat immobile was shown repeatedly on local and network television for the next forty-eight hours—all day Sunday, and then again on the Monday morning and evening network news programs. It had captured a rare moment in a political campaign—an instant of genuine drama that no media consultant could have plotted. Against it, all the candidate adver-

tising paled. The reality was that Ronald Reagan had taken
George Bush over the jumps.

Looking back at the episode a year later, Bush was not hesitant
about agreeing that it was "rather devastating" to his campaign
in New Hampshire, although he was also convinced his campaign all along had underestimated Reagan's "fundamental
strength" in the state. "As I think about it," he said in an interview, "I've got several thoughts, one of which is that I clearly
could have handled it better. I'm not sure I felt that then but I
now, in retrospect, think that. And, secondly, I think that it was
some political maneuvering on the part of Sears that you can say
was effective or you can claim that it was the basic sandbag, however you want to look at it."

The reaction in the opinion polls was almost instantaneous.
Reading the results of his canvassing early Sunday, Wirthlin saw
a landslide in the making. "At that point," he said, "the thing just
exploded." Where Reagan might have expected his pre-Nashua
lead of 7 or 8 percentage points to level off in the final days of
the campaign, it climbed rapidly in the last forty-eight hours to
the 27 points it proved to be on election day.

Bush did nothing to rescue himself in those final hours. His
complaint that he had been "sandbagged" by Ronald Reagan
only added to the impression that he was out of his league competing against the conservative from California. As George Romney had discovered twelve years earlier, when he admitted to
being "brainwashed" on the Vietnam issue, the voters do not
take kindly to the notion that a presidential candidate is susceptible to being taken. Bush's managers tried to repair some of the
damage by running radio advertisements urging voters to read
the *Nashua Telegraph* account of the debacle to get the accurate
story. But those protests only reinforced the notion that this had
indeed been a critical, and telling, event.

Then Bush compounded the felony by making a blunder that
Reagan had made four years earlier (when he lost the state by
only 1317 votes). At the behest of the same local campaign manager, Hugh Gregg, Bush left New Hampshire for home. Gregg
didn't like to have candidates around during the final days of a
campaign. He argued that they got in the way of his political mechanics, diverting resources that might be better used in getting

out the vote. And he had made it a condition of his agreement to run the Bush campaign that he would have absolute control over the candidate's schedule there.

Bush said later that he had considered remaining in New Hampshire for those final two days but then decided it would be seen as a sign of "weakness and uncertainty" on his part.

So while Reagan remained on the scene to accept the voters' accolades, Bush was shown on television back in Houston complaining he had been sandbagged. What Wirthlin would call "the most devastating visual" of the campaign was a film on network news of Reagan shaking hands in the cold of New Hampshire, his breath frosting in the air, while Bush jogged in the warm sunshine of his home city. Although Bush put up a brave front in the final days of the New Hampshire campaign after Nashua, its meaning was clear enough to him two days after the votes had been counted in the primary. Taping notes for himself then, he described the scene at Nashua as "a real blow" and said: "We just got mowed over . . . we were just brutalized by the proceeding."

Thus, the final days of the New Hampshire campaign had shown Ronald Reagan at his public best—on a stage, thinking on his feet, and instinctively performing in a way the voters would applaud. But there was still another small drama to be played out, this one in private, that showed another side of Reagan—an ability to make a hard decision for the most pragmatic reasons when it seemed in his self-interest to do so.

John Sears's position in the Reagan campaign of 1980 had always been a somewhat tenuous one. His skill four years earlier in bringing his candidate to within an ace of denying the presidential nomination to the incumbent Gerald Ford had been widely admired among politicians—to the point that when the first stirrings of the 1980 campaign began, he was sounded out by several candidates on the possibility he might direct their efforts.

The conservatives who made up the core of Ronald Reagan's support, however, were not among Sears's admirers. They suspected he had far more commitment to winning than to conservative principles, which was undoubtedly accurate. They had never forgiven him the ploy in 1976 of enlisting Richard Schweiker of Pennsylvania as Reagan's choice for vice president, even though history showed that was what had kept Reagan's candidacy alive until the convention. Indeed, a few of Reagan's backers from 1976, such as former Governor Jim Edwards of South Carolina (later secretary of energy), had joined Connally rather than Reagan because of Sears.

The Californians who had been with Reagan long before Sears came along—Lyn Nofziger and Mike Deaver, for example—had other objections. They resented Sears's assumption of total control of the campaign, and they objected to the highly public role of the interloper from the East. (At one point in Iowa, for example, Sears had flown into Des Moines and held a full-scale press conference of his own—to explain why he was limiting Reagan's exposure there.) One long-time Reagan ally described it this way: "There was concern as to who the candidate was. John was getting more television and ink than the candidate and speaking for the governor on issues, and the feeling was the governor was being relegated to a back position, a Charlie McCarthy sitting on John's lap."

Reagan himself was ambivalent about Sears. On the one hand, he did not share Sears's consuming interest in the theory and practice of politics. On the other, he was impressed enough by Sears's expertise to accept him. At staff meetings and in quasi-social situations, the former actor would listen open-mouthed to Sears's accounts of the political machinations of Richard Nixon in the campaign of 1968, in which Sears had been a leading strategist. Some of Reagan's friends suspected that, as one put it, the candidate felt subconsciously that he was being patronized by his campaign manager.

But both Ronald and Nancy Reagan were pragmatic enough to value Sears, and Reagan himself was convinced that differences in personalities and clashes of egos could always be resolved with a little display of goodwill on all sides. More to the point, he was secure enough in himself not to feel threatened. So he kept reassuring both the Californians and the conservatives that although John Sears was needed, he would not actually run the campaign. And late in 1978 he approved the concept of a "management team" that would include Sears and his two principal lieutenants, Charlie Black and Jim Lake, and the three Californians—Deaver, Nofziger, and Edwin Meese. The idea was accepted even by the man with the most persistent doubts about Sears, Senator Paul Laxalt of Nevada, the politician closest to Reagan on a personal level. But the "team" approach didn't work. "John, through the force of his personality, filled the vacuum and ended up running the show," Laxalt said.

Reagan, however, continued to accept the tensions, even after Sears forced Nofziger out of the campaign in the early fall of 1979. And when Sears and Deaver locked horns a few weeks later, Reagan summoned them to his home at Pacific Palisades, hoping to resolve their differences, then acquiesced in Deaver's departure when it was clear they could not do so. There were signs then, nonetheless, that there were limits to Reagan's patience.

After showing Deaver to the door of his home Reagan came back into the living room where Sears, Lake, and Black were waiting with Nancy Reagan. "The biggest man here just left the room," he told them angrily. "He was willing to accommodate and compromise and you bastards wouldn't." And when the three left he told his wife: "They'll be in here again and next time they'll be after Ed Meese. And, goddammit, I'm not going to let that happen."

His remark proved to be prescient, because the tensions between Sears and Meese continued to build through the fall and winter. And the muttering from Laxalt and other congressional supporters of Reagan about Sears became louder. But not until Reagan had lost in Iowa did Sears become vulnerable in the way politicians always become most vulnerable—by making a strategic error that leads to defeat.

The problem between Sears and Meese—and earlier between Sears, and Deaver and Nofziger—was to some extent predictable. Nofziger, Deaver, and Meese were old Reagan hands who had been with him for years, in Sacramento and elsewhere, and it was not surprising that they resisted being pushed away. At the same time Sears was running the campaign of the front-running candidate for president and felt entitled, even obliged, to rely on the best political professionals available. In his eyes that meant, among others, Charles Black as political director and James Lake as press secretary.

The complaints Sears had about Meese, and vice versa, apparently had some validity. Meese, who had worked for Reagan in Sacramento first as a legal adviser and then chief of staff, had a reputation as a masterful synthesizer of information and situations. He had a genius for presenting complex issues to Reagan in a way that spelled out all of his options and the probable consequences of each. Moreover those who knew Meese's work attested that he was a totally honest broker and, as such, had earned Reagan's total confidence. Indeed, Reagan was often quoted as saying Ed Meese was the first man he would turn to in time of crisis.

On the other hand Meese did not have equivalent talents as an administrator, and even his friends joked that "the best way to kill something is put it in Ed Meese's briefcase." From Sears's standpoint, what this meant was that Meese was not carrying through on campaign responsibilities that he, Sears, expected him to accept.

By the same token, Sears had a well-deserved reputation for his own kind of genius—the ability to come up with innovative political approaches (such as the Schweiker ploy in 1976) and then carry them out to success. And beyond that, he was one of those politicians who could assess instantly all the implications of any development, strategic or tactical, in a campaign.

It was also true, however, that Sears could be uncommunicative and moody. And as the tensions continued inside the Reagan campaign, he seemed to be relying almost totally on Black and Lake, even to the point that he had relatively little contact with Reagan. "Sears remained virtually behind locked doors most of the time," said one insider, "and there was no communication between him and the candidate. Reagan was totally frustrated."

Early in February 1980 the situation came to a head. The first incident occurred in East Orange, New Jersey, where the Reagan people had stopped for the night. Sears was using a bathroom between two staff workrooms when he heard Meese on the telephone with David Fischer, Reagan's personal aide. The way Sears heard it, Meese was promising that Sears, Black, and Lake were shortly to be fired. Meese insisted later that the conversation "never happened." But he did recall trying to reassure Fischer (who was threatening to resign because of his difficulties with Nick Ruwe, another old Nixon hand whom Sears had brought into the campaign as scheduling director), telling him, "Let's just everybody keep doing what they're doing and get through New Hampshire. At that point we've got to get some of these things adjusted."

Whatever Meese actually said is, of course, lost in the mists of that motel room in East Orange. But Sears was plainly outraged, and a few mornings later he went to Nancy Reagan in New Hampshire with a proposal. Why not bring in William Clark, who had been Reagan's first chief of staff in Sacramento (and later was to become deputy secretary of state), to serve as chief of staff again, for the campaign? Although Sears didn't phrase it quite so bluntly, his idea was clearly to put a layer of insulation between Reagan and Meese and, not incidentally, between Meese and Sears. Then, after a decent interval, Meese would be eased out.

The use of Nancy Reagan as a broker in such a situation told a great deal about her role in her husband's campaign. Even at the tensest moments, she had maintained a friendly, easy relationship with Sears, Black, and Lake, as well as with Ed Meese. And she never took her eye off the principal objective: the success of Ronald Reagan in winning the presidential nomination. Moreover, at times when her husband seemed to expect that awkward situations would resolve themselves, Nancy Reagan understood the necessity for nudging them along.

But Clark, then a state supreme court judge in California, was unwilling to accept the assignment. So Sears, he said later, suggested William J. Casey, a New York lawyer who had been working part-time in Reagan's campaign, principally on developing positions on issues. But the bottom line was still that Meese eventually would have to go, and that was something Ronald Reagan was not prepared to accept.*

The climactic meeting was held late one night a few days be-

---

*Meese said after the campaign he believed it was Reagan himself, rather than Sears, who originally came up with the idea of bringing Casey into the campaign management. But the critical point was that Sears saw Casey as a potential buffer and Reagan saw him as a potential replacement as campaign manager.

fore the New Hampshire primary in a suite at a hotel just over
the line in Andover, Massachusetts. Sears, Black, and Lake, and
Ronald and Nancy Reagan, went over what had become familiar
ground inside the campaign. Sears believed that Meese was not
fulfilling his assignment of preparing Reagan adequately on the
issues, but instead was too involved in decisions that properly
should rest with the political team. Sears was convinced that the
campaign ahead, whether against President Carter or Ted Kennedy, would be difficult, and he argued that Reagan needed to
be better equipped to handle it. Otherwise, Sears said, he would
have to leave.

Reagan blew up. "I know what you're doing," he said. "You're
after Ed." At one point he leaped out of his chair, his face flaming red, and raged at Sears in strong enough terms that it crossed
Lake's mind the candidate was about to punch the campaign
manager. Lake, Black, and Nancy Reagan tried to cool the situation down, and the meeting broke up without any resolution.
But Reagan was not mollified. The next morning, riding on a
campaign bus with Black, he pounded the back of a seat in front
of him and told the political director: "Charlie, you guys just
don't understand Ed."

At the urging of Black and Lake, however, Nancy Reagan continued to play the broker. They flew to Chicago with her, where
she telephoned Bill Casey in Florida and asked him to come up
to New Hampshire to take a bigger part in the campaign. And
she agreed she would set up another meeting for the three with
her husband right after the New Hampshire primary.

Reagan himself, however, was becoming increasingly restive,
complaining at one point that "every morning I wake up with a
lump in my stomach." On Sunday night, two days before the
New Hampshire primary, he summoned Meese and Casey and
told them: "This is an intolerable situation. It can't go on any
longer. I've decided to make a change."

The candidate compared the idea of replacing Sears with the
frequent firings of professional baseball managers and football
coaches, arguing that like the sports situations it would not be a
reflection on Sears's ability but instead a product of the need for
better chemistry in the campaign.

What he was seeking, Reagan said after the election, was a system under which Sears would devise strategy and Casey would be responsible for administration of the campaign. But Sears would not agree. "There was a flat refusal," Reagan said. "He would not hold still for that." In Reagan's eyes, Sears had delivered an ultimatum: he would run the campaign his own way— meaning without Meese, among other things—or not at all. And Reagan was not going to let go of Ed Meese. "I had made it plain," he said, "that that was not going to happen."

The plan was to announce the change late enough on Tuesday so that it would not influence the result in New Hampshire but early enough so that it would not be seen as a reaction to that result.

If Sears was concerned on primary day, there was no indication of it as he ate lunch with us and Tom Ottenad, the national political reporter for the *St. Louis Post-Dispatch*, at Gunther's, in downtown Manchester. On the contrary, the campaign manager was unusually ebullient, laughing about George Bush's discomfiture at Nashua seventy-two hours earlier and predicting an easy victory when the votes were counted that night. Shortly before 2:00 p.m. Ottenad drove Sears back to the Holiday Inn just across the Amoskeag Bridge. Black and Lake were waiting for him because Governor Reagan wanted to see them in his suite on the third floor.

From the moment they walked into the suite the three understood what was happening. Reagan was sitting on a couch, and Bill Casey in a wing chair nearby. But Nancy Reagan, Charlie Black noticed, was sitting across the room, uncharacteristically out of the group. "We've been having some problems and we want to get them solved," Reagan said. Then he handed Sears a single sheet of paper.

"Ronald Reagan today announced," it read, "that William J. Casey has been named executive vice chairman and campaign director of his presidential campaign, replacing John Sears who has resigned to return to his law practice. . . .

"In announcing the change in his campaign organization, Reagan said, 'The campaign requires a sharp reduction in expenses and restructuring of our organization to intensify the people-to-people type of campaigning I have been doing here in New Hampshire. Bill Casey has my complete confidence and full authority to carry out his work.'

"Reagan has also accepted resignations from Charlie Black, national political director, and Jim Lake, press secretary, who are returning to private business. Reagan expressed appreciation 'for the effort John Sears, Charlie Black, and Jim Lake have put into my campaign.' "

Sears, now seated on the couch next to Reagan, read it and, without a word, passed it on to Lake. From the corner of the room, Nancy Reagan looked inquiringly at Sears. "Well, John?" she said. "Well?"

"I'm not surprised," Sears replied.

Then Lake looked up from the statement at Reagan. "Governor," he said, "you don't realize this, but Ed Meese manipulates you, he manipulates you." He passed the statement over to Black, who turned it face down on a table. "I don't know what's in this," Black said, "but I want to say that I quit."

The news of the firings hit the political press corps with explosive force that afternoon. Sears, Lake, and Black, after all, had been the leading professionals in Reagan's operation. And all of them were respected, trusted, and liked by most of those who made their living off presidential campaigns. They could not imagine Ronald Reagan succeeding without that gray presence Sears offstage giving directions.

What the reporters did not understand then was that, once the votes were counted in New Hampshire that night, the campaign for the Republican presidential nomination would be essentially over. Reagan had 50 percent, Bush 23, Baker 13, and Anderson 10, and the die was cast.

Howard Baker withdrew a week later, after finishing fourth in both the Massachusetts and Vermont primaries. John Connally was buried four days later when Reagan polled 54 percent of the vote in South Carolina to his 30. Anderson enjoyed a brief vogue when he finished second in both Massachusetts (to Bush) and Vermont (to Reagan). But he, too, was brought down by Reagan less than a month later, and in his home state of Illinois. (And, once again, Reagan's skill on the debating platform was a critical

factor. The most memorable moment of that primary came
when Reagan, needling Anderson over his reluctance to promise
support for any Republican nominee, leaned over, placed an
avuncular hand on his arm, and said in tones of sorrow rather
than anger: "John, would you really find Ted Kennedy preferable to me?")

The only survivor of New Hampshire was George Bush, but he
was fatally compromised by those vivid images of that Saturday
night in Nashua, destroyed not by the machinations of political
technicians but by Reagan's skill in a moment of genuine stress.
David Broder, political reporter and columnist for *The Washington Post*, summed up the result in a campaign song to "Joshua
Fit the Battle" that included these stanzas:

> *Nashua's the battle where they bagged Big Mo,*
> *Slowed him so. Hear 'em crow.*
> *Nashua's the place Hugh Gregg said go.*
> *But the polls came a-tumbling down . . .*
>
> *Bush was such a stickler for games with rules,*
> *The kind they play in better schools.*
> *He thought the interlopers would just look like fools*
> *If he kept his word and cool . . .*
>
> *Nashua was the battle that lost the war,*
> *Lost the war, lost the war.*
> *Nashua was the battle that lost the war,*
> *To Reagan and the Gang of Four.*

Bush's troubles multiplied. Moderate Republican politicians
still harboring doubts about Reagan decided, nonetheless, that it
would be prudent to remain on the sidelines. Enough moderate
Republican voters defected to Anderson to make it impossible
for Bush to score the kind of upset he needed for a fresh start.
And the few victories he won were robbed of their luster by other events. Bush won in Connecticut on March 25, but the same
night Reagan swept most of New York's delegates. Bush won the
popular vote in Pennsylvania late in April but lost most of the
delegates. And then, when he won the Michigan primary in

May, ABC News dealt him a final blow by announcing that what had really happened that night—because of delegates elected elsewhere—was that Ronald Reagan had clinched the nomination. "It was a body blow," Jim Baker said later. "We got the results [of the Michigan primary]. We were ecstatic." But the next morning in Cleveland, after watching television prematurely proclaiming Reagan the nominee, Baker told Bush: "I think we'd better take another look at this."

George Bush, tenacious as always, persisted, campaigning in Ohio and New Jersey where—along with California—primaries were to be held June 3. He finally withdrew several days later only after Jim Baker and Keene, without consulting him, cut the ground away by announcing they were closing down his operations in California because they lacked the money to continue.

Meanwhile Ronald Reagan had assembled most of the organization that was to take him to the White House. Nofziger and Deaver returned to his staff. Dick Wirthlin took over more of the responsibility for strategy. Ed Meese became the ascendant figure.

And in the end, even John Sears was philosophical about the whole thing. "We might have thought the campaign could have been run better," he said one bitter cold afternoon much later. "But, hell, it won."

7.
"Damaging to Our Country"

Although the Iranian crisis commanded the nation's attention from the start, the Russian presence in Afghanistan also occupied much of President Carter's time as Senator Kennedy and Governor Brown mounted their challenges to him, beginning in Iowa. And when Carter in early January 1980 imposed an embargo on the shipment of American grain to the Soviet Union in response to the Afghan invasion, both Kennedy and Brown—as well as all of the Republican candidates except John Anderson—quickly criticized the move. Taking issue with Carter on the grain embargo *in Iowa* could hardly be called an act of political courage, of course. Indeed, the President's decision to impose the embargo less than three weeks before the first precinct caucuses there seemed to be politically risky.

"All of us want strong action against the Soviet Union," Kennedy said, pouncing on what he clearly saw to be a new presidential vulnerability. "But a grain embargo won't work and it's unfair to farmers. The Soviet troops won't leave Afghanistan and the American farmer will pay the price for an ineffective foreign policy."

That the embargo was downright foolhardy was a view shared by many diplomats in the State Department. That action, and subsequent efforts to rally a world boycott of the Summer Olympics in Moscow, "was just understood to be a disaster from beginning to end," Hodding Carter recalled much later. "But the various steps were taken because they were considered to be symbols of a real American outrage, and an attempt to extract some penalty for it. There was no illusion it would make the Soviets pull out. It was an attempt not to repeat the post-Czechoslovak, post-Hungarian Western response, which was first rhetoric, then passivity, then acquiescence, all within three months of the event. This was not going to be Hungary and Czechoslovakia all over again."

It was this determination that led Carter characteristically to rhetorical overkill, for he went on to call the Afghan invasion "the most serious threat to world peace since World War II." Carter's penchant for hyperbole was a never-ending source of embarrassment to those around him. One attributed it to a basic small-town inferiority complex: "Where he comes from, if you've got a mule you say you've got the best damned mule in Georgia." As Hodding Carter acknowledged, "Some of the rhetoric that was used thereafter was an attempt to contain the political damage." But the American people were caught up in the crisis atmosphere and that turned out to be as true in Iowa as anywhere else. If the President of the United States said a grain embargo was required to underscore American displeasure toward the Russians, Iowa's farmers would fall in behind him. No score for Kennedy, even on that one.

Indeed, there might be an opportunity here for Carter's campaign to give Kennedy a political black eye. Vice President Mondale, in Des Moines as the President's chief campaign surrogate, wasted no time going after Kennedy. In remarks that obviously had been carefully prepared, he charged that the senator was motivated in his comments by "the politics of the moment." Like Carter, Kennedy had to make up his mind "whether to do the political thing or the thing that best serves this nation," and Kennedy obviously had chosen the former. In the shorthand of political exchange, wire-service reports informed the country that Mondale in Des Moines had impugned Kennedy's patriotism, and Kennedy was furious. He cited the service of his family to the country, which cost the lives of his three brothers, and said he didn't need a lecture in patriotism from anyone.

Much later, in his office in the West Wing of the White House, Mondale recalled the episode. It had never been his intention to convey the idea that Kennedy was unpatriotic, he said, and indeed he told him so by phone the day after the Democratic convention: "The one thing in this campaign that I really regret is the thought that you thought I would say that about you. I didn't say it. I wouldn't say it." But Mondale is no country bumpkin and he certainly had not gone to Des Moines to give Kennedy a bouquet.

The day before Kennedy declared his candidacy, Mondale recalled, he had told him: "Ted, I'm sorry for you and I'm sorry for us and I'm sorry for the Democrats, because I've been through so many of these fights. As civil as you and I think this is going to be, it won't. We don't intend to leave voluntarily. You wouldn't. And the Republicans are going to benefit from this."

Kennedy did not soon forget Mondale's remarks in Iowa, but whether he really was as wounded by the remarks as he claimed was open to question. His swift invoking of the public service record of his family was not without political nuance either; Mondale had thought that response was a clear effort to make the most of some political in-fighting. "My assumption all along was that the people around Ted knew I didn't say that. . . . I figured he had a nice issue and he was building it, trying to get us on the defensive." Indeed, several nights later Kennedy was making light of it all when he presented Mondale with a New England Patriots' football jersey at a dinner in Waterloo, Iowa. But one of Kennedy's aides traveling with him at the time said the senator had been "amazed" that Mondale would make such an attack, and assumed that he hadn't intended to go that far. But with the old Boston adage, "Don't get mad, get even," in mind, Kennedy also thought he could give Mondale a political black eye by calling attention to his family's considerable service to the country. "He'll always think of that when he thinks about Mondale," the aide added. "But at the same time there were plenty of other memories, and I think he feels Mondale wasn't the point man, a hatchet man against Kennedy, except for that one slip. I think he appreciated that Mondale took the high road and that it was all the more noticeable the one time he departed."

For all that, Kennedy learned from the exchange that he would have to be exceedingly careful about what he said concerning the Iranian and Afghan crises, lest his remarks be used against him by a President too busy doing his job to engage in partisan politics. Paul Kirk later referred to this time as "the kid gloves period" of the Kennedy campaign. "Even on the leadership question," Kirk said, "Kennedy felt constrained by the public sense that the only individual who could cope [with major crises] was the President of the United States himself. All the insecurity that people felt about their own lives that had brought him [Kennedy] into the campaign in the first place was transferred into fears for the hostages."

That constraint endured through most of Kennedy's bid for the Democratic nomination. Not only Carter's and Mondale's political moves, but the voters' own, and real, nationalistic response to the events in Iran throttled Kennedy's efforts to engage Carter in a debate about the country's domestic ills.

On caucus night in Iowa, January 21, voters gathered at designated neighborhood locales across Iowa—school and church basements, clubrooms, living rooms in private homes—to support the candidates of their choice. Delegates to later county caucuses then were chosen by a formula based on the proportion of turnout for each candidate. Ordinarily the turnout is low at precinct caucuses because the process is more complicated and, to many, more intimidating than simply casting a ballot by pulling a lever in secret. But Iowans shattered expectations. "They think," said one veteran Iowa politician, "they're going to meet Walter Cronkite in their neighbor's living room." And so, in spite of a vigorous and well-executed campaign by Kennedy and his aides that was geared to a reasonable turnout, the abnormally high participation diluted Kennedy's organizational effort, delivered Iowa to Carter by a margin of more than two to one, and further eroded Kennedy's reputation as a vote-getter.

Later, in assessing why he had lost in Iowa so badly—59 percent to 31—Kennedy said: "Just every single evening there was twelve, fifteen, eighteen minutes of national television focused on the hostages and the administration's reaction to it. It was the dominance of that issue in the news, and not just any issue but an issue of foreign policy that touched the hearts and souls of the American people, and also reached the matter of national honor and national prestige as that prestige and power is institutionalized in the presidency.... And of course as one who shared those same kinds of emotions, I probably didn't anticipate it could be that divisive in terms of the political implications vis-à-vis the administration and myself."

The resounding defeat in Iowa forced Kennedy to take a hard look at whether it made any sense to go on. The first test on New England home ground, the Maine caucus, was approaching, and a defeat in New England would certainly trigger demands that he abandon the campaign, and complicate his already severe fund-raising problems. When the Iowa returns made clear he was a heavy loser, he went from his home in suburban McLean to his headquarters in the old Cadillac showroom in downtown Washington to confer with Steve Smith and other aides. Some thought Kennedy should quit, but he was not persuaded. Finally he summoned Parker and Bob Shrum, another speechwriter, into the privacy of the small bathroom in Smith's office. "Okay," he said to them, "what wonderful words do we have?" They scribbled him a statement that struggled with only modest success to be upbeat. "Well," he told his supporters a few minutes later, "we could have done a little better." But he predicted better times to come. "Tonight, according to my count, President Carter needs 1643 delegates more to win the nomination," he said. "We need 1657, and we're going to get it." The supporters cheered, as they always do, even when they have nothing to cheer about.

The next few days were critical for Kennedy. Already he had paid a severe price for spending so much time and attention on the question of whether he should run and practically none on how. His paid television commercials were abysmal and money had been wasted on other things, too, like the chartering of a jet campaign plane without calculating the cost and effect. Now the plane was given up and key aides sought to bring some order out of the chaos. But the problem was more than one of poor organization; Kennedy himself, his speeches, and his whole campaign lacked sharp focus. A planned trip to New England was canceled so that Kennedy, and his advisers, could do some serious soul-searching.

Two nights after the Iowa caucuses Carter delivered his annu-

al State of the Union message to Congress. In it he said, among
other things, that the United States was prepared to use military
force to rebuff any Russian incursion into the Persian Gulf, and
he called for resuming draft registration. Kennedy, sitting on the
House floor with Senate colleagues, was appalled. On the way
out a reporter asked him about the draft, and he said he was
against registration. Back at his office, aides asked him why he
had bucked the President so openly, and he told them: "If I'm
going to stay in this race—and I am—I'm going to do it on my
terms."

The result of that attitude was a major speech given by Kennedy at Georgetown University in Washington five days later. In
it, he sought at last to spell out the rationale for his campaign in
words that would inspire his flagging troops, and give stronger
justification to his challenging an incumbent of his own party.
He insisted that severe differences with Carter across the range
of domestic and foreign affairs were motivating him, not simply
a naked ambition to reinstate Camelot.

"Forty years ago, when the Nazis swept across the Low Countries and France, a far more urgent threat to our security, there
was no suspension of the public debate—or the presidential campaign [between Roosevelt and Willkie]," Kennedy said. "If we
could discuss foreign policy frankly when Hitler's Panzers were
poised at the English Channel, surely we can discuss foreign policy when the Soviet Union has crossed the border of Afghanistan.
If the Vietnam war taught us anything, it is precisely that when
we do not debate our foreign policy, we may drift into deeper
trouble. If a president's policy is right, debate will strengthen the
national consensus. If it is wrong, debate may save the country
from catastrophe."

Having said that, Kennedy did not mince words. He blamed
Carter directly for the crises in Iran and Afghanistan. He recalled that in the fall of 1979 Carter had said the presence of Soviet combat troops in Cuba was "unacceptable" but then backed
down. "The false draw in Cuba," he said, "may have invited the
Soviet invasion of Afghanistan." And of the seizure of the American hostages, he said, "The time has come to speak the truth
again: this is a crisis that never should have happened. In the

clearest terms, the administration was warned that the admission of the Shah would provoke retaliation in Tehran. President Carter considered those warnings and rejected them in secret. He accepted the dubious medical judgment of one doctor that the Shah could be treated only in the United States. Had he made different decisions, the Shah would doubtless still be in Mexico, and our diplomats would still be going about their business."

Kennedy went on: "The 1980 election should not be a plebiscite on the Ayatollah or Afghanistan. The real question is whether America can risk four more years of uncertain policy and certain crisis—of an administration that tells us to rally around their failures—of an inconsistent nonpolicy that may confront us with a stark choice between retreat and war. These issues must be debated in this campaign. The silence that has descended across foreign policy has also stifled the debate on other essential issues. The political process has been held hostage here at home as surely as our diplomats abroad."

That night the Georgetown speech was televised over several channels in New England, where Kennedy was facing the party caucuses in Maine and then the New Hampshire primary. Kennedy opened with a special statement for the television audience he had written himself about Chappaquiddick, saying he knew many people didn't believe his account but that it was "the only truth I can tell because that is the way it happened." The brief statement was a candid recognition that the crises in Iran and Afghanistan were not the only specters hanging over his candidacy.

Several of Kennedy's campaign workers in Maine gathered at the Hourglass restaurant and bar in downtown Portland to watch their candidate on television—among them Peter Meade and Bill Ezekiel, two street-smart young professionals from Boston; Connie LaPointe, political adviser to Governor Joseph Brennan; and Mary Duffy, a young press assistant who moved from one battleground to another all through the winter and spring.

When the broadcast began the bar was thick with nervous apprehension, and it persisted while Kennedy talked about Chappaquiddick. But when he began speaking with greater assurance about liberal issues and the failures of Jimmy Carter, the atmosphere began to change. "All right! All right!" the aides called out in the exaggerated accents of the sports world. "Tell it like it is, Teddy, tell it like it is!" And when their candidate finished they erupted in applause. "The good news," shouted Meade, "is that we have a campaign." What the reaction might be among voters, no one could tell, but Meade was confident of its meaning within the campaign. "Now the troops know what they are fighting for, they know what the battle is about," he said, "and they believe in the general."

Three months into his campaign, Ted Kennedy at last had answered the question Roger Mudd had asked: Why do you want to be president? And he had breached the moratorium on crisis debate that Carter had tried to impose. In the second real test of 1980, the municipal caucuses in Maine, Kennedy ran a close second to Carter—45.2 percent to 39.4, with 11.6 for Brown. And in another major speech, at Harvard, Kennedy kept up the attack, charging that "no president should be reelected because he happened to be standing there when his foreign policy collapsed around him." Starkly, he warned that "the last gasp of a failed foreign policy is war," and that war in the Persian Gulf would mean "a nightly television body count of America's children." In his campaign to force Carter out of his "Rose Garden strategy," Kennedy said the meaning of the Maine result "is that the presidency can never be above the fray, isolated from the actions and passions of the time. A president cannot afford to posture as the high priest of patriotism."

Kennedy soon learned that the incumbent President was not without the means to exact a heavy political price for the senator's newly proclaimed license to speak out. In a press conference the night after Kennedy's Harvard speech, Carter laid it on the line: "The thrust of what Senator Kennedy has said throughout the last few weeks," he intoned, "is very damaging to our country and to the establishment of our principles and the maintenance of them, and to the achievement of our goals to keep the peace and get our hostages released." Powell called the Harvard speech "a disgraceful exhibition of political ambition that was unconstrained by either accuracy or responsibility," and Secretary Vance charged that Kennedy "still fails to recognize the seriousness of the Soviet action" in Afghanistan.

Kennedy the very next morning struck back. In a tough speech at Exeter High School in New Hampshire, he deplored Carter's use of the presidential press conference to attack him and said: "We will all rally around the flag. But we need not, we must not, rally around the failures of a president that threaten the real interests of the nation. . . . In 1980 I will reject the course of false patriotism. I will continue to express my views on foreign policy with candor and with a commitment to what is best for our country." But the White House counteroffensive had hurt, badly. Kennedy himself was aware from polling data that he was skating on very thin ice, and as a result he began to put more emphasis on Carter's refusal to campaign or debate than on his actual handling of the two foreign-policy crises. His allegation that the President was using the crises as a convenient excuse to stay off the campaign trail was now demonstrably true. But instead of being able to drive the point home, Kennedy was obliged to cope with a perception that his criticism was simply personal political ambition pushing him to irresponsible conduct.

One episode illustrated graphically how the new strain of American patriotism, generated by the hostage crisis and Carter's tough rhetorical line toward the Russians, could be tapped for political advantage by an imaginative, some might even say unscrupulous, White House. Four days before the New Hampshire primary, at the 13th Winter Olympic Games at Lake Placid, New York, the American hockey team scored a come-from-behind 4–3 upset victory over the defending champions of the Soviet Union. The Russians had not lost a single hockey game in Olympic competition in twelve years and had been beaten only three times since first entering the games in 1956. The triumphant scene was marked by an incredible outburst of patriotic fervor, with the crowd chanting "U.S.A.! U.S.A.!" as the last minutes ran out, and a delirious winning team singing "God Bless America" when the game was over. Also, as fortune would have it, the telephone rang in the winners' locker room, and who was calling but the President of the United States, congratulating them and inviting them to the White House the following Monday.

Before that meeting could take place, however, the American team had to win one more game, against Finland, to capture the gold medal. This time Vice President Mondale was on hand, and when the Americans came from behind in the final period again and posted a 4–2 victory, the arena erupted once more, American flags waving wildly and more chants of "U.S.A.!" Mondale quickly repaired to the winners' locker room and picked up a telephone, conveniently wired for the occasion. When Carter's voice came on expressing the country's pride in the American hockey team, it could be clearly heard by the millions of fans—and voters—who had watched the climactic game on television.

Carter also told the team that all crisis work had stopped at the White House while he and his closest advisers watched them whip the Finns. Ironically, this was the same President who was insisting on a boycott of the Summer Olympics in Moscow as retribution for the Russians' invasion of Afghanistan. While playing the heavy among American summer-games athletes, Carter was making himself a conspicuous part of the great outpouring of patriotism. And again ironically, it was a patriotism stimulated in part by the public's frustration over his failure to resolve the hostage crisis or affect the Russian presence in Afghanistan.

The next day, on the eve of the New Hampshire primary, Carter welcomed the American Olympic hockey team to the White House. One by one, as the Olympians climbed the stairs on the South Portico and as television and still cameras captured the scene, he shook their hands and embraced them. It was a most serendipitous moment for a politician looking for a little extra boost at the polls, especially in hockey-crazy New Hampshire. Who needed to debate about Iran, the Russians, 18 percent inflation, and climbing interest rates when he had the nation's latest sports heroes on his doorstep?

Carter scored a clear-cut 49 percent to 38 victory over Kennedy in the New Hampshire primary—an outcome that probably would have occurred no matter what happened at Lake Placid, or what the President did in response. But the whole affair demonstrated again what Kennedy was up against. Subordinated in the public mind for the moment was the fact that Khomeini had just said he did not intend to release the hostages before April. If Carter needed a pressure valve to vent the national frustration just then, this surely was a convenient one.

Quite beyond the advantages of incumbency, the calendar now favored Carter. He could afford to lose to Kennedy in the Massachusetts primary (and did) because it was the senator's home ground, and because there then ensued a string of Southern primaries in which Kennedy's chances were now so hopeless that his organization made little more than a token effort in them—South Carolina, Florida, Georgia, and Alabama. And a week later, in Illinois, the President beat Kennedy by more than two to one in their first confrontation in a neutral northern industrial state.

That primary was marked most notably by the scene of Kennedy and his wife, Joan,* marching through a heavy, chilling snow in Chicago's annual St. Patrick's Day parade the afternoon before the voting. The Kennedys walked at first with his chief local supporter, the beleaguered first woman mayor, Jane Byrne, but gradually allowed a diplomatic distance to develop as the crowd's lusty boos descended on her, and some on Kennedy as well. Ever since her upset victory over Daley-machine Mayor Michael Bilandic in 1979, the acerbic, independent-minded Jane Byrne had struggled through a series of city strikes, fiscal crises, and intramural party feuds and conspiracies. In the process she slipped badly in the public-opinion polls but lost none of her defiance and feistiness toward her critics. She proved to be an additional burden Kennedy could not carry, along with a heavy Catholic vote against him. Chappaquiddick and "the moral issue" clung, and could not be shaken, in spite of television commercials depicting Kennedy as a man who had been visited by tragedy and had endured and survived.

The dimensions of Kennedy's defeat in Illinois made the New York primary a week later imperative for him; if he lost there, he would have little rationale left to continue his challenge to

*During the Illinois primary, a Kennedy advance man checked Joan Kennedy into a hotel suite in Chicago. Shortly afterward she came down to the lobby and smilingly told the young advance aide: "The Carter people arranged that suite for me." The advance man was puzzled. "No they didn't," he replied. "It was arranged through the Merchandise Mart [owned by the Kennedy family]." But she was adamant. "No, I'm sure the Carter people did," she said. "There was a six-pack and a bottle of my favorite white wine in the refrigerator." She was, of course, making a joke.

Carter. By this time, Kirk recalled later, "we had basically been backed into an industrial-state strategy"—meaning Kennedy had to demonstrate he would be a stronger candidate than Carter in most of the big industrial states from New York through Illinois, the states that are essential to any Democrat's election. And with Illinois a disaster, he said, "New York at this point was really make-or-break."

Up to now, Kennedy had suffered from a series of foreign-policy events and administration decisions beyond his control. But now, finally, he became an unwitting beneficiary. On the Saturday before the Massachusetts primary, the United Nations Security Council had taken up a resolution calling on Israel to dismantle civilian settlements in occupied Arab territories, including Jerusalem. The United States, which had abstained on two similar votes in 1979, surprised the Council—and infuriated the Israelis—by voting for the resolution, making it unanimous. Two nights later President Carter put out a statement explaining that the vote had been a mistake, a "failure to communicate" between the American mission to the U.N. and the White House. The vote had been approved, Carter said, "with the understanding that all references to Jerusalem would be deleted."

This "explanation" only worsened the embarrassment for Carter—the Israelis and the American Jewish community were not placated by the excuse, and critics of the Israeli settlement policy were quick to read domestic political motives into the switch. Including a reference to Jerusalem in any such Security Council resolution, the totality of which was offensive to the Jews, was objectionable to them because it did not acknowledge that the western half of the city had been part of Israel before the 1967 war, in which the other Arab territories had been taken.

The U.N. vote did not attract great publicity until the primary schedule had moved south, where the controversy caused Carter no trouble. Nor did it have any appreciable political bearing in Illinois, although Kennedy was quick to exploit it in fiery speeches to Jewish leaders in Chicago about the American commitment to Israel. Carter's campaign chairman, Robert Strauss, while acknowledging to them that the handling of the whole thing was "a terrible mistake," argued that Carter ought to get some credit for admitting it. Afterward, there were the usual postmortems to sort out how a "failure to communicate" was possible on a sensitive diplomatic and political matter. To one administration insider, however, the gaffe was easy to understand. Different viewpoints on what the policy should be among Carter, Vance, and United Nations Ambassador Donald McHenry, and Carter's failure to make his requirements known firmly enough, probably resulted in the snafu, he said. "It would have been almost unbelievably stupid to attempt to have it both ways by casting a vote and then rescinding the vote. Perhaps even more damning than the cynical interpretation is that it was just another screw-up."

In any event, Carter's easy victory in Illinois made the New York primary the last chance Kennedy had to stop Carter's campaign steamroller. Well before this juncture, in fact, some Democrats were calling on Kennedy to quit before the damage to the party's chances in November was irreparable. Within the Kennedy camp, too, there had been concern prior to Massachusetts. "I don't think everybody assumed he was going to win Massachusetts," Kirk said. "Coming in, the numbers looked tough, and there was some fear expressed that if you lost Massachusetts, what would it mean in terms of '82 [when Kennedy would be up for reelection to the Senate]." In addition, the campaign had little money, and few influential Democrats were rallying to Kennedy.* Also, the whole Kennedy strategy had been based on the expectation of some early victories, not necessarily to knock Carter out but to sustain the campaign for a more protracted fight. So, Kirk recalled, the thinking was that "there was a possible danger of losing Massachusetts, and at least it ought to be considered what that would mean. You know, 'Maybe we're just up against a brick wall here that we'll never be able to break through.'"

As already noted, Kennedy's home state had not let him down, however, so he pressed on, convinced that in any event Carter couldn't be reelected, and that sooner or later the President would have to abandon the Rose Garden strategy, and come out and discuss the issues.

---

*Among the few who did were Senators George McGovern, Paul Tsongas, John Durkin, Howard Metzenbaum, and Don Riegle; Representatives Barbara Mikulski and Morris Udall; and United Auto Workers president Douglas Fraser.

After the Illinois setback, however, the question of quitting inevitably had to be faced again. "Had he lost New York, he would have had to get out," Kirk later acknowledged. The polls indicated more bad news. One had Kennedy 27 percentage points behind with only a few days to go, in spite of the fact that before Jewish audiences he had been hitting Carter hard about the United Nations vote. Parker and Shrum, preparing for the worst, wrote a withdrawal statement for their candidate—a brief concession with congratulations to Carter and a call for a Democratic victory in November. "But he didn't even look at the thing," one staff aide said later.

In the final days before the New York primary, a massive surge developed for Kennedy, in part because of the U.N. vote controversy, but also quite probably because the first serious expression of negative feelings among voters about Carter himself. His "mistake" on the Israel vote was considered by many New Yorkers as an initial failure to assess the political consequences of the original vote, and of a subsequent "correction" by his political strategists. And there was suspicion, shared by Democratic Mayor Edward Koch among others, that federal aid to New York City might suffer in Carter's efforts to balance the federal budget.

Later, at least one member of Carter's political circle argued that if it hadn't been for the "mistaken" U.N. vote, Carter would have won the primary, Kennedy would have been forced to quit the race, Anderson would not have run as an independent, and in the fall the President would have carried New York and been reelected. That, of course, was a barrelful of ifs. Not only was Carter hurt among Jewish voters in New York, this insider said, but the last-minute intensive wooing of that bloc alienated others in the state. "I can remember spending so much time doing spots with Koch and on the U.N. thing," he said, "and trying to get the Jews back, and getting calls from Dan Horgan [a campaign aide upstate], who was picking up New York City television in Buffalo and saying, 'What are you doing for my people?' We spent so much time bringing back the Jews that we also neglected going after the Catholics and the rest of the vote, which we had. And the flip-flop on the vote hurt us because the big thing Carter still had was honesty and being a good man."

Kennedy, for his part, contended later that the switch on the U.N. vote and the uncertainty about Carter's commitment to New York City "demonstrated two of the points we were trying to make there—the [lack of] competency and consistency and predictability in the area of foreign policy, and the back and forth about the cities. All of those elements that I thought were fairly typical of the administration generally really came together and permitted me to really get a focus and attention on the issues. Things really took hold that were not as evident in some of the other places."

In any event Kennedy not only upset Carter in New York and Connecticut as well, but his New York margin was a virtual rout over an incumbent on a winning streak—about 16 percent. As a result of the Democratic Party's proportional allocation of delegates, Carter won nearly half of New York's and Connecticut's national convention delegates and was still in a commanding position for the nomination. But now for the first time the foreign crises were not enough to carry the day for a President who declined to campaign. Carter was not yet ready to abandon the Rose Garden strategy—indeed, he seemed to be locked into it by his commitment not to campaign until the hostages were freed. Also, one insider said later, after the loss in New York, "it would have looked so desperate to come out." So, although Carter state coordinators around the country, and field director Tim Kraft, were clamoring for an end to the Rose Garden strategy, still the President clung to it.

"New York really shook everybody up quite a bit," a Carter campaign strategist said later, "not because we thought there was a significant chance of the thing unraveling, but because there was that concern that all those people who said, 'If they ever cut the guy [Carter], he'd bleed to death,' might be right. Carter could become the issue, and we felt that whoever became the issue would lose. Wisconsin, the next important primary, would be the test of whether he was hemorrhaging." Wisconsin was considered critical because it was going to be a test of whether or not the New York vote had been an aberration, a "Metroliner phenomenon," as the Carter people referred to an Eastern seaboard aversion to Carter. "Pat Caddell's data in New York and Connecticut," this same strategist said, "indicated that in fact Jimmy Carter had again become the issue, along with the economy. . . . Attitudes toward Kennedy were softening and were hardening toward Carter, and the impact of Iran and Afghanistan was lessening." The reality of the Carter record had intruded, and whenever that happened it was bad news for the President.

There was to be still one more dramatic, political exploitation by Carter of the hostage crisis, however. During recent weeks, a U.N. commission had been negotiating with the Iranians, and the administration was hopeful that a breakthrough might at last be at hand. President Abolhassan Bani-Sadr had indicated privately that he was mustering the votes in the Iranian Revolutionary Council to order the hostages' captors to turn them over to the jurisdiction of the government. That action in turn was seen as a necessary first step toward their eventual release. Carter had been considering the imposition of economic sanctions against Iran but had agreed to hold off, pending this possible transfer.

Such was the background in the early morning hours of April 1—"April Fool's Day," as Paul Kirk noted wryly—as most of the nation slept, including the voters of Wisconsin and Kansas, whose primary polls were to open in several hours. At about 4:00 a.m., according to Jody Powell, the President and his principal foreign-policy and political aides met in the Oval Office. Among those present at that odd hour were Secretary of State Cyrus Vance, Deputy Secretary of State Warren Christopher, national security adviser Zbigniew Brzezinski, Powell, and Hamilton Jordan. News had just come from Tehran, in Powell's words, "that the government control was greased, that it was going to happen, that Bani-Sadr was going to meet with these people [the Council] and they had a majority. And that once they voted he was going to make a public statement to that effect."

As matters turned out, Powell acknowledged, although Bani-Sadr gathered a clear majority for the move, "they caved at the last moment" and there was no transfer at all. But Carter did not wait for the apparent good news to be confirmed, or give it time to turn sour. After three hours of digesting all the information at hand and satisfying himself that Bani-Sadr had said what the White House had been told privately he would say—that the hostages would be transferred if the United States would refrain from "all propaganda and agitation" toward Iran—Carter simply called a press conference.

The unusual hour—it was 7:13 a.m. when he began—itself signaled some major announcement and guaranteed live, nationwide television network coverage on the morning news programs. Standing behind his desk in the Oval Office, Carter proclaimed that Bani-Sadr's statement constituted a "positive step" that removed the necessity for imposing economic sanctions against Iran. In response to questions the President acknowledged that "we have no assurance that this will be done except that the President of Iran has announced that it will be done." And while he did not say the step would lead to the hostages' release, his response to a question permitted that inference to be drawn.

Reporter: "Do you know when they will be actually released and be brought home?"

Carter: "I presume that we will know more about that as the circumstances develop. We do not know *the exact time scheduled* at this moment."

It certainly sounded like very good news, particularly because the word came directly from the President, from the Oval Office, and at that unusual hour. Americans across the Eastern and Central time zones were just getting up, having their coffee, and watching the morning television news shows—Americans in New York and Ohio, and in Wisconsin and Kansas. Many in the latter two states got dressed and went out to vote in their primaries, and an overwhelming majority of those who voted Democratic voted for Jimmy Carter over Edward Kennedy and Jerry Brown. They probably would have done so anyway, but this little early-morning television encouragement surely didn't hurt.

Jody Powell later denied there had been any politics in the timing of the press conference. It was, he said, simply that Carter was up and about, and the news was at hand, so why wait? "It just seemed like the natural thing to do," he said. "This whole three months we were building toward that morning. We had this stuff directly and indirectly from the Iranians. Their meet-

ing was supposed to take place, the statement was supposed to
be made about midnight our time. We came down to see if
[Bani-Sadr] said what we had been told he would say. He did,
and the ball was now in our court to react to it. We could have
waited until nine o'clock or I suppose I could have read a statement rather than the President make it. We didn't come down
here at four o'clock in the morning because it was the day before
the primary. We came at four o'clock in the morning because
Bani-Sadr met with the Revolutionary Council." Had the promise of a transfer occurred a day earlier or later, he said, "I don't
think we would have handled it at all differently." And, Powell
went on, he didn't believe Carter's optimistic statement had anything to do with the result in the Wisconsin primary—though
Caddell acknowledged in a Milwaukee press conference a day
later that "the fact that the Iranian thing surfaced in a public
way focused attention on the fact that he [Carter] is working on
the problem."

   Still, voters had some grounds for being skeptical, for, as another insider observed later of Carter: "He has been known to
exaggerate things, and he might very well have taken what was
a legitimate although perhaps less than monumental change in
the situation, seen the potential for some political gain from it,
and maximized the potential. Once the hostages had been taken
and once the campaign had begun, it was impossible to talk
about either totally independent of the other. In fact the campaign *was* having an impact on the hostage situation, whether
we liked it or not. The Iranians were watching the developments
of the campaign, and the hostage situation was inevitably influ-
encing the course of the campaign. I don't think there was . . .
a cynical attempt to manipulate the hostage situation to advantage, but I think there was and had to be a recognition of the
connection. I think Carter's number-one concern was, and always had been since the hostages were taken, to try and do
whatever he felt was necessary to successfully get them out of
there. But he was not operating in a political vacuum, and he
knew that."

   Another insider brought up an additional factor, which was
shortly to change drastically. Carter had given up "his most valu-

able political instrument," he noted, in electing very early on not to use force to resolve the Iranian crisis, which would have been popular. And once having done that, he could not be blamed for making other gestures to preserve his political position at home. "To complain about him playing politics with it is to ignore that he didn't use the chief political instrument he had," he observed.

Others were not so charitable. Indeed, what came to be known in political circles as the "Wisconsin primary press conference" was to haunt Carter for the rest of the election year. Kirk argued later that while the episode may have been of short-term benefit to the President, it "sowed the seeds of cynicism" that blossomed on the final weekend of the fall campaign with the suspicion that Carter had also somehow manipulated the "October surprise" feared and rumored by the Reaganites.

Indeed, Carter strategists agreed. They acknowledged later that the memory of the skepticism bred by the "Wisconsin primary press conference" caused them to pause in timing Carter's televised remarks on the hostage situation on the Sunday night before the election. In any event, however, Carter's actions on that early morning—revealed almost at once to be premature, when Bani-Sadr would not or could not effect the transfer of the hostages—did not harm his steady progress toward renomination.

Yet some of the President's aides had been convinced since the Maine caucuses that the Rose Garden strategy would not hold up indefinitely. Greg Schneiders, the former White House aide who joined Rafshoon's advertising and consulting firm before the campaign, told later of radio and television ads prepared to cope with criticism of Carter's not campaigning. "We did some spots for Maine and New Hampshire with the President saying himself, on tapes and also on camera, that he was sorry he wasn't able to campaign, which we hoped would mitigate the negative impact of not being up there," Schneiders said. "Each state that he didn't campaign in, it seemed that more and more people became convinced that we were being hurt, until it finally got to the point that there really weren't any dissenters."

But the problem remained, however, that Carter had said at the outset of the Rose Garden strategy that he would not campaign until the hostages had been released. Powell recalled saying to him in December, "If we do this, it will play hell on getting back into the campaign." What finally got Carter out of the Rose Garden, ironically, was not a release of the hostages but a military operation that ended in fiasco and made their release more unlikely than ever.

Ever since the taking of the American embassy in Tehran, contingency planning had been under way in the Pentagon to rescue the hostages, but the President had insisted that peaceful measures would bring their return. When Bani-Sadr failed to obtain his government's control over the hostages, however, Carter decided it was time to use force, although, as one insider put it later, he "by nature is almost a pacifist."

The plans for extricating the Americans in Tehran in a daring helicopter raid were reviewed at one Camp David meeting and were sent back to the Pentagon for revisions before a countdown finally was begun in the third week of April. The mission was a high-risk one for political as well as military reasons. Powell recalled that after a meeting in which Cabinet members were informed of the planned raid, somebody said on the way out, "God, I hope to hell this works." To which a Cabinet member replied: "Well, if it doesn't, it could also be the end of the Carter presidency." Of all of them, however, only Secretary of State Vance voiced strong objections. In fact, he told Carter in advance of the mission that he was going to resign afterward, regardless of the outcome.

On the night of April 24, six C-130 American transport planes took off from a base in southern Egypt for a refueling rendezvous in the Iranian desert some three hundred miles southeast of Tehran. Also, eight American helicopters were launched from the aircraft carrier *Nimitz* in the Gulf of Oman. One helicopter developed mechanical troubles and was forced to land well short of the rendezvous point; one got lost in a sandstorm and returned to the *Nimitz;* a third had a hydraulic problem at the refueling point and couldn't take off again. Because the plan called for a minimum of six operating helicopters, the commander recommended that the mission be aborted, and Carter, following the progress closely at the White House, agreed. But as the five remaining helicopters and the six transports prepared to take off to return to their bases, a helicopter and a C-130 collided on the ground, causing a fire in which eight men were killed and four others burned. The survivors abandoned the scene, leaving the dead behind in the flaming wreckage. It was an unmitigated disaster.

Carter, looking shaken, went on television the next morning, again at seven o'clock, to report to the nation on what had happened. Nobody accused him this time of timing his appearance for political benefit. Indeed, after the election Hamilton Jordan wrote in *Life* magazine that the news Carter announced that morning cost his boss the presidency. "The hostage crisis had come to symbolize the collective frustration of the American people," Jordan wrote. "And in that sense, the President's chances for reelection probably died on the desert of Iran with eight brave soldiers who gave their lives trying to free the American hostages."

In the long run, perhaps Jordan was right. In the short term, however, the failure—which Carter, a believer in accentuating the positive, characteristically called "an incomplete success"— only served once again to rally public support behind the beleaguered President. Just as Americans rallied behind President John F. Kennedy after the Bay of Pigs fiasco in 1961, Carter accepted full responsibility for the failure—and won public support in return.

By now Carter had lost, though very narrowly, in two more major industrial states—the primary in Pennsylvania and caucuses in Michigan. Concern mounted among his supporters that the President might indeed be a political hemophiliac. In terms of the national convention delegate count, the President was steadily accumulating the voting strength he needed for renomination. But there was considerable disagreement within the Democratic Party about whether delegates, once selected to support a specific candidate, were legally bound to vote for him at the convention. The Kennedy strategists were hoping that late major-state primary defeats for the President would convince his delegates they would be nominating a certain loser in November, and would turn to Kennedy when the nomination roll call came in New York in August. And beyond that, the truth of the political situation after the failed raid was that there no longer was any valid reason for Carter not to campaign, and everybody knew it. "One of the reasons that [attacks on] the Rose Garden strategy . . . had not cut very much was that they weren't particularly credible," Powell explained later. "I think most people judged up to that point that the President had a considerable amount of logic on his side, but in fact it wouldn't be credible anymore because it wasn't true anymore."

Powell and other Carter aides recognized as well that the President's reputation for integrity was his greatest political strength, and that Kennedy could undermine it, as he was striving mightily to do, by labeling as phony Carter's contention that he was too occupied with foreign-policy crises to campaign. "It was an obvious point of attack," Powell noted. "If you claim you can't campaign when in fact you know and everybody else knows that you can, then you're asking for trouble."

The next question was how to end the Rose Garden strategy with the minimum damage to the credibility of a President who had vowed he would not campaign until the hostages were released. A press conference was scheduled four days after the aborted rescue mission. Powell and others in the White House assumed that a question would be asked about campaigning, and they prepared the President for it.*

"I frankly recommended," Powell said later, "that he really not get into explaining or justifying . . . but just simply say, 'I have decided that the situation permits me to conduct a limited campaign schedule, and I'll intend to do that as long as that remains the case.'" It was "almost always" the practice in pre-press conference briefings, Powell explained, for aides to suggest the exact words that the President might use in response to sensitive or politically important questions. They did so on this occasion, but as is often the case, the question never was asked.

If the matter was to come up in any but a happenstance way, a dependable interrogator would have to be found. And as it turned out, finding one, and an occasion for him to ask the ques-

---

*Not to leave the matter to chance, one of the President's political strategists sought out a kindly member of the press with the idea of planting the question. But by the time the aide walked into the room, the reporter was already seated with a group of other reporters, and the "plant" was abandoned.

tion, was not difficult. On the very next day Carter held a meeting in the East Room with "community leaders" from around the country. One of them was Charles Manatt, former Democratic state chairman in California who was now finance chairman for the Democratic National Committee (and later, in February 1981, elected Democratic national chairman). It occurred to Manatt, with some advance information from the White House staff on what the answer would be, to ask the President whether he might now be able to get out and meet the voters. Carter didn't hesitate. "Yes," he said, as applause broke out in the room. "It's been a long time. I have stayed in the White House under extraordinary circumstances. But times change and a lot of the responsibilities that have been on my shoulders have been alleviated."

The raid, though aborted, was behind him; American allies were supporting political and economic sanctions against Iran; American sanctions against the Russians for the Afghanistan invasion were in place; and support was building for his economic and energy proposals at home. "None of these challenges are completely removed," he said, going beyond what had been planned for him to say, "but I believe they are manageable enough now for me to leave the White House for a limited travel schedule, including some campaigning if I choose to do so, in order to explain to the American people how these things can be brought to a successful conclusion." This, remember, was only five days after the failed raid that already had resulted in a reported dispersal of the hostages to various other locales in Iran, thereby making any mass rescue much more difficult.

Kennedy, campaigning in Indiana, was quick to respond. "Is an inflation rate of 18 percent 'manageable' for the American people?" he asked. "Are our interest rates of 18 percent 'manageable' for young people who would like to buy a home?" Now that Carter finally was coming out, Kennedy lost no time renewing his challenge for the President to debate "any place in this country, any time in this country." But Carter just as quickly declined. Resuming campaigning *on a limited basis* meant just that—a few token appearances somewhere.

The phrase "manageable enough" was not, of course, in the script, and Powell later acknowledged that "it was certainly an unfortunate way to put it, but the substance of it was entirely accurate." Carter had said what he had been supposed to say, all right. The trouble was he went on and added a phrase—another example of his penchant for always putting the best face on things, for maximum political benefit.* Rosalynn Carter was infected with the same rhetorical virus. Campaigning in Indiana, she reported that the failed rescue mission "has made a dramatic change [in the hostage situation] because now the Iranians realize we can do something about it. They are very nervous men now." It was as if George Orwell's novel *1984,* in which the characters talked "newspeak," had arrived four years early. (The Random House Dictionary defines "newspeak" as "an official or semiofficial style of writing or saying one thing in the guise of its opposite, especially in order to serve a political or ideological cause while pretending to be objective.") Mr. Orwell, meet Mr. Carter.

Thus, in any event, ended the Rose Garden strategy. On his first outing ten days later, advertised as nonpolitical, the President dusted off his most "presidential" format, the "town meeting" that had been so successful—and politically safe—during his term. At Temple University in Philadelphia, he stood before a huge American flag that would have done justice to General Patton as played by George C. Scott and answered questions that were pointed but "manageable enough" for an old pro.†

It was not until three weeks later—only five days before the

---

*That observation, and Carter's press-conference characterization of the desert disaster as an "incomplete success," were reminiscent of his remarks when he was campaigning in North Carolina in 1978, facing tobacco farmers who were outraged at the anti-smoking campaign of Secretary of Health, Education and Welfare Califano. On that occasion Carter had unabashedly reported in tobacco country that Califano's campaign was out to make cigarette smoking "even safer than it is today."

†Shortly before this "town meeting" Carter had named Senator Edmund Muskie to succeed Vance as secretary of state, and at the meeting the President told a questioner, "I see Ed Muskie as being a much stronger and more statesmanlike senior citizen figure who will be a more evocative spokesman for our nation's policy; not nearly so bogged down in the details of protocol, like meeting with and handling the visits of a constant stream of diplomats who come to Washington." Reporters immediately interpreted this as a slap at Vance, but Carter denied it. Vance, one close aide said later, "felt betrayed and assaulted" and never forgot the incident, although Carter wrote to him saying he hadn't meant to be critical—to which Vance replied with "a fairly stiff" note of thanks for his trouble.

end of the entire primary period—that Carter actually made an overt, acknowledged campaign appearance. In Columbus, Ohio, he demonstrated that he had lost none of his talent as a political alchemist. With a promise that "we will always talk sense, we will always give it to you straight," he told the crowd that "America is turning the tide" in dealing with its economic, energy, and foreign-policy problems. If Edward Kennedy hoped that by driving Jimmy Carter out of the Rose Garden the President would crumble politically under the weight of a sick economy and failed foreign policy, he was sadly mistaken.

On June 3, the final day of the primary season—with more than a third of the total delegates needed for nomination at stake in eight different primaries—Kennedy defeated Carter in five, but by now it was too late. Carter picked up enough delegates in the three states he won, and through proportional allocation in the five he lost, to assure his nomination—unless, of course, what he had could be pried loose from him by convention time in August.

From November until June Kennedy had been out on the firing line trying, with success only at the last hour, to get Carter to join him. But all that Kennedy, his strategists and media managers could do could not make up for public concern about a foreign-policy crisis, even when Carter had proved demonstrably that he could not solve it. Kennedy was plagued, too, to the very end of the primaries, by money woes, a media campaign that was too little and too late, and by the deficiencies of his own organization. "We didn't have a Jordan," one insider said later. "The best thing about the campaign was the senator. There was no thematic organization. The strength of it was him. Any creative things on the schedule he added on the road."

In a sense, though Carter's strategists longed in vain for the day the wounded Kennedy would drop out of the race, his persistence through the long string of primaries was a political godsend to Carter. It gave him the recurrent image of a winner, in spite of the obvious vulnerability of his own record. "The only good thing for Jimmy Carter in 1980," said Paul Kirk after the primaries, "was Tuesday nights, when he could say he beat Ted Kennedy. All the rest was bad."

8.
Cronkite's
Co-Presidency

Ronald Reagan's unimpeded march to the Republican nomination—George Bush having conceded defeat when there were still twelve primaries to go—gave him more time than is often afforded a presidential nominee to select his running mate. This fact seemed particularly fortuitous because, given Reagan's age, there was a more than normal actuarial possibility that the individual he picked, if the Republican ticket were elected, would become president.

How Reagan made use of that time—or, rather, failed to make use of it—offers a classic case history in how not to choose a running mate. But perhaps even more notably, the way the news media, television especially, reported the story at the Republican National Convention in Detroit is a case history in perception overtaking reality—the appearance of things being accepted so widely as fact that it threatens to become fact.

It all really began, according to Dick Wirthlin, as early as May of the election year, when some of Reagan's strategists started to discuss the possibility of a seemingly far-fetched but intriguing idea: Reagan should try to get Gerald Ford to run with him. What encouraged them, Wirthlin said later, was the fact that a similar idea "was emanating from people very close to Ford, and it was difficult for us to tell whether he was sending us a message through intermediaries or whether these individuals were acting pretty much on their own volition." Some of these friends of Ford, Wirthlin said, implied they had discussed the possibility

166

with the former President, and others "flatly told us, 'No, he is not interested in getting back into politics, and clearly not interested in running as a vice-presidential contender.'" In fact, Reagan himself had broached the subject with Ford at a meeting in Palm Springs around this time, and Ford had told him he wasn't interested. "I thought it was a firm turndown," Ford said in an interview after the election.

Among those who nevertheless talked up a Reagan-Ford ticket to the Reagan people was Bryce Harlow, who had been a White House aide under Eisenhower, Nixon, and Ford. On his own Harlow circulated a petition for the "dream ticket" among prominent Republicans and discussed it directly with Ford and former Secretary of State Kissinger.

In any event, Wirthlin in late May and early June conducted some polls that indicated that in each category tested, Ford rated ahead of all other Republicans being mentioned as possible running mates, including the eight actually on Reagan's "short list" of prospects: Bush, Howard Baker, William Simon, Donald Rumsfeld, Richard Lugar, Jack Kemp, Guy Vander Jagt, and Reagan's old friend Paul Laxalt. Ford's rating was not surprising. He was clearly the best known of the pack.

Armed with these polls, Wirthlin went to Bill Casey and Ed Meese with the idea. His rationale went like this: "One, Ford brought something right out of the box. Two, he appealed to a different coalition. Three, he didn't need any start-up time; he could begin campaigning the day after he was selected. Four, it would be a sufficiently dramatic event to capture the focus of the press in a positive way. Five, and this was the clincher, given the fact that it was a close election, Ford might make the crucial difference between our winning and losing."

Casey and Meese thought enough of the idea to have Wirthlin present it to Reagan. Again Wirthlin spelled out these five arguments for a Reagan-Ford ticket and told Reagan: "There are a lot of things in politics you cannot control. There are a lot of things out there that are handed to you on your platter. But the one thing you have absolute control over is who you ask to be your vice president. This is probably going to be one of the most critical decisions you're going to face." Then Wirthlin reviewed the polling data and concluded his presentation with this question to Reagan: "Suppose that in 1976, in spite of the signals that were sent to the Ford people that you didn't want to be vice president, President Ford came to you in a private way and said, 'Governor, I need you. The country needs you. Your being on the ticket can make the difference between my beating Jimmy Carter and my losing to him.' Governor, what would you have done if that kind of appeal had been made in that way?"

Reagan replied: "Dick, I would have accepted."

Then Wirthlin said: "Governor, can you afford not to give Gerald Ford the same opportunity?"

And Reagan said: "No." The candidate instructed Wirthlin to discuss the idea with more of his aides, but in the strictest secrecy. Reagan himself meanwhile sounded out members of his California "kitchen cabinet," and they were enthusiastic.

Reagan's reply to Wirthlin's hypothetical question was not, by the way, in keeping with what his closest aides had sworn was his position at the time of the 1976 convention in Kansas City. John Sears, then his campaign manager, had in fact told Ford's aides that Reagan would meet with Ford after the presidential nomination *only* if he would *not* be asked to be Ford's running mate. However, Reagan rewrote this bit of political history only ten days after Ford's defeat in November 1976. He told a business group in Boston that if Ford had asked him, he would have accepted second place on the Republican ticket. "What if he [Ford] had come with the party leaders," Reagan posed to his listeners, "they had come together and said to me, 'You have to do this'? Nancy and I both agreed that would have been an almost impossible situation to say no to." Many with suspicious minds reasoned then that Reagan, knowing he would try again for the Republican nomination in 1980—and would need the help of Ford and his supporters, or at least not their active opposition— was trying already to improve the atmosphere. It was no secret that Ford blamed his defeat in part on Reagan's refusal not only to run but to campaign vigorously for him.

Wirthlin, of course, knew all this, too, when he posed the question. He is not an attorney, but he was following the cardinal rule of the criminal lawyer: Never ask a witness a question the answer to which you don't already know.

One question that Wirthlin did not have to put to Reagan, the answer to which he also knew, was whether Reagan would like an alternative to the choice that political logic, and many fellow Republicans, were already pressing on him—George Bush. Ever since the episode in Nashua in February, Reagan had come to hold the preppy Yankee transplant in, as the late Senator Robert Kerr of Oklahoma used to say, minimum high regard. "Reagan is a very gracious contestant," one of his inner circle said, "and he generally views his opponents with a good deal of respect. The thing he couldn't understand [was that behavior]. It imprinted with Reagan that Bush was a wimp. He remembered that night clearly when we had our vice-presidential discussions. He couldn't understand how a man could have sat there so passively. He felt it showed a lack of courage. And now that it was time to think about a running mate, the prospective presidential nominee gave a sympathetic ear to those who objected to Bush for reasons that ran, one of the group said later, from his behavior at Nashua to "anti-Trilateralism" (a reference to Bush's membership in the Trilateral Commission). The Commission, an organization of businessmen, bankers, academicians, and politicians from North America, Western Europe, and Japan, founded in 1973 by the American banker David Rockefeller, had Jimmy Carter as a member before he was elected President. Carter later called on some fellow members, most notably Columbia professor Zbigniew Brzezinski, to join his administration, leading some conservatives to talk of a "conspiracy" backed by Rockefeller to gain control of the American government. Bush had resigned from the Commission by the time he ran for the Republican presidential nomination, but many conservatives continued to view him with suspicion.

Other insiders, however, made the obvious strong case for Bush. By now he was well known, and he had demonstrated strength in precisely those industrial states—notably Pennsylvania and Michigan—where Kennedy had shown Carter to be weak and that figured to be key battlegrounds in the fall campaign. Drew Lewis, Reagan's agent as deputy chairman of the Republican National Committee, argued that he needed Bush in the Eastern states and urged that Reagan settle on his choice before he got to the convention. If Reagan waited, Lewis said, he would come under too many pressures and would end up with a politically neutral running mate. (That was exactly what had happened to Ford in 1976 when, after a long night of weighing various possibilities, he had settled on Senator Bob Dole of Kansas. Lewis had told Ford then, "You just lost the election." But Ford had replied that the imperative had been to choose someone whom he could get the convention, filled with disappointed Reagan supporters, to accept with a minimum of controversy.) Although either Ford or Howard Baker also would have fulfilled Lewis's requirement for a candidate who would broaden Reagan's base, he argued forcefully that Bush was the most palatable and practical choice.

Reagan, however, continued to resist. He told several staff members and advisers that he still harbored "doubts" about Bush, based on Nashua. "If he can't stand up to that kind of pressure," Reagan told one intimate, "how could he stand up to the pressure of being president?" To another, he said: "I want to be very frank with you. I have strong reservations about George Bush. I'm concerned about turning the country over to him." And to several he had added, as he said to one, obviously with Paul Laxalt in mind, "I don't know why I can't pick somebody who's always been for me." There was, moreover, a personal element in Reagan's feeling about Bush. Neither he nor Nancy Reagan was entirely comfortable with George and Barbara Bush; the gulf between life in the Eastern establishment and in Pacific Palisades was too great.

As the convention approached, though, Reagan was beginning to face the inevitable: that it would have to be Bush—unless he could persuade Ford to become the first former president to run for vice president, a job he had also held. About two days before leaving for Detroit, one Reagan strategist said, "He came to the conclusion that it would be Bush, but he wasn't all that happy about it." As Reagan began to analyze the situation, another insider said, "The governor began to see that while Nashua may have been a negative, Bush showed a certain toughness while a lot of other people fell by the wayside." If there was a good option, though, Reagan was ready to seize it.

A few days before the convention formally opened in Detroit, while hearings about the Republican platform were being held,

Bob Teeter, whose office is in Detroit, flew home from Washington on the same plane with Casey, Meese, and his fellow-pollster Wirthlin. They brought up the subject of Ford with the surprised Teeter, one of a select group of political advisers who met with the former President periodically to discuss politics and his future. "It was clear that they all were very enthusiastic about Ford," Teeter recalled. "Wirthlin had tested it and Ford showed best." But the Reagan men also asked Teeter about Bush, for whom he had done some polling and whom he had supported for the nomination. "Bob said he didn't think Ford would do it," Wirthlin said.

Meanwhile, Stuart Spencer, Ford's 1976 campaign manager, had been contacted by Casey, Meese, and Mike Deaver and asked to sound out Ford. He did so, asking the former President: "Want me to pursue it?" Ford replied, "Hell, no." He had already thought about the idea because Bryce Harlow had discussed it with him and Reagan himself had raised it at that earlier meeting in Palm Springs.

On Saturday, July 12, Ford arrived in Detroit for a round of public appearances and a speech to the convention on Monday night. He didn't want to be on the ticket, and at one point told Teeter he was contemplating going home from the convention after his speech "because he was concerned about somebody trying to pull a draft on him." Teeter talked to Ford daily over the next three days, and each time Ford emphasized that he wasn't interested.

On Monday Reagan arrived on the same plane from Los Angeles with Stu Spencer, who had signed aboard for the fall campaign. Reagan asked him how Ford had reacted to the feeler. "Ron," Spencer said, "Ford ain't gonna do it, and you're gonna pick Bush." But judging from Reagan's reaction, Spencer recalled later, "There was no way he was going to pick Bush," and the reason was simple: Reagan just plain didn't like the guy. "It was chemistry," Spencer said.

Once in Detroit, Reagan received the customary nominee's welcome and began the nominee's routine. One of the first orders of business was a courtesy call paid by Ron and Nancy Reagan on Jerry and Betty Ford in Ford's suite at the Detroit Plaza Hotel. Reagan was well aware that Ford could not but recall that four years earlier Reagan had pledged support and then, in Ford's view, had extended precious little of it. Ford, in fact, was in Detroit with a distinct coolness toward Reagan and had set his mind on helping the Republican ticket more out of loyalty to party—and a keen desire to kick Jimmy Carter out of the White House—than out of any yearning to see Reagan elected. (When Ford earlier had gathered his advisers in Palm Springs to consider and finally reject the idea of challenging Reagan himself, he had launched into a tirade against Carter. And then, one participant recalled, as Ford was leaving the room he held up his hand with his thumb and forefinger about an inch apart and said: "And Reagan's about that much better.") So the atmosphere was clearly strained as Reagan greeted the former President. To get off on the right foot Reagan handed a surprised Ford a handsomely wrapped gift. "Reagan seemed kind of anxious for him to open it," said David Kennerly, the official photographer in Ford's White House, who was there on assignment for *Time.* The gift was an old, authentic Indian peace pipe. "It was a thoughtful thing to do, and it gave Ford a good feeling about their first meeting," Kennerly said. The foursome exchanged small talk for a short while and then the Reagans left.

That night, Ford addressed the convention with one of his best speeches ever. He gave the Democrats in general and Jimmy Carter in particular a pummeling, and he pledged his support to Reagan in terms so extravagant that the convention erupted with joy at this signal that the simmering Ford-Reagan feud seemed at last to be at an end. Reagan's men thought they might be hearing a more significant message—an encouragement to offer Ford the second spot on the ticket. "When Ford spoke," Wirthlin said later, "we thought he was sending us some very strong signals. We thought in essence he was saying, 'The door's open.' "

Ford's words certainly gave that impression. "Some call me an elder statesman," he began. "I don't know. I don't mind telling you all that I am not ready to quit yet. I've got news for this convention and for Jimmy Carter. This Republican is going to do everything in his power to elect our nominee to the presidency of the United States. We've got a lot of work to do, and you are looking at one volunteer who will try harder, work longer, and speak with more conviction to get this country a competent president again. Elder statesmen are supposed to sit quietly and smile wisely from the sidelines. I've never been much for sitting. I've never spent much time on the sidelines. Betty'll tell you that. This country means too much to me to comfortably park on the bench. So, when this convention fields the team for Governor Reagan, count me in."

Having heard that invitation, Reagan definitely decided he would do just that and make one more try. ("I must say, we all got swept away with the idea," Reagan told us after the election.) Around noon the next day, Tuesday, a delegation of senators, congressmen, and governors supporting Reagan came by his suite to discuss the matter of his running mate. Reagan broke in at one point and asked what they thought about Ford. The group was surprised because all had thought there was no possibility, but they were clearly in favor. They advised Reagan to approach Ford directly, which he had already decided to do.

William Timmons, Reagan's convention manager, meanwhile had suggested that Reagan meet with each of the vice-presidential prospects so that he could explore with them questions about their backgrounds, qualifications, and attitudes toward campaigning and governing. "But he said, no, he was not going to parade them through his suite because he felt that a number of good Democrats were misused by candidate Carter in Plains when he paraded them down for publicity purposes, and he didn't want to use those candidates that way. He thought that was demeaning, and he wasn't going to do it." Timmons said frankly he favored the exercise, to make sure Reagan was comfortable with the individual he chose if it wasn't going to be Ford, and "I was not unaware of the publicity value in moving people up and down the hotel."

That afternoon, this time in Reagan's suite, Reagan and Ford met again, just the two of them, and Reagan popped the question again, this time more earnestly. "I know what I'm asking," he said to Ford, "and I know that you've made it plain already that you didn't want anything of this kind, but I'm asking, will you please reconsider?"

Ford replied, "I don't think there's any chance of it." He could be of more help to Reagan, he said, off the ticket. Besides, there were complications, such as the fact that they both were now residents of California, and the twelfth amendment to the Constitution prohibits electors from voting for both a president and vice president from their own state.

Ford for months had been using this fact to rule himself out. It always seemed like a disingenuous alibi, since all he would have had to do was change his legal residence back to Michigan, or to Colorado, where he had a vacation home in Vail. Reagan was ready for the excuse. He handed Ford a legal memorandum on how the twelfth-amendment problem could be handled, asked him to look it over, think about the whole idea, and get back to him the next morning, Wednesday. That was the day of the presidential nomination roll call, and Reagan wanted to make his selection after its conclusion. Ford said he didn't think anything could be worked out, but he would look at the memo.

Reagan's very deferential manner toward Ford, begun with the presentation of the peace pipe, was paying dividends. When Ford returned from the second meeting he told Kennerly, "Do you know, I'm really beginning to like the man."

To Kennerly this remark was significant. "He [Ford] was pretty bitter going into that whole deal," he said later. "I think Ford had just decided that because he disliked Carter so much . . . he really would go to any lengths to defeat Carter. And if it meant swallowing some of his pride in getting back together with Reagan, I'm sure that was part of it. But then it went beyond that, for there did become between the two of them a kind of affection."

Reagan came away from the second meeting thinking he might be able to get Ford after all. That night Casey phoned Henry Kissinger and invited the former secretary of state to his suite at the Plaza. When Kissinger arrived, Casey, Meese, and Deaver asked their visitor to intercede with the former President, knowing that few people more impressed Ford and carried more weight with him than Kissinger. He agreed to do so. That night Ford began to feel the pressure in earnest. He and Betty went to a party on the yacht *Global Star*, owned by John McGoff, a Michigan newspaper publisher, and returned late to his suite, where Kissinger was waiting. It was now around midnight, as Kissinger, Ford, Jack Marsh, an old Ford White House aide and friend, and Alan Greenspan, former chairman of the Council of Economic Advisers, discussed Reagan's overture. Again Ford's answer was no. But when Kissinger and Greenspan began to weigh the possibilities for Ford to have a significant role in policy he didn't cut off the discussion.

Even later that night, as Teeter was leaving the Detroit Club, where his firm, Market Opinion Research, had given a reception, he got a phone call and was surprised to hear the voice of Bill Brock, the party's national chairman: "Can you come to breakfast tomorrow morning in my room to talk about this Ford situation?"

Teeter was befuddled. "I didn't know what he was talking about," he said later. "I was astounded to hear this. The reason I was baffled was that I had talked to Ford several times and every indication I had from him was that not only was he totally not interested, but he was trying to prevent the possibility of this thing ever getting warmed up."

What Teeter did not know was that Brock had been watching the night's convention events on television with Reagan and had taken the opportunity to urge him to go after Ford. Reagan had expressed considerable enthusiasm. And so Brock—not knowing whether Ford would be more interested than he had been before—began to contact for breakfast some of the leading Republicans he thought might be willing to join him in appealing to Ford.

After a few hours' sleep Teeter went to Brock's suite. On the elevator with him was Bob Dole. "Exciting, isn't it?" Dole said. Teeter, still in the dark, mumbled, "I guess so." At the breakfast, in addition to Brock, Teeter, and Dole, were House Minority Leader John Rhodes, Assistant Minority Leader Robert Michel, Howard Baker, Governors Jim Thompson of Illinois and Bill Clements of Texas, pollster Tully Plesser, former Senator Robert Griffin of Michigan, and Greenspan. Some had seen Ford that morning on the *Today* show and were intrigued by his answer to a question about whether pride would interfere with his taking the second spot on the ticket. "Honestly," Ford had replied, "if I thought the situation would work, if all the other questions could be resolved, the problem of pride would not bother me in any way."

What Greenspan now told them intrigued them even more. He reported on his meeting with Ford of the night before and said that as a result of it he thought the odds on a Reagan-Ford ticket had shortened from something like 100 to 1 to about 10 to 1. The group was highly enthusiastic about the idea, except for Teeter and Rhodes. (Rhodes left early, after saying he didn't think the group ought to ask Ford to run, and he would not be a part of any effort to pressure him, because to do so would not be fair to Ford.) They decided to go as a delegation to see the former President and urge him to consider the idea for the good of the party. At this point Teeter suggested that Representative Richard Cheney, Ford's White House chief of staff, be recruited, so Brock called him and Cheney joined the group.

As these friendly conspirators talked, a wild summer thunderstorm suddenly hit downtown, rattling windows high in the glass skyscraper of the Detroit Plaza Hotel, the centerpiece of the city's new Renaissance Center. The winds were so furious that Reagan was evacuated to a lower level. But the breakfast group ignored the storm and continued plotting.

Meanwhile, Reagan's staff asked to meet with Ford's representatives to talk the matter out. Ford instructed his negotiators— Kissinger, Greenspan, Marsh, and Bob Barrett, Ford's personal aide—to find out what the Reaganites really had in mind. Ford said he would not be interested in being simply a standby vice president. Kissinger and Greenspan had some ideas about how the job could be made more fruitful, and they were to explore them with the Reagan people.

Most of the participants at the breakfast meeting wanted strongly now to try to talk Ford into going on the ticket. But the two younger men closest to the former President since he had left office, Teeter and Cheney, were cool to the idea and doubted he could be persuaded. Cheney cautioned the others: "Look, boys, there are two possible approaches to take. One is to say, 'They're going to make this a meaningful job and beef it up,' and I don't think that would work. The other way is to say, 'This is a really rotten, stinking job, but we want you to do it for the good of the country and the party.' That would be the only way he'd do it. We're talking to a guy who has been Vice President and has been President. If some of us think it is his responsibility to the country to take a crummy job for four years, to assure getting Carter out of there, then fine. Let's go in there and tell him that. But don't go in and try to tell him it's going to be a wonderful job. He knows better. He's been Vice President."

By this time the group had learned that Ford had sent his four negotiators to meet with the Reagan side, and the excitement grew. "It was a hell of a ticket and it guaranteed victory," one of the participants remembered thinking. But then he added: "In retrospect, too, there were a few guys around there who were in line [as possible running mates]. I think there was a kind of feeling in the meeting that if it wasn't Ford, it might well be George." In other words, if they couldn't have the nomination they preferred Ford to Bush. Clearly Ronald Reagan wasn't the only prominent Republican in Detroit that day who held Bush in minimum high regard.

By now, news of the efforts being made to put together a Reagan-Ford ticket began to leak out on television. Brock's delegation finally saw Ford in midafternoon, after Senator Strom Thurmond had made an appeal of his own for Ford to accept. Ford went around the room asking his visitors to give their views. Each urged the scheme on him, and no one more emphatically, Kennerly later recalled, than Howard Baker. "You have a blank check if you take this," Kennerly said Baker told Ford. The chorus of voices urging him to take the job persuaded the former President to prolong the discussion, but in the end Ford told the group: "I've been Vice President. I don't want to do it again. I know what the job involves." As Teeter recalls it, he told them: "My position is definitely no, always has been and still is. But it's important enough that if Reagan wants to pursue these discussions, I'm willing to do it." Teeter said later he didn't believe, regardless of what went on, that Ford ever wavered from his disinclination to be a candidate. "I don't believe that Ford was ever close [to accepting], to tell you the truth," he said.

That impression, however, was not the word that suddenly was spreading rapidly through the convention headquarters hotel. Republicans close to Reagan kept saying that the governor, searching almost desperately for an alternative to Bush who could mollify all factions of the party, had decided to go hard after Ford. With so many people enlisted to build pressure on the former President, it was inevitable now that the story would be out, although the Reagan insiders hoped otherwise.

People in the Reagan operation reported that the candidate was going to try to induce Ford to join him with assurances that as Vice President he would have responsibility "for a major segment of government." If Ford really was not at all interested, why was he permitting these discussions to go forward? That was the one ingredient that elevated the whole business from convention rumor to electric anticipation.

Ford said later he had permitted the talks to go on "only in deference" to his party's prospective presidential nominee. But he acknowledged too that he had come to the independent conclusion long before that better use ought to be made of the vice presidency, such as making the vice president the White House chief of staff, implementing the president's decisions. "I prefer an elected officer in that position rather than an appointed one," he said. "I saw the frustrations of a vice president. I saw some of the evils of a nonelected officer being chief of staff. As President I thought we ought to use the Vice President more effectively." The evils, he said, were demonstrated by the tenure of Richard Nixon's chief of staff, H. R. Haldeman—though three men, Alexander Haig, Donald Rumsfeld, and Richard Cheney—all appointed officials—subsequently carried out the job in his own administration to his satisfaction, he said. With this idea in mind, and because "I felt so strongly that Mr. Carter ought to go," Ford said, he let the talks go on. "If they could prove to me that this would be the best ticket to change administrations, that was a sort of beneath-the-surface reaction."

By chance, we ran into Reagan in a hotel corridor as he was walking within a circle of protective Secret Service agents and aides from one meeting to another on that Wednesday afternoon. Was it true he was trying to get President Ford to run with him? "Oh, sure," Reagan replied in his matter-of-fact way, grinning. "That would be the best." Well, was there any chance? "I don't know," he said, as the aides tried to hurry him along. "I only know what he said at Palm Springs." The aides, obviously chagrined at Reagan's continuing inability to snub reporters' questions even at such delicate times, hustled him off. But that brief exchange was enough to give the whole story indisputable authority.

All this while, Kissinger, Greenspan, Marsh, and Barrett were deep in discussion with Casey, Meese, and Wirthlin. As one participant explained a short time later: "First we had Phase One, which was the dream ticket from now to November. To the Reagan camp, that obviously was the priority phase. But for Ford, Phase Two was the governing one. He wanted to know, 'Will it work? I would have to have strong input on the economy and foreign affairs. But how would you do it? What are the staff requirements? You can't give the vice president certain decision-making responsibilities where the law requires the president to act.'" Reagan emphasized later that it was Ford's negotiators, not Ford himself, who were probing. "They were coming to our people," he said. "They were coming back with, 'Look, we think maybe we can get him if we could tell him *this*'; then they'd come back with, 'What if we could tell him *this*?' . . . He had not changed."

Reagan's people came up with a list of ten "talking points" to satisfy Ford. Some who saw the list, about a page and a half typed double-spaced, said later that Ford would have been given a special role in dealing with the Office of Management and Budget and on the National Security Council. But the Reaganites sought to minimize the document's importance, and anyway it didn't seem to budge Ford—except that he did authorize his four negotiators to continue talking. And that fact in itself kept tongues wagging all over the convention headquarters hotel.

Once the discussion went past the election to the actual governing arrangement, as Ford insisted it do, and once the new ideas were committed to paper, some of the Reagan insiders began to ask themselves what they were getting themselves, and Reagan, into. At one point Wirthlin took the ten points to Bill Timmons, who had had long White House experience under both Nixon and Ford, and asked him: "If we fulfill all these, do we impinge on any of the rights and prerogatives of the president?" Timmons said he didn't think so. Mike Deaver, however, was not so sure, and he told Wirthlin forcefully at one point: "Dick, as you go into those bargaining sessions, I want you to remember one thing: Reagan is going to be the President, and in no way do we want to limit or create any constraining conditions on his exercising the full powers of the presidency." Wirthlin replied: "Mike, I agree with you one hundred percent."

Wirthlin said later that one of the ten talking points explicitly stated "that there would be nothing done to change the prerogatives or the Constitutional powers of the President." But, he went on, Ford apparently feared that Reagan on his own would be unable to put together an effective Cabinet and White House staff, so the Ford negotiators began to talk of a special role for Ford in recommending appointments. "If we had acceded to them," Wirthlin said, "I think [the concessions] probably would have changed and limited some of the powers of the presidency. Once we got into that discussion, it was over."

Meese said afterward, however, that while there was "a healthy skepticism on both sides" about the workability of the whole notion, all the later speculation "that we were bartering away the presidency" was erroneous. "At no time was there any request on their part nor desire on our part," he said, "to give away any of the ultimate responsibility of the President."

Kissinger later told *The Washington Post* how discussions on the means by which an expanded vice presidency would be implemented was the sticking point. "We got to the point," he said, "of saying he [Ford] would have a major input on all decisions. At that point everybody agreed. But then, what does major input mean? When you say the paper goes through the V.P., what does that mean? If all he does is be a bottleneck, then how does he contribute? Does he have a staff? Can he stop something? Can he send a paper back?" These were questions nobody had really thought about.

In the press at least, Kissinger's presence in these negotiations raised natural suspicions that as usual he was looking out for Kissinger—this despite the fact that the Reagan people were the ones who had asked him to get involved in the first place. Kissinger, in first broaching the whole subject with Ford, reportedly ruled himself out of returning as secretary of state, and counseled Ford not to let personalities or possible appointments enter into the negotiations.

At any rate, in late afternoon Ford placed a call to Reagan, saying he wanted to see him. Reagan asked him to come right down to his suite one floor below. The meeting was brief, presumably to discuss how Ford's vice presidency would work, and inconclusive. *Time* reported in its post-convention issue that Ford had asked Reagan point-blank at this meeting to appoint Kissinger secretary of state, and that Reagan had declined. But both sides, and Ford personally in a later interview, denied any such conversation had taken place.

Meese told us later that as he understood the Ford-Reagan conversations, Ford said that "Greenspan was the kind of guy who ought to be secretary of the treasury and that Henry was the type of person they ought to have as secretary of state, but it was in no way a condition of his [Ford's] taking the thing." Also, one of the Reagan negotiators said that Richard V. Allen, the Reagan foreign-policy adviser who had worked very unhappily under Kissinger in Nixon's White House, was beside himself at the time with concern that some deal might be struck to bring Kissinger into a Reagan administration, and repeatedly warned against it. "Dick Allen was in absolute, unbridled fear of Kissinger," this insider said. "Every time we'd leave the room [to resume negotiations], I could see poor Dick Allen's blood pressure jump about a hundred points."

Up to this point, the whole Reagan-Ford saga had basically been inside politics. Now, however, came an episode that brought the matter into the open and for several hours transformed the entire convention into a beehive of activity and rampant speculation. In minutes, the convention nerve center moved from a few security-tight suites on the sixty-ninth and seventieth floors of the Detroit Plaza to the wide-open world of television.

Sometime earlier, Ford had agreed to go on the CBS evening news live with Walter Cronkite. The former President and his wife went to the CBS booth at the convention hall, the Joe Louis Arena, with Barrett and Kennerly, apparently with nothing special in mind to say. As Ford was waiting to go on the air, however, he caught sight of Dan Rather on a television monitor in the booth talking from the convention floor about the progress of the dream-ticket talks. According to Kennerly, Ford was distressed about how everybody seemed to be saying he was going

to agree to run, in spite of his insistent, repetitious "no." Or
more accurately, his "no, but—." Ford himself said later, "I was
quite shocked, because there was nothing substantive that coin-
cided with Rather's predictions. And so on the show with Walter
I tried to balance it out so there wouldn't be any misunderstanding. . . ."

"Balancing it out" hardly did justice to Ford's performance
with Cronkite. The interview started unremarkably, but as
Cronkite pressed him about the possibility of a draft from the
convention floor, Ford conceded that such a development
"would be tough" to reject. Then, to the amazement of everyone
within earshot of a television set tuned to CBS, he proceeded to
lay out conditions under which he might accept:

"I really believe that in all fairness to me, if there is to be any
change, it has to be predicated on the arrangements that I would
expect as a vice president in a relationship with the president.
I would not go to Washington . . . and be a figurehead vice president. If I go to Washington, and I'm not saying that I am accepting, I have to go there with the belief that I will play a
meaningful role across the board in the basic and the crucial and
the important decisions that have to be made in a four-year period. For me to go there and go through the ceremonial aspects,
it wouldn't be fair to Betty, it wouldn't be fair to me, it wouldn't
be fair to the president, and it wouldn't be right for the country.
So I have to, before I can even consider any revision in the firm
position I have taken, I have to have responsible assurances. . . ."

Cronkite obviously knew he was on to something. "In my
mind," Cronkite said later, "I felt, hearing it all at that very moment, that Jerry Ford himself was so disingenuous that he simply
was telling the story because I asked. But I think subconsciously
he was putting on record probably what his requirements were
to take the job, so that there would be no misunderstanding in
the first place, and reneging. In effect, 'I can't do this unless I get
this and this.' "

What about "the question of pride," Cronkite asked the former President, whether for himself or for Reagan, who would
have to accept a former President "who . . . has said, 'It's got to
be something like a co-presidency' "? Ford, in fact, had never

used the term "co-presidency." It was Cronkite's. But the former President did not dispute it at the time.

"That's something Governor Reagan really ought to consider," Ford answered. "Neither Betty nor myself would have any sense that our pride would be hurt if we went there as Number Two instead of Number One. We've been around this city [Washington] for a long time, Walter, and I think we're big enough, we're self-assured enough, that that problem wouldn't affect us in any way whatsoever. But the point you raised is a very legitimate one. We have a lot of friends in Washington. And the president-to-be—and I would hope it's Ronald Reagan—he has to also have pride. And for him not to understand the realities and some of the things that might happen in Washington is being oblivious to reality."

A few blocks away at this precise moment, in the candidate's suite at the Detroit Plaza, Reagan, Wirthlin, Marty Anderson, Lyn Nofziger, Dick Allen, and other aides were randomly watching the convention television coverage without any notion that Ford would be on the air. As Wirthlin tells it, Reagan "sat up on his chair like this [coming up straight] and said, 'Did you hear what he said about a co-presidency?' He was real shocked. It wasn't an angry response. It was just a sense of real surprise, because we had tried to hold that whole thing very close to the vest. . . . He was just taken aback." Another in the room described Reagan as "aghast" and "perturbed" that Ford would talk so openly about the matter.

The interview, Reagan told us after the election, "was part of what was making me realize that this thing was out of hand." Of that expression "co-presidency," he said, "I knew it had grown out of all the conversations that our two groups were having, and I knew that such a thing could not work. And this was probably the first time I began to wonder if all of us in our belief in the dream ticket, if we had thought beyond the election. Everything we were doing was based on the election; it was not based on thinking about how it would work."

Word of the Cronkite interview swept through the convention. The phrase that startled everyone, of course, was "co-presidency," just as it had startled Reagan. But Ford, Cronkite said

later, "seemed to accept it as the way it should develop." However, Ford told us that the phrase was exactly contrary to what
he had in mind. "I don't know where he got it," he said. "It was
nothing I ever said. In fact, everything I've said was to the contrary, that the president is the chief executive officer who makes
all the final decisions. And the vice president ought to be the
chief operating officer as the chief of staff in the White House."

Among those who saw the interview, probably with more
emotion than most others, was one of Cronkite's prime network
rivals, Barbara Walters of ABC News. She had interviewed Ford
earlier in a routine session, and now here was one of her best,
most important sources delivering up the scoop of the convention to the opposition. Walters not only knew Ford well but had
dated Alan Greenspan for a long time, and here she was out in
the cold. She hustled over to the CBS booth, waiting for Ford to
come out. What happened when he did is best told by Kennerly:

"She literally pleaded with him to come and do another interview with her. She said, 'Mr. President, you've got to come talk
to me, you've got to.' Ford said, 'Well, Barbara, I really have to
go to this other meeting.' And she says, 'Oh, Mr. President,
you've got to do it. . . . For old times' sake. . . . For Alan's sake.' "

Kennerly could not believe what he had heard. "That quote is
imbedded in my mind," he said later. "Begging is the only way
I could put it. I wished I would have had one of those little airline barf bags, because I just about lost it. It was the single most
disgusting display by a newsperson that I've ever seen in my life.
And Ford said, 'Okay, Barbara.' You know the way he is."

Ford benignly went with Walters to the ABC booth, where,
again according to Kennerly, she frantically tried to get set for
her interview. At one point, Kennerly recalls, a technician
walked by and tripped over the cord from the tiny microphone
pinned to her clothing, ripping the mike off as she let out a yell.
"The President leans over, puts his hand on her arm, and says:
'Now, Barbara, calm down. I'm not going anywhere.' " Walters
got her interview, but it didn't touch Cronkite's.*

---

*The next day, at a small lunch where both Cronkite and Walters were also guests,
Ford said to some of the men present, "Don't shake my hand too hard. My shoulder's
out of joint from Barbara twisting my arm to get me over to her booth."

Ford returned to his suite at the Detroit Plaza and had dinner with his wife. By this time, Cronkite's interview was being accepted on the convention floor as confirmation that the Reagan-Ford ticket was a sure thing, and still the Ford and Reagan negotiators were struggling with the details of how it would all work. The longer they talked, the more complicated they recognized the matter was. Kissinger and Greenspan, however, seemed determined to find a way.

On the convention floor, the rumors were now flying wildly. Laxalt said later of the scene: "I personally witnessed the networks putting together their own team [of Reagan and Ford]. Starting with the Cronkite interview, they smelled a clean beat on everyone else. A couple of CBS people told me the ticket was already put together and they [Ford and Reagan] were coming to the hall. They [CBS reporters] felt it was coming and they wanted to be ahead of it."

Ford and Kennerly were watching television in Ford's suite when one television reporter came on and said he understood that at that moment Ford and Reagan were on their way to the Joe Louis Arena to announce that they would run together. Kennerly turned to Ford and asked: "Are we on our way over to the convention hall?" Ford replied: "Not to my knowledge."

To other viewers, however, the word was gospel. With telephone lines hopelessly tied up, television becomes a vast communications network for the convention itself—as well as an intercom system of sorts through which even principal players in the drama can convey messages to each other. That, indeed, was a subject of speculation in the press corps now. Was Ford, by going public, trying to put pressure on Reagan to accept his terms?

In the Michigan delegation, former Governor George Romney, himself a presidential aspirant in 1968, started working up a resolution to draft Ford as the vice-presidential nominee. "Look," Romney told us at the time, "Reagan's got two problems. He's an amateur. He's not experienced in Washington. And he's ultraconservative. Ford would answer both questions, and [the ticket] would sweep the convention." When Laxalt heard of this development he went to Romney. "George, don't do that," he urged. "Don't create pressure on the governor." But Romney, full of his usual enthusiasm, still favored the idea.

Bill Timmons, on the convention floor also, observed later how Ford's comments on the Cronkite interview "began to stampede the delegates. And each network and all the working journalists were trying to scoop each other, and it was a snowball. It was almost uncontrollable." He went to Reagan's trailer, just off the floor, and called the candidate's suite to warn Reagan and to find out what was really going on.

In the suite everyone already knew that matters were getting out of hand. Reagan, sitting in his shirtsleeves watching the convention on television, also saw the reporter saying "that he absolutely had it as a fact that I was coming over to the convention to make the announcement." It was clear now that matters had gone far enough. And when Kissinger told Meese that the Ford side might not be able to have an answer until the next morning, if then, because there were still many questions about how the arrangement might work, Reagan acted. At about nine o'clock, he called Ford and pressed him for an answer that night. According to sources on the Reagan side, Ford repeated that he still had reservations about the scheme and asked to have overnight to think about it. Reagan in effect told him: "Well, we just can't do that because the convention is expecting you to be the Vice President, and if tomorrow it doesn't come to pass, it'll be a tremendous letdown. And also, the other candidate I select will be handicapped some with that sort of publicity. So I really have to have a decision now."

"There was a deadline," Wirthlin said later. "The concerns being raised had got us into this whole issue of presidential territorial imperative in such a fashion that we were asking him [Ford] to either do something that was impossible or to put us in a position which was absolutely unacceptable. I'm not talking about bargaining away any powers of the presidency. It was always understood that that was not an area for discussion. But when we got into the issue of staffs and specific roles that he would fulfill, it then became more and more evident that he could not say yes, and time simply made the decision for us."

As Nofziger said later, "It was impossible to give them a few more hours without throwing the whole convention into a state of turmoil. And I don't mean just from the standpoint of the mechanics of the convention, but also from the standpoint of all the shock over there on the floor. You were fast reaching a time where, had it gone much longer, it would have been very difficult to not go with Ford irrespective of the conditions he might lay down. It would have looked like a double-cross.

"What happened really," he went on, "was that the Ford negotiators were really asking for more than Reagan could comfortably give or might even have the right to give. You can't give away the operational details of the presidency. What we finally came down to was, 'Hey, we don't think this is going to work, and these guys are kind of stalling for time here,' almost as if they would have put us in a corner, but I'm not accusing them of that." In any event Reagan decided he couldn't wait any longer, so he dispatched Nofziger and Deaver to pull his own people back.

In Ford's suite, at about 10:30, Gerald Ford turned to his wife and told her he was going to see Reagan to "give him my decision, and my decision is no." The former President put on a clean shirt and tie and went out. In about ten minutes he was back upstairs. "I've done it," he said. He gave his obviously relieved and happy wife a hug, sat down, and just looked off silently, pondering what he had done.

Reagan himself had been apprehensive about having to tell Ford that he had concluded that the ticket just wouldn't work out, and was relieved when Ford announced his decision. "His first statement," Reagan recalled to us, "was, 'Ron, I've believed from the first, as I told you, this is wrong, and I feel even stronger about it, and I just don't think it's the right thing to do.' And by this time he'd convinced me. I said to him, 'Mr. President, I think if anything good has come out of this, I think it is that you and I have established a much closer relationship than we ever had.' And he put his arm around my shoulders and he said, 'We absolutely have. And I want you to know that I want you to win and I will do anything and everything I can to help you win.' He said, 'I feel a deep feeling of affection and respect for you.' And any hangovers from '76 were all gone."

As Ford left, Reagan wiped his brow and said, "Now where the hell's George Bush?" He had decided that afternoon, Meese said, that if something couldn't be worked out with Ford, his choice would be Bush.

Reagan was not the only one to face that alternative without joy. Still, having made the effort to get Ford made accepting Bush easier for him, as well as enabling him to leave Detroit with a truly unified party. The wounds of 1976, if not forgotten, were at least well along toward healing now. Ford, incidentally, told us after the election that one of his prime objectives at the convention had been "to subtly help George Bush get the [vice-presidential] nomination." He had helped him, all right, in the long run, but there was nothing subtle about the whole business.

Bush, who wanted the vice-presidential nomination badly, was deliriously happy to take the assignment under any conditions, and in spite of the obvious and extravagant effort Reagan had made in another direction. Bush, too, had taken Ford's interview with Cronkite as a pretty good indication that Ford would be Reagan's running mate. He had addressed the convention earlier that evening, and now, in his hotel suite, had changed into a red sports shirt and was sipping a beer rather disconsolately and watching the convention on television when the phone rang. Jim Baker, his campaign manager (and later Reagan's White House chief of staff), picked up the receiver. "Is Ambassador Bush there?" a voice asked. "Yes," Baker said. "Who's calling?" "Governor Reagan," the voice (of Drew Lewis) said. "Just a moment," Baker said, and handed the phone to Bush, who took it, still seated, and faced the wall.

"The feeling on the part of most people in the room," Baker said later, "was that [Reagan] was calling to tell George he had done the deal with Ford. George got on, and he said: 'Hello. Yes, sir, how are you? Yes, sir.'" There was a long pause, and then Bush turned, and with his familiar crooked grin breaking out, raised his thumb in the air as a signal to his wife, Barbara, and family sitting morosely across the room. Then he listened to Reagan again. "Why, yes, sir," he said in a moment. "I think you can say I support the platform—wholeheartedly!"

Reagan told Bush he was going to the convention hall to announce his choice—a move obviously being taken to stop the Reagan-Ford dream ticket in its tracks in the most upbeat way now possible under the circumstances—and asked him to keep the news confidential for a short while.* Bush agreed, and to make sure, Barbara Bush marched out into the hallway where Bush staff workers and supporters were waiting and announced with a long face that she was going to bed. But a moment after she left a yell went up down the corridor, where someone had just heard the report on television.

When it was all over, both Kissinger and Greenspan argued publicly on television that if only they had had some more time, even a few hours, the Reagan-Ford deal might have been worked out. Ford seemed to feel the same way in an interview after the election, when he told us: "We made a lot of progress but could not in the time allotted make it specific enough to satisfy me." But Wirthlin disagreed. "The longer we discussed the issue," he said afterward, "the more evident it [was] that that would not have been a good thing.

"Politicians don't like each other almost by definition," he went on, "but there is a real antagonism between a Ford and a Carter, and there was the belief that [Reagan] wouldn't win this election. Here was an opportunity for Ford ... to make a difference, but the price to be paid was something he couldn't come to grips with. They [Kissinger and Greenspan] saw that reluctance. They saw that door ajar and they said, 'If we'd only had time.' But that was absolutely wishful thinking.

"The problem with it was, if Ford had said, 'Yes, I will do it,' and then took a leap of faith, it would have happened. But everything I saw that night, everything I felt, said the longer the discussion, the more clear it is that it'll never work."

As matters turned out, Reagan didn't need Jerry Ford. But nobody knew that then. Most notable about the episode was the effect of television. By broadcasting the hint that he might agree to go on the ticket, Ford moved the most important business of the 1980 Republican convention into public view. The resulting pressures in turn became a real factor in the deliberations. The

*Actually, the Reagan campaign intentionally leaked the news about Bush several minutes in advance of Reagan's appearance, to condition the delegates to the fact that they weren't going to get the "dream ticket" after all. "We didn't want them to have any sort of massive expression of regret or joy either way on the governor's decision," Timmons said later. "So we scooped him a little on the floor to settle the delegates down, and the audience, and word spread very quickly."

delegates to the convention had been sent into a state of great anticipatory excitement, which Reagan had to address, or be stampeded into a decision that both he and Ford came to understand would have created more political problems than the one it had been conceived to solve. For all the private meetings and shuttling back and forth of advisers, it may have been that Walter Cronkite's pithy summation of the arrangement as "something like a co-presidency" best crystallized what was at stake, and may have been what warned Reagan off.

This whole confusing pursuit of a "dream ticket" was widely criticized in the press at the time as an exercise in folly—as the encouragement of a notion that never took into account Ford's oft-stated disinclination to be a candidate. Yet in the long run the affair had some tangible positive results. Ford's cool, somewhat resentful attitude toward Reagan ended, and Republican Party harmony was encouraged. After all, in reaching out to Ford, Reagan not only enhanced the prospect that the former President himself would campaign energetically for the Republican ticket, but also enabled all the convention delegates, and party loyalists around the country, to embark on the fall campaign with a sense of solid party unity. Some even began to think not only of a Reagan-Bush victory, but of taking a giant step toward control of the United States Senate for the first time in twenty-six years. After all, a bumper crop of liberal Democrats was up for reelection, and no illusions were harbored on the Democratic side that Jimmy Carter's political coattails would offer any of them much help.

That pessimistic appraisal of the incumbent President's appeal, in fact, was very much in the minds of many delegates to the approaching Democratic National Convention. And although Carter, by every count, had enough delegates pledged to him to win nomination for a second term, Ted Kennedy and his liberal supporters were still hoping for some kind of political miracle that would convince a majority of the convention delegates to change their minds in New York. They didn't, but before that convention was over, Carter would have reason to wonder who had "won"—and just how much the Democratic nomination was worth.

9.
"The Best They Can Do in Unity"

When Jimmy Carter concluded the speech in which he accepted the Democratic National Convention's nomination for a second term, a predictable demonstration erupted before him on the floor of New York's Madison Square Garden. The band played "Happy Days Are Here Again" and the delegates cheered and waved their green-and-white Carter-Mondale signs. The floor was even hotter and more crowded than it had been all week. The crush had been deliberately increased by the distribution by Carter's managers of extra floor passes, to assure the appearance for the television cameras of an enthusiastic response to the nominee as the convention reached its climax and its close.

On the platform Carter, grinning broadly, waved to the crowd, posing now with his family, now with his running mate Fritz Mondale, their hands joined and held aloft. The applause rolled down from the galleries to his right and left, which also had been packed with supporters of the President.

After seven or eight minutes the demonstration seemed to be losing steam, but a signal was sent from the podium to the band to keep playing. And when, a few minutes later, the cheering once again died away, Bob Strauss started summoning prominent Democrats—governors, mayors, members of Congress, party officials—to the platform for a bow. Soon it was packed with people embracing, shaking hands, waving to their less fortunate friends in the crowd.

The convention was over, and all that remained to be done of-

ficially was for the chairman, Speaker of the House Thomas P.
(Tip) O'Neill, Jr., to bang his big gavel and declare the convention adjourned. But there was one more bit of unofficial business
to be transacted—the traditional embrace of victor and van-
quished, Jimmy Carter and Ted Kennedy, to symbolize the unity
of the party entering the general election campaign. But where
was Ted Kennedy?

As the wait lengthened—fifteen minutes, then twenty—the
party officials on the platform grew anxious. Where the hell was
he? How long could Strauss keep finding people to introduce? In
the press galleries, the reporters speculated among themselves
about just how long Kennedy intended to keep the Leader of the
Free World in limbo.

Kennedy had left his suite at the Waldorf-Astoria just after
Carter finished his speech, thinking he had plenty of time to get
to the convention. The demonstration would surely run at least
thirty minutes, as the one for Kennedy himself had two nights
earlier. But as his car made the trip of twenty-two blocks, he
learned there was an incident in the making. "We were going
down in the car," Paul Kirk recalled later, "and we heard a woman reporter on the radio say Kennedy was keeping Carter waiting. Kennedy was angry."

When Kennedy did arrive, after what had seemed an excru-
ciatingly awkward delay, he pointedly avoided giving Carter the
satisfaction of that traditional closing-night tableau—the winning candidate and his rival standing together, their hands
clasped and raised to demonstrate their shared commitment to
a unified campaign against the common Republican enemy,
Ronald Reagan.

On the contrary, Kennedy seemed to go to conspicuous
lengths to avoid it. When he came out onto the platform, setting
off a new wave of cheers on the floor, he shook hands with Carter in an almost perfunctory way, waved to the delegates briefly,
and then walked around the stage for a few minutes—it seemed
endless on television—while Carter and party officials pursued
him in an obvious quest for something more demonstrative. The
President, an intimate said later, "looked like a puppy dog" trot-
ting after Kennedy.

The closing tableau is one of the rituals of American politics. And, like most of those rituals, it is one that becomes important only if someone chooses, quite deliberately as Ted Kennedy did, not to play the part expected of him. To those inside politics, the incident spoke volumes. To the voters watching on television sets across the country, it may have suggested only that there was something slightly amiss. But there were, of course, television commentators and newspaper writers there to tell them what was missing, and to explain why it happened and what it meant.

To the men and women on the platform, it was not quite apparent at the moment just how clearly the picture had been projected—of a president, ostensibly the leading actor in this mock-drama, playing the supplicant, and an unsuccessful one at that. Fritz Mondale, for example, was startled when reporters stopped him as he left the hall to ask what he thought of "the insult" Kennedy had delivered. But none of them mistook the implications of the scene as it appeared on the television screens. "It looked like hell," a reporter suggested later to Strauss. "It looked worse than hell," Strauss replied. At the very moment when Jimmy Carter should have been most in control of the situation, he seemed instead to fit the picture the country had developed of him over the previous three and a half years—somehow smaller than life.

Looking back at that awkward scene, and particularly at the careful way Kennedy moved around the stage, some of the President's men suspected that Ted Kennedy might have had a few drinks before he left the Waldorf. "I thought Ted had a couple of pops," one of them said. "You know, I didn't blame him, what the hell. And you know, sometimes that leads to excessive dignity, especially when the cameras are on you."

Whether or not he had enjoyed "a couple of pops," the fact was that Kennedy made a calculated decision not to participate in that traditional tableau, and he took pains to avoid it. "We anticipated it might happen," Kirk said, "and he was wary. It was like walking on ice."

The previous night, when Carter had been officially nominated, Kennedy had told members of the Massachusetts delegation that he wanted them to move to make the vote for Carter unanimous. And he had asked the convention chairman, Tip O'Neill, to read his endorsement to the delegates, but it was pointedly brief and cool: "I congratulate President Carter on his renomination. I endorse the platform of the Democratic Party. I will support and work for the reelection of President Carter. It is imperative that we defeat Ronald Reagan in 1980. I urge all Democrats to join in that effort." Finally, he had sent word through his staff that he would indeed appear with Carter on that final night.

The terms of his appearance were not settled, however, without several conversations between Kirk, Kennedy's chief political lieutenant, and his opposite number, Hamilton Jordan. The possibility of Kennedy sitting in the gallery to listen to the acceptance speeches was discarded right away. There was still too much emotion among the Kennedy delegations and too great a likelihood of an embarrassing distraction. Similarly, Kennedy was unwilling to go to the convention hall early and wait out of sight in a holding room until Mondale's and Carter's speeches, and the film on Carter sandwiched between them, were over.

Each side had its own special concerns. Jordan, for his part, wanted to be sure that Kennedy did not leave his hotel during the President's speech or the film, and thus draw network television cameras away from what the Carter campaign saw, correctly, as an hour-long free commercial on all three networks. What Kennedy should do, they agreed, was wait until the speech ended and then drive downtown. The trip would take less than fifteen minutes, and the demonstration on the convention floor would occupy the time.

It was, of course, a measure of the mistrust and suspicion between these two Democratic leaders that these negotiations were required at all. And it was a measure, as well, of the lingering personal bitterness from the campaign. Kirk made it clear to Jordan that Kennedy would not take kindly to any personal references either to him or to his family during the speech. He was clearly still smarting about such things as the television commercial that had shown Carter helping his daughter Amy with her homework—implying a contrast between the family lives of Carters and Kennedys.

Late on the final morning of the convention, eating sandwiches at P. J. Clarke's, Kennedy, Kirk, and several other members of the staff discussed the plan for the night and speculated on Carter and that closing tableau. "We had a little fun kidding about it," Kirk recalled. Kennedy told his staff there were "too many people out there" who had supported him through the primaries and now wouldn't find it credible if he were too demonstrative in support of the President. He was willing to work for the ticket in the general election campaign—indeed, there was no way out of that—but he wouldn't go overboard tonight. He didn't want to get trapped in a mob scene on the stage while "every freeholder from New Jersey" was summoned to take a bow.

As it turned out, Kennedy could not avoid the freeholders, but he did avoid Carter. And later he observed privately that the President, "for a guy who said, 'I don't have to kiss his ass,'" had been extraordinarily solicitous.

In a perverse way it was a fitting final moment for the contest within the Democratic Party of 1980. The difficult business of dealing with Kennedy had preoccupied Carter and his campaign managers throughout the summer, at a time when they should have been turning their attention instead to planning the general election campaign against Ronald Reagan. Kennedy's refusal to withdraw, and his continued attacks on Carter after the last primaries on June 3, left what one White House insider called "deep and lasting bitterness."* They had beaten "the fat rich kid," as some Carter strategists called Kennedy, but he had refused to acknowledge it.

Carter had driven in the last nail in those final primaries. Al-

---

*The tension between the Carterites and Kennedyites continued during the fall, even after Kennedy agreed to campaign for the President. It was heightened on the Carter side by the suspicion that the Kennedy managers were taking advantage of them to help pay their own campaign bills, particularly to the Kennedy media adviser David Sawyer. When it came time to make some Kennedy-for-Carter commercials, the Kennedy staff insisted that Sawyer film them, and arrangements were made to do the filming in a New York studio. There were to be five "talking head" television ads plus two for radio, and Gerald Rafshoon, Carter's media man, figured "the cost on that, stretching it, would be $1500" or perhaps $2000 to allow a small profit. But Sawyer billed the Carter campaign for $45,000 and, only after a squawk and a decision to cut out one ad, agreed to accept $32,000. The Carter campaign was required to wire the money to New York before the tapes would be delivered.

though Kennedy won in California, New Jersey, Rhode Island, South Dakota, and New Mexico, Carter had prevailed in Ohio, West Virginia, and Montana. He had won twenty-four primaries to Kennedy's ten. He was assured of the support of 300 more delegates than the 1666 he needed to win on the first ballot. And although Kennedy's managers continued to insist that many of the Carter delegates were "soft" and could be converted by convention time, they never produced any evidence of substantial defections. On the contrary, it seemed more likely that the counts of Carter's votes underestimated his real strength.

Jimmy Carter was, however, damaged goods, and the problems that plagued him throughout his time in the White House made him appear far more vulnerable, or potentially vulnerable, than the figures would indicate.

All along, for example, he had been betrayed politically by those he called his "closest friends" straying into politically embarrassing situations—Bert Lance, Hamilton Jordan, Peter Bourne, Andrew Young. Now, as the convention approached, there was his brother Billy. He had accepted $220,000 as the first installment of a "loan" from the Libyans, and investigations were under way in both the Senate and Justice Department to see if Billy Carter had violated requirements that he register as an agent of a foreign government. And, more important, there were questions as to whether Jimmy Carter and his White House had behaved improperly in either Billy Carter's affairs or the inquiries into them. "There was great fear in the White House," said one of those who worked there, "that the Billy thing, if it escalated, could have been a real problem."

Moreover, except in that innermost of inner circles around the President, no one really knew what to expect from the inquiry into Billy Carter's affairs. In the end it came to nothing, but as the convention approached Democrats faced the possibility that they might nominate the President for a second time, then discover a "smoking gun" in the Billy Carter case that would leave them with a compromised candidate leading their ticket.

Signs of Carter's political weakness, and uneasiness in the party, were epidemic. There were embryonic movements to draft Senator Henry M. Jackson or Secretary of State Edmund S. Muskie. There was talk of enlisting "favorite-son" candidates from major states who might hold away enough delegates from Carter to leave open the possibility of another nominee. At a meeting in Denver shortly before the convention, the Democratic governors avoided reaffirming the endorsement of Carter they had voted a year earlier. There were rumors that women delegates might form a bloc to withhold their support temporarily, to pressure the President on issues of importance to them. On the eve of the convention, plans were disclosed for Representative Ronald V. Dellums of California to become a candidate and rallying point for black delegates, and for Roberto Mondragon, lieutenant governor of New Mexico, to do the same for Hispanics.

All of this, of course, was a result of Carter's extraordinary weakness in the opinion polls. He was running 25 to 28 percentage points behind Ronald Reagan, and in some states third behind both Reagan and independent candidate John B. Anderson, who had abandoned his party to lead what he called a "national unity" coalition.

The issues were no more promising. Inflation and unemployment rates were both rising. The country was still powerless to resolve the crisis with Iran. The Russians were still in Afghanistan. All that Carter had left was his reputation for honesty and personal decency, and now "the Billy thing" was threatening even that.

There was more involved in Carter's weakness, however, than even this litany of bad news. The President was paying the price for paying too little attention to his party, for being too self-involved, for failing to do the little favors that are the bricks and mortar in building a loyal political following. He had the support of many Democratic mayors and governors, who relied heavily on the administration for federal assistance, but he had built few alliances with influential members of Congress, to whom he was still a distant enigma.

The relationship between Carter and his party colleagues in Congress was exemplified by an incident the previous April involving Senator Robert C. Byrd of West Virginia, then the majority leader.

Carter telephoned Byrd one afternoon and asked if he could

come to the White House. Byrd replied that the legislative calendar was heavy and wondered aloud if he could wait until morning. But the President pressed him, and a meeting was arranged for about 9:00 p.m. at the White House.

After the briefest exchange of small talk, Carter asked Byrd what the attitude on the Hill might be about the use of military force in Iran. The majority leader, startled, replied that the time for that had long since passed. Anything of that nature, he cautioned, should be undertaken only after the broadest possible and most thorough consultation with the Senate.

Then Carter asked: What about a military operation to rescue the hostages? Such a plan had been drawn, he said, and the mission rehearsed repeatedly in the desert in the far West. This time Byrd was more receptive. Such a mission, he told Carter, might very well win approval on the Hill, but it would be important for the White House to consult in advance with the right people there—himself, of course; Howard Baker, the Republican minority leader; and the chairmen and the ranking Republican members of the Foreign Relations, Armed Forces, and perhaps Intelligence committees. If such a plan were feasible, and if Carter decided to go through with it, Byrd went on, he would be prepared to advise the President on who should be informed and to help make the arrangements. Carter thanked him, and Byrd left.

The next morning, however, there was another telephone call. "That subject we were talking about last night," said Carter without being specific, well, Byrd could forget about it. The mission had been aborted.

Thus it was that the Senate majority leader learned that even while he and the President had been meeting the previous night, the operation about which Carter seemed to be seeking his opinion already had been under way for several hours. But the President had not been willing to take Byrd into his confidence, even then.

That story, unsurprisingly, soon circulated among other Democratic senators, who took it as another confirmation of the distance that had been established between them and the President of their own party. As the convention in New York approached, there was another, more immediate concern for many of these Democratic officeholders: the real possibility that they would be challenged by serious and well-financed Republican opponents while their ticket was led by a politically crippled president. Continued Democratic control of the Senate seemed assured, but for many incumbents it was going to be a difficult year.

All of these things encouraged Kennedy to remain in the contest even though the delegate realities had been inevitable for weeks. "The arithmetic began to hurt Kennedy even before those final primaries," Paul Kirk said, making it far more difficult to enlist any of the uncommitted or convert the Carterites. "But we didn't think we were on a kamikaze mission," he said. "By the time the primaries were over, people would reflect on what happened. They would look back and say, 'There really hasn't been a dialogue, the hostages aren't back, and the economy isn't better. Kennedy did better in the industrial states, and with all that we have to look ahead and see what we do in November.'... We thought an argument could be made that politics were more important than the delegate selection."

During the weeks leading up to New York, Kirk met regularly with Richard Moe, Mondale's chief of staff and a political professional of long experience with conventions, to negotiate the procedures for the convention. The White House emissary never sought a withdrawal, and it was clear all along that none would be forthcoming. Although Carter clearly had the votes, he lacked the political strength to dictate terms—at least, if there was to be any hope of leaving Madison Square Garden with any semblance of party unity. It was an anomalous situation: The President had won the primaries and almost certainly would win the nomination, but the defeated Kennedy was the one with the power to shape the convention.

The device for the Kennedy campaign would be an attack on a convention rule—section F (3) (c)—that required delegates to vote at the convention for the candidate under whose banner they had been chosen in primaries or caucuses earlier in the year. The assumption was that some of Carter's delegates might be having second thoughts now, given the opinion polls and the

Billy Carter case, and might be lured into supporting the principle of an "open convention" even if they were not prepared to back Kennedy. What the key strategists in both camps understood was that a political convention, and particularly a Democratic convention, could be extremely volatile; if an emotional enough issue could be injected, anything might happen.

By late July the "open convention" idea began to gain some support. It had the backing of many liberal supporters of Kennedy, a few prominent Democrats officially neutral at that point, and even a smattering of Carter supporters. Carter and his principal advisers at the White House remained adamant against it, but it became apparent they were losing the public-relations war. The notion of "freedom" for the delegates was an attractive one, and the President was depicted as trying to use technicalities to hold his majority together.

Campaign chairman Strauss, playing the horses on a vacation in California, was summoned back to try to turn it around. He quickly held a series of meetings on Capitol Hill and press conferences to argue that "open" was the wrong word; the delegates would be betraying their constituents if they abandoned their commitments. It was not a totally persuasive case, of course, but the White House operatives began to find their support firming up in the final days before the convention.

The President had held a sixty-minute televised press conference to deal with the questions about his brother Billy and the Libyan connection, and that seemed to have resolved some of the doubts. In retrospect, Kennedy was convinced that this press conference had stiffened the support for Carter on the "open convention" issue.

Some of Carter's delegates and some state leaders, their nerves rubbed raw by the long and bitter contest within the party, were angry at Kennedy for pursuing the challenge and, by their lights, trying to rewrite the rules of the game. Simply because most of Carter's backers had qualified for the convention only after a brawl in their own states over Kennedy, they were not inclined to be susceptible to his charm at this point. Contrary to what Kennedy's managers had been suggesting, there was no great underground reservoir of enthusiasm for their man at all. Instead, the delegates accurately reflected their party. They might not be wild about Jimmy Carter but they didn't consider Ted Kennedy an improvement.

Even with these assurances, Strauss was unyielding; the rule would be enforced and the delegates held to it. "There's no possibility," he said in New York, "of our releasing the delegates after the rules vote, none whatsoever." It was, he explained later, too risky. "A convention's too dangerous, too dicey, to take a chance."

The Kennedy strategy covered the first two nights of the convention—Monday, August 11, when the rules issue would be settled, and Tuesday, when the platform would be considered. If Kennedy won the first, Kirk thought, the convention "might take on a life of its own." If he didn't, the platform debate offered an opportunity for the liberals to win a kind of consolation prize by imposing their views on Carter on such issues as abortion, defense spending, and economic policy. Kennedy was sponsoring a series of proposed planks that were clearly provocative to the President. One called for wage and price controls, which Carter had ruled out without qualification. Another demanded a $12-billion-dollar program to create new jobs, which Carter had rejected as inflationary. Another would have given a higher priority to combatting unemployment than dealing with inflation, the obvious implication being that Carter was following quite different policies.

Kennedy and the liberals were playing a mischievous game here. The opinion polls generally showed the public closer to Carter than to his challenger on these issues, and the primary results had seemed to confirm that. Quite beyond that, as the likely nominee Carter had to design a campaign against the conservative Reagan in which it would be far more important to occupy the great center of the ideological spectrum than the left. But Carter lacked the authority as a political leader, or the force of personality, to persuade the liberals to put aside their own agenda for the moment. He had the votes, but he lacked the broad base of affection and respect that is any politician's most prized asset.

As part of an agreement on convention procedures, spelled out in a twelve-page memorandum that clearly reflected the distrust on both sides, Kennedy had won the right to address the delegates at some point. Some advisers urged him to do it Monday night, to reinforce the attempt to upset the rules. But Kennedy said that would be "too political" and that he would be better off speaking Tuesday night on the economic issues he had claimed all along were the real rationale for his challenge. Besides, it was becoming clearer almost hourly that the Carter delegates were holding firm on the rules.

That proved accurate. Carter won the rules test with only minor defections, 1936.4 votes to 1390.6, and Kennedy knew his candidacy was finished. Back at the Waldorf, his speechwriters, Bob Shrum and Carey Parker, were preparing a brief statement of withdrawal that would take him out without yet delivering the endorsement of the President. "I'm a realist," said Kennedy, "and I know what this result means. The effort on the nomination is over."

His effort to dominate the convention was far from over, however. Tuesday night, speaking for his platform proposals, Kennedy ignited an emotional firestorm with a speech that seemed to touch every liberal nerve and revive every liberal memory on the floor. The delegates cheered when he warned they could not sit by and see "the great purposes of the Democratic Party become the bygone passages of history." And they erupted into a forty-minute demonstration when he closed by saying: "For all those whose cares have been our concern, the work goes on, the cause endures, the hope still lives, and the dream shall never die."

But Kennedy also demonstrated that he was sensitive to the accusations that had followed him all year, that he was espousing 1960s liberalism that no longer had any relevance to American politics and, on the contrary, reflected the intellectual poverty of his campaign. In a key paragraph, he said: "The commitment I seek is not to outworn views, but to old values that will never wear out. Programs may sometimes become obsolete, but the ideal of fairness always endures. Circumstances may change but the work of compassion must continue. It is surely correct that we cannot solve problems by throwing money at them; but it is also correct that we dare not throw national problems onto a scrap heap of inattention and indifference. The poor may be out of political fashion, but they are not without human needs. The middle class may be angry, but they have not lost the dream that all Americans can advance together."

It was, of course, the kind of statement Kennedy should have been prepared to make when he sat down with Roger Mudd ten months earlier. The Kennedy delegates seemed to recognize that, defeated, he had at last been able to articulate their cause, and the cheers rolled over the floor in waves: "We want Ted! We want Ted! We want Ted!" Even many of the Carter delegates, recognizing he was no longer a threat, wept and cheered. And when Kennedy left the podium he laughed and told Kirk: "You were right. I should have given the speech last night."

Among other things, Kennedy's speech had been—by unmistakable implication—a summary of his case against Jimmy Carter. But the President, mindful of the necessity for bringing Kennedy along with him, responded with characteristic hyperbole that ignored those implications. It had been, he said, "one of the greatest political speeches I've ever heard."

The voting on the platform planks was essentially sham, the product of negotiations behind the scenes by the two candidates' ambassadors. Kennedy would abandon the wage and price controls plank, and Carter would yield on the other three dealing with the economy—including that defiant demand for a $12-billion-dollar program to create 800,000 new jobs. On the podium Tip O'Neill quickly called up the planks, called for voice votes, and, without waiting for responses, gaveled the decisions into the record. It took only minutes, so little time that Walter Cronkite couldn't be diverted from his line of analysis long enough for CBS cameras to catch the scene. Later the White House did manage to block a plank attacking funding of the MX missile, but only after Carter, who had come full circle in four years to demanding more defense spending, reminded delegates of his role as "commander in chief." But two planks the President opposed, on the Equal Rights Amendment and federal funding of abortions, were approved.

Platforms don't have any intrinsic importance, of course, but the results in this case were extraordinary. An incumbent president, his renomination assured, had been forced to accept a document that on both important economic issues and sensitive social questions represented a repudiation of his own policies. Much later Jody Powell would question his side's willingness to seek unity at almost any price. "If anything," he said, "I think we probably overdid the efforts to appease those people." But at the time Jimmy Carter didn't seem to have any option in the matter. The weaknesses in his record and his demonstrated inadequacies as a political leader had forced him on the defensive within his own party. He was a general struggling for control of his own troops. And if the voters did not follow all the machinations on the platform, neither could they avoid seeing the image of weakness being projected from Madison Square Garden.

From the outset the veteran Strauss had worried about what he called "the rhythm of the convention" and Kennedy's role as the protagonist. "I felt," he said later, "that we let the convention events take over from us too much. They were making all the news and we were making none, and we were chasing him." At one point Strauss even suggested that Carter might break the pattern simply by gimmickry, leaving his hotel to cross the street to the Stage Delicatessen, a New York landmark, for some lox and bagels. What the President needed was anything that would turn the attention of the news media away from Kennedy—and counter the impression of Carter as a passive figure being manipulated by the man he had defeated in all those primaries.

Now, with Kennedy's speech and the platform behind him, Carter had forty-eight hours to regain the initiative. But even his nomination on Wednesday night was less than an unqualified success. In the gallery Rosalynn Carter and son Jeff marked their ballots as the roll call progressed, cheering at the appropriate moments. And in his suite at the Sheraton Centre Carter was photographed while following the count on a television set with Strauss and two long-time allies, Mayor Tom Bradley of Los Angeles and consumer affairs adviser Esther Peterson. But the vote was only 2129 for Carter, 1146.5 for Kennedy, and 55.5 scattered. That meant that although Kennedy's name had never been placed in nomination, he lost only about 100 delegates from those he had captured during the primaries. It was still another clear warning that many Democrats were far from reconciled to supporting the President with the kind of enthusiasm an incumbent might expect at that moment. He had captured the nomination but not the convention or the Democratic Party.

Now Carter's last chance would be his acceptance speech, in political terms the single most important moment of this week on center stage. The speech was carefully composed by Carter and Rick Hertzberg, his chief writer, with guidance only from those closest to the President—Jordan and Powell, of course, Pat Caddell and Jerry Rafshoon. It was perhaps the most closely held speech of his presidency. Even Stuart Eizenstat, Carter's chief adviser on domestic policy, didn't see the text until it was finished.

Late in the day Jody Powell tried to condition the press to see the speech as the White House wanted it to be seen. The two acceptance speeches, Mondale's as well as Carter's, had been prepared as a package, he explained, and should be viewed that way. "The Vice President's speech," said Powell, was "designed to raise the spirits, to get the people to cheer, to sound the bugle"—largely an attack on Ronald Reagan. Carter's speech was "designed to get people to think about the serious nature of the choice they face in the fall." The President, the press secretary said, had invested more "personal time" in this speech than any other because he was determined "to establish what this election is all about."

Mondale, as announced, let Reagan and the Republican Party have it with both barrels. He employed a favorite rhetorical device of his old mentor, Hubert Humphrey, who at the 1964 Democratic convention at which he was nominated to be Vice President shouted a list of Democratic achievements. Then he noted the Republican presidential nominee, Barry Goldwater, had been against all of them. Mondale did the same, asking who supported this and that Democratic program. "Not Ronald Reagan!" he shouted after each, as the crowd cheered.

The strategy was straightforward enough. Because Carter could hardly run on his record, the focus would be on the dangers of turning to Ronald Reagan in the next four years. The election, said the President, "is a choice between two futures." He offered a future of "security, justice, and peace" in contrast to one of "despair" and "surrender" and, most of all, "risk—the risk of international confrontation; the risk of an uncontrollable, unaffordable, and unwinnable nuclear arms race."

"No one, Democrat or Republican either, consciously seeks such a future," Carter said. "I do not claim that my opponent does. But I do question the disturbing commitments and policies already made by him and by those who have now captured control of the Republican Party.

"The consequences of those commitments and policies would drive us down the wrong road. It is up to all of us to make sure America rejects this alarming, even perilous, destiny."

Carter also had a warning about the future at home under Reagan. "I see despair," he said, "the despair of millions who would struggle for equal opportunity and a better life—and struggle alone. I see surrender—the surrender of our energy future to the merchants of oil; the surrender of our economic future to a bizarre program of massive tax cuts for the rich, massive service cuts for the poor, and massive inflation for everyone."

In light of the actions the Reagan administration took immediately after the 1981 inaugural, Carter's speech correctly identified a momentous political fact—that Ronald Reagan if elected indeed intended to move the country onto a radically different course, rejecting the basic guideposts that had marked life in America under Democratic Party dominance since the days of Franklin D. Roosevelt. As subsequent events proved, Carter was right that Reagan meant in a very literal sense to turn back the clock on the role and scope of the federal government, particularly in the area of social welfare—just as he had repeatedly promised in all those speeches since 1964 about "getting the government off your backs." But Carter's emphasis on Reagan as a man who could not be trusted with his finger on the nuclear button obscured the equally threatening specter, from a liberal Democratic point of view, of Reagan as a social engineer insufficiently sensitive to the needs of the nation's poor.

The speech was carefully crafted to rally Carter's fellow Democrats, but even so there were sour notes. The inevitable "personal word" to Ted Kennedy seemed too supplicatory:

"Ted, your party needs—and I need—you. And I need your idealism and your dedication working for us. There is no doubt that even greater service lies ahead of you—and we are grateful to you and to have your strong partnership now in the larger cause to which your own life has been dedicated. I thank you for your support. We'll make great partners this fall in whipping the Republicans." And the obligatory reference to Hubert Horatio Humphrey became a small disaster when Carter shouted "Hubert Horatio Hornblower—(gasp) Humphrey."* What was more important, however, was that Carter somehow sounded more strident and less sure of himself than the words themselves would suggest. And to whatever extent that image was projected, it was reinforced an hour or so later when Ted Kennedy finally arrived on the podium and made such an obvious point of preserving his political chastity. As Reagan himself, watching television in California, observed: "If that's the best they can do in unity, they have a long way to go."

As Tip O'Neill banged the gavel to signal adjournment, it was clear that the convention—and particularly that final scene on the podium—had become a distillation of all of Jimmy Carter's vulnerabilities as a President, leader of his political party, and candidate for reelection.

An incumbent president's staff should be able to write the party's platform, not obliged to negotiate it. An incumbent president with the votes for renomination should strike some fear into his party rivals, not casualness bordering on contempt. If Lyndon Baines Johnson had been waiting that final night for Ted Kennedy, it might well have crossed Ted Kennedy's mind that he had better cooperate or run the risk of every post office in Massachusetts being shut down the next morning. Most of all, however, an incumbent president should be able to use a national convention as a celebration of his performance in office—and as a message to voters that the risk of losing him was one they

---

*There were conflicting explanations later about why this happened. Some sources suggested that "Hornblower" was a derisive name used for Humphrey within the White House inner circle; others said it was simply a natural mistake made by Carter because, a navy man himself, he was devoted to the Horatio Hornblower novels by C. S. Forester.

dare not take. For Jimmy Carter the four days in Madison Square
Garden had been none of these things. Instead, they had been
a desperate attempt to paper over his failings.

By that standard, of course, the convention was something of
a success. Carter's standing in the opinion polls rose sharply after
he left New York, just as the standing of any politician rises when
he has been given intensive media exposure. And Carter's men
were deceived into believing that the worst was now over. Hamilton Jordan was telling anyone who would listen that Carter not
only would win the general election but win "big" November 4.
Even Strauss found himself carried away. Meeting with the editors of *Time* magazine, he confided: "I have little doubt that the
people will reelect the President. I felt confident enough to
make a couple of pretty good bets on it, and I bet with my head."

The prime source of this optimism, of course, was the fact that
it was Ronald Reagan they would be facing in the general election. The "internals" of Pat Caddell's opinion research suggested
that the voters had many doubts about this one-time movie actor
in the White House. He was perceived, for one thing, as more
of a risk on the basic question of them all—his ability to keep the
country out of war. And what sustained Carter's strategists most
of all was their knowledge that Reagan had never before endured the pressures of a national general election campaign and
had a well-documented penchant for putting his foot in his
mouth.

It was, they told themselves, only a matter of time before the
attention of the electorate could be turned away from the un-
happy reality—Jimmy Carter's record—and focused on the already widespread perception that Reagan did not qualify as a
safe alternative to him. In the days immediately following the
Democratic convention, it became clear the President's men
were right about that, at least.

10.
"I'll Stick to the Script"

On Thursday, September 4, near the end of the first week of the general election campaign, Ronald Reagan's crowded chartered plane was flying out of Jacksonville toward another stop in New Orleans. The heat in Jacksonville had been stifling, but it had been a good day for the candidate nonetheless. He had given two speeches there—actually, the same speech twice—and he had been cheered enthusiastically when he accused President Carter of a "cynical misuse of power and a clear abuse of the public trust" because he had allowed news of the new "Stealth" aircraft to leak out during the campaign. "The breach of secrecy was blessed and sanctioned by the Carter administration itself clearly for the sole political purpose of aiding Mr. Carter's troubled campaign," Reagan had said in identical words on both occasions.*

What was important about that was that Reagan had managed to stick to his text. He avoided any gaffes that would have distracted from his purpose of stressing national defense in a state with seventeen important electoral votes where defense is always a good issue. This discipline was the new priority, and press secretary Lyn Nofziger, who had been protecting Reagan in such situations for fifteen years, helped by good-humoredly but firmly interposing his not inconsiderable bulk between the can-

---

*A report by the Democratic-controlled Intelligence Subcommittee of the House Armed Services Committee agreed with Reagan in February 1981.

209

didate and any reporters who wanted to raise a different topic.

Reagan was buoyant, standing in the front cabin of the jet surrounded by members of his staff. At the next stop, he began, he might spice the speech a little with a few ad libs. But then Stuart Spencer, sitting at one of the work tables built into the cabin of the plane, caught Reagan's eye and stared at him hard, raising his expressive eyebrows in an unspoken question. And Reagan, laughing suddenly, interrupted himself. "Okay, Stu, okay," he said, "I'll stick to the script."

Reagan's difficulty in doing that was, of course, the principal reason that Stu Spencer, a fifty-three-year-old professional of uncommon skills, was now riding the campaign plane with him. Indeed, the candidate's weakness for making the extemporaneous, and politically unfortunate, remark had been demonstrated so often recently that the press was now beginning to write far more about his "bloopers" than they were about his message. It had reached the point that the whole campaign was being threatened even as it began.

In a speech to the national convention of the Veterans of Foreign Wars in Chicago, Reagan had added his own assessment that the war in Vietnam had been "a noble cause." In a series of meetings with the press he had renewed his insistence that the United States should have "an official relationship" with Taiwan. At a meeting of Protestant fundamentalists in Dallas he had suggested he had some doubts of his own about the theory of evolution. And three days earlier he had slandered Alabama in particular and the South in general by criticizing Jimmy Carter for opening his campaign in the home territory of the Ku Klux Klan.

Reagan had always had a tendency to say things that might be acceptable in a board room or over dinner at Chasen's but clearly were unacceptable, and potentially damaging, coming from a candidate for president of the United States. And he had a reputation, well-founded, for accepting as fact, and then retelling, almost anything he came across in his reading matter. "It wasn't that he wouldn't read things," a former staff member once said. "The problem was getting him so he wouldn't take *everything* as gospel."

In one sense, this artlessness was one of Ronald Reagan's most attractive qualities. There are many decent people who retail rumors and half-truths, things they have heard or read somewhere, without seeming to worry too much about their accuracy. Reagan was one of them. His standard speech in fifteen years in politics had been a collection of "horror stories" about the excesses of government and mindless stupidity of the bureaucracy, all of them noted on four-by-six cards he carried in his pocket. Many of them were exaggerated, of course; it really wasn't quite accurate to say that General Motors was obliged to employ more than 23,000 workers for no other reason than to fill out federal forms, as Reagan suggested. And many of them were essentially beyond verification—how could you determine there were exactly 103 taxes on a loaf of bread? But they made his argument, and only nitpicking reporters occasionally raised the question of his playing fast and loose with the facts.

Reagan was always sensitive to these complaints. What the reporters called "gaffes," he told us later, "were bits of knowledge that I transmitted in speeches at various times and someone would rush out and get someone to give them an opposite story. Ever since then, and from pretty reputable sources, all that I've said has been proven true.

"For example, when I said, and I was a New Deal Democrat and very active in my support of it, but when I said that the New Deal was patterned after Mussolini's state socialism—fascism, and long before fascism became a dirty word in the lexicon of the liberals—that this was true, that it was based on private ownership but state management and control. And I remember a very distinguished historian from one of our Eastern universities, a lone voice that rose to my rescue and confirmed [it] from his own studies, and at the same time said he was surprised that I had such a sophisticated knowledge of history, that it was true."

Similarly, Reagan was, as he put it, "annoyed" when the press kept describing as errors such things as his remarks about how many GM employees were caught up in regulatory paperwork. He had a letter, he said, from a GM executive saying the actual number was even higher, 26,600, but still he was being accused of "talking out of turn."

"I had been on the mashed potato circuit so long," he said, "and I always did my own speeches. I had so much research material that I was sure of those bits of information of that kind when I used them."

But there were two characteristics of these remarks that Reagan was given to saying that he seemed not to recognize. One was the way he so often implied more than his facts would justify. Whenever he mentioned those GM workers, for example, he seemed to conjure up a vision of an army of people sitting at desks doing nothing but filling out forms. The other was that it is a political hazard for a presidential candidate to say certain things that might be perfectly acceptable coming from someone else. A historian may safely discuss parallels between the New Deal and Mussolini's state socialism, but not a partisan politician.

In some cases, of course, these politically counterproductive remarks were nothing more complicated than a reflection of his strong views on issues. His attitude on the war in Vietnam, for example, had been conditioned by the anger he felt about the demonstrations against the war in the late 1960s. His skill at voicing the frustrations of the middle class and middle-aged had been one of his prime assets in running for governor of California in 1966. Similarly, in common with most conservative Republicans, Reagan had been a devoted admirer of Taiwan, and he was outraged when U.S. diplomatic recognition was withdrawn as part of the price of rapprochement with the People's Republic of China.

On other occasions, Reagan would get into deep water because he read so uncritically. Members of his staff used to joke among themselves about Mike Deaver, the aide closest to Reagan, hiding copies of *Human Events*, a right-wing newspaper, when an issue contained something particularly outrageous. Newcomers to Reagan's staff were astonished to hear him talking seriously about how great quantities of nuclear wastes could be reduced to concentrations "the size of baseballs" and then simply dropped into the deepest part of the ocean. A conservative columnist helping Reagan prepare a speech was startled when he began musing about how driver's licenses really shouldn't be required because people had a Constitutional right to drive their cars.

Reagan maintained a wary distance from reporters. Because he had come to politics so late in life, he didn't understand them very well, and he seemed to regard them as not very substantial people. At the same time he was unfailingly courteous and apparently incapable of simply smiling and turning away if someone thrust a microphone in front of his face or called out a question to him. When Nofziger would advise him he didn't have to answer every question put to him, Reagan would reply that "it looks worse" if you walk away.

On some occasions he would simply be off guard, either forgetting or ignoring the presence of reporters bent on measuring his every dimension. That was what happened, for example, when he told that joke about the duck at the cockfight back in New Hampshire. It would happen later when he began speculating about the hidden benefits to health in an oil slick that had covered the Santa Barbara Channel at the turn of the century. He would say to himself, one long-time intimate said, "This is not important, I'm just chatting." But presidential candidates do not enjoy that luxury.

In the spring of 1979 he had invited a reporter, along with three of his campaign advisers, to dinner at his home in Pacific Palisades. It was just a few days after President Carter had appeared in Los Angeles and a derelict in the crowd had been arrested when federal agents discovered he was carrying a starter's pistol. It had been reported that day that the FBI had placed charges against the derelict, but the agency also made it clear that this was done only to allow time for a thorough investigation of the highly unlikely possibility it had been an assassination plot. But Reagan saw it differently. He didn't hesitate to speculate that Carter "might be so inhumane" that he would seek the prosecution "to get the sympathy vote like Ford did"—a reference to the serious attempt that had been made on President Gerald Ford's life while Reagan was competing against him for the 1976 Republican nomination.

Later that same evening the conversation turned to whether Ted Kennedy might seek the Democratic nomination. That led, inevitably, to the question of Kennedy's personal safety if he became a candidate. A Secret Service agent once assigned to Kennedy, Reagan blithely recounted, had told him that Kennedy was "a physical coward," so perhaps he wouldn't run. It wasn't said in a judgmental way, and Reagan never indicated he shared that view or, if he did, that he would be inclined to criticize Kennedy for it. It was hardly prudent, nonetheless, for a man running for president of the United States to pass on gossip from the Secret Service to a reporter he scarcely knew. But Ronald Reagan was hardly the conventional politician, either.

Now, however, the situation in August 1980 was quite different. Reagan was not just *a* candidate but *the* Republican nominee for president. As such, he would be living under much brighter light than he ever had as an actor or conservative spokesman or even governor of the nation's most populous state. The press coverage would be sometimes ridiculous, always relentless.

In one sense, Reagan understood that he had what his advisers called "an image problem" because of his strong conservative views on domestic matters and his history of saber-rattling on foreign-policy questions. Indeed, at a press conference right after the Democratic convention, he joked about being considered "a combination of Ebenezer Scrooge and the Mad Bomber." But what Reagan didn't understand at this stage was how his freedom of speech and action alike would be limited by the necessity to convince the voters he wouldn't be too much of a risk in the White House.

Thus, going over the text of a speech he would deliver to the Veterans of Foreign Wars in Chicago, Reagan himself inserted the reference to the Vietnam war as a "noble cause." That is what he believed, and some primordial political instinct told him that was also something the members of the VFW would like to hear. For any actor, applause lines are basic sustenance. What Reagan did not foresee, however, was that those few words would be viewed as an attempt to open up national wounds that had scarcely healed. And what he did not recognize, because the insertion of the phrase slipped by his staff, was that making this point would divert the press from the main point of his speech— that Jimmy Carter was following policies of "weakness, inconsistency, vacillation, and bluff" on national defense issues.

In some cases, Reagan's staff had failed him by putting him

into situations a more prudent candidate might have avoided. On August 22, for example, Reagan flew into Dallas to speak to a national conference of evangelists, which he might very well have bypassed. At the least, it was clear later, he should have whipped into the convention hall, delivered his speech, and then fled without allowing any opportunity for him to be identified with the fundamentalists' more controversial positions. But instead he held a press conference and found himself confronted with a question about the theory of evolution. He was, an adviser observed later, "trying to pick his way" between offending his hosts and the press. "Like a lot of people, he forgets he doesn't have to answer a question."

Reagan might simply have said that he couldn't see the relevance of the debate over Darwinism to the presidential campaign and left it at that. But, eager to please, he suggested instead that there were indeed "great flaws" in the theory of evolution and it might be a good idea if the schools taught the "creationist" theory as well. It was hardly the thing to say for a candidate who was trying to resolve widespread doubts about his intellectual capacity. And although his remarks never provoked a major controversy, they were not overlooked by voters paying close attention to the campaign. A week later we were conducting random interviews in a largely Jewish neighborhood in Queens and found that almost everyone had heard about it. "What does he think?" a waiter in a delicatessen asked rhetorically. "Science has been wrong all these years? It makes you wonder."

The controversy that developed over United States policy toward Taiwan was considerably more serious, if only because it involved foreign policy, and Reagan was a candidate whose credentials in that area had by no means been established. It gained added weight, too, because it made a disaster of one of his campaign's first political exercises.

Again, this was a case in which Reagan was failed by his staff. Shortly after the Republican convention the candidate and his strategists began to discuss the idea of sending George Bush, the vice-presidential nominee, to Peking. At first blush it made some political sense. Bush had served fourteen months as the head of the United States liaison office there before normalization of dip-lomatic relations, so he knew the Chinese leaders. It would pres-ent an opportunity to raise Bush's visibility somewhat while reinforcing, or appearing to reinforce, the foreign-policy creden-tials of the Republican ticket. But what the strategists clearly un-derestimated was the difficulty inherent in the conflict between Bush's role in the opening to China and Reagan's long-standing support of Taiwan. Nor did they fully understand that what was important politically was not the travels of a vice-presidential candidate but the views of a presidential nominee.

Reagan had never wavered on this issue. He was given to call-ing Taiwan "the Republic of China" or even "the free Republic of China." Moreover, during an appearance in Cleveland back in May, Reagan had said: "One of the things I look forward to most if I am successful in this election is to reestablish official relations between the United States government and Taiwan." Such a step, of course, would be a violation of the agreement with Pe-king, which declared "there is but one China and Taiwan is part of China." And it would also violate the Taiwan Relations Act of 1979, which created an ostensibly private but government-staffed and government-funded American Institute in Taiwan—a de facto embassy.

The press, inevitably, remembered what Reagan had said in Cleveland. At an August 16 news conference that was supposed to be a kind of *bon voyage* media event for Bush, reporters man-aged to elicit from Reagan that, yes, he did indeed still believe in an "official government relationship" with Taiwan. Even after Bush arrived in Peking and the Chinese were very publicly ex-pressing their anger at Reagan's comments, Reagan told report-ers "I guess it's a yes" after they pursued him to the wall on the same question. The controversy doomed Bush's mission; the Chi-nese complained that Reagan "has insulted one billion Chinese people" and had "failed to reassure" the Chinese leadership on the nature of the relationship between the two powers in the fu-ture. Bush's trip, rather than representing the play of a high card, was being viewed at home as an example of the pitiable naïveté of the Republican ticket.

Finally, on August 25, Bush was flown back to Los Angeles to join Reagan at the Marriott Hotel near the airport for a press conference that was intended finally to resolve the issue. Reporters were given a nine-page statement in which Reagan's foreign-policy expert, Richard V. Allen, had labored mightily to reconcile the candidate's well-known views with the realities. In both the statement and in answers to questions, Reagan took the position that President Carter was being "hypocritical" by maintaining the fiction that the U.S.-Taiwan relationship was private and unofficial. What he was objecting to, he said, were "the petty practices of the Carter administration which are inappropriate and demeaning to our Chinese friends in Taiwan"—such as the policy of requiring meetings between officials of the American Institute and of the Taiwan government to be held somewhere other than in the offices of either. But, of course, as President, Reagan fully intended to abide by the Taiwan Relations Act. In short, nothing would change except for some reduction in the hypocrisy quotient.

It was a lame story. The real one was that, presidential candidate or not, Ronald Reagan was not ready to let go of an emotional commitment he had shared with his friends on the Far Right. And he had allowed that commitment to lead him into a political blunder that raised all over again with new force the questions about his capacity on foreign affairs. Moreover, in case anyone had missed it, the United States ambassador to Peking, Leonard Woodcock, took the extraordinary step of holding a press conference to say: "To endanger the carefully crafted relationship between the People's Republic and the United States is to run the risk of gravely weakening the American international position at a dangerous time."*

Reagan's problems had now reached the point where they seemed to dominate the campaign. Even minor irregularities were being fit into the context of the bumbling candidate out of control. For example, two days after the press conference with

---

*Woodcock insisted that was all his own idea rather than a suggestion from the White House or the Carter-Mondale Committee. But, as a former president of the United Auto Workers, Woodcock was also obviously sensitive to the political content of his press conference.

Bush in Los Angeles, Reagan altered his text to tell an Ohio Teamsters' conference at Columbus that the country was in the grip of "a severe depression" rather than simply "a severe recession." Before the speech he had met with Governor James A. Rhodes, one of the rhetorical free spirits of American politics, and it was clear Reagan was trying to fit his assessment to that of his Ohio sponsor. It didn't really matter, of course, but when Alan Greenspan, one of Reagan's economics advisers, admitted that he didn't consider that conditions fit the classic definition of "depression" the press focused on the difference of opinion. And the Reagan people found it necessary to issue still another clarification. The old jokes were revived, and the memories of George Romney running for President in 1968. Romney had made so many misstatements and issued so many clarifications that a reporter claimed his typewriter was equipped with a special key that would print, at a single stroke, "Romney later explained . . ."*

On the campaign plane and back at headquarters in Arlington, there was obvious alarm. James Baker, one of the few people in Reagan's camp with experience in a general election campaign, wrote a memorandum warning that especially intense scrutiny had to be expected; it wouldn't solve the problem simply to say it was unfair and blame the press. "I think the problem was," Baker said later, "that the campaign didn't recognize that's the way the process works." Again, it was a matter of perception rather than reality. "The perception out there," said Baker, "was that he was sticking his foot in it every time he opened his mouth."

Others were similarly concerned. William Timmons, another veteran of the Ford days serving Reagan as political director, said later: "In and of themselves, I didn't take them [the gaffes] very seriously. But the aggregate effect was of grave concern, because at some point people would start thinking that he's incompetent. If you have one a week and the press plays 'em up pretty strong and people start laughing, then you've got a real image problem."

---

*Reagan eventually turned the "recession" vs. "depression" flap to his advantage by telling audiences: "A recession is when your neighbor loses his job. A depression is when you lose your job. Recovery is when Jimmy Carter loses his job."

Ed Meese quarreled with the definition of these incidents as "bloopers" but not with the potential problem they represented. "My own feeling was that you're bound to have that in any campaign," he said later, "and that it was good to have it early. And the second feeling was that we had to do some things to change it so that it didn't continue to grow, because most of it was press-inspired rather than actual, it was perceptive rather than actual."

Nofziger was convinced, correctly, that the early "bloopers" would be forgotten, but he recognized the focus had to be turned on more basic issues. "I kept telling people," he said, "this stuff is nothing, that nobody's paying any attention, and that it's not going to have a serious effect on the campaign if we put it behind us and talk about the things people are interested in."

The obvious answer, it was soon apparent, was to "put someone on the plane" in addition to Mike Deaver (who was managing both the tour and the candidate) and Nofziger (whose prime responsibility was dealing with the huge and difficult press corps that travels with a presidential candidate and greets him at every stop). At meetings in Arlington and with Reagan at Wexford, Virginia, where he was renting a home temporarily, the possibility was discussed. Campaign manager William Casey suggested at one point that a roster of senators and congressmen be compiled and that they rotate on the plane. But others argued that a full-time professional was required. There was some talk of using the campaign chairman, Paul Laxalt, but he had his own duties in the Senate and his own campaign for reelection back in Nevada. Nofziger and Deaver on the plane, and several of those back at headquarters, including Timmons and Baker, were convinced that Spencer was the ideal choice, if he could be persuaded to do it.

Then, as the general campaign opened more or less officially on Labor Day weekend, another gaffe brought new urgency to the question.

Reagan began this final phase of his quest for the presidency at Liberty Park in New Jersey, a waterfront site that provided the cameras with a backdrop of New York harbor and the Statue of Liberty. He had deliberately chosen to go into "enemy torri-tory" to emphasize his concern for blue-collar workers and his determination to seek out converts among the Democrats.

The President, meanwhile, had opened his campaign in Tuscumbia, Alabama, at an outdoor rally. There had been about twenty robed members of the Ku Klux Klan there, protesting his appearance, and Carter had not missed the chance to put them in their place. "These people in white sheets do not understand our region and what it's been through," he said, to the cheers of the rest of the crowd. "They do not understand that the South and all America must move forward."

Reagan noticed that Carter had chosen to open his campaign in "safe" home territory while he was opening his on Democratic ground in New Jersey and then Michigan, where for years Democrats began their campaigns. "I was going to the lion's den and he was going to where, you might say, he would have the warm blanket of security around him," he told us later. On the plane to Detroit Reagan and his advisers discussed this contrast and, he said later, "someone happened to bring up" the point that Tuscumbia was some kind of center for the Ku Klux Klan. They even discussed whether he should mention this at Detroit, then decided he should just let it pass. But while he was speaking at the Michigan state fair later that day Reagan noticed "a woman down front who was wearing a Carter mask and who was kind of heckling." And that was enough to trigger a reaction. "Now I'm happy to be here," he told the crowd, "while he [Carter] is opening his campaign down there in the city that gave birth to and is the parent body of the Ku Klux Klan."

Reagan himself knew he had made a mistake. "I shouldn't have said it because the minute after I said it, I knew this was what would be remembered, and I knew that it didn't sound like [what he had intended]. . . . When it was over and we got into the car, the first thing I said to our own guys in the car there, I said, 'I could have bitten my tongue off.' "

He was right that time. Aside from getting his facts wrong—Tuscumbia was not the birthplace of the KKK—Reagan evoked an angry reaction from politicians, press, and, presumably, voters who took it as an insult to Alabama and the Deep South. Seven governors from Southern states quickly sent him a telegram of protest, and Reagan was obliged to call both the governor of Alabama and the mayor of Tuscumbia to offer his apologies.

But the KKK gaffe also galvanized his campaign. Nancy Reagan was particularly alarmed, and became insistent that more help was needed on the plane. Two days later at a meeting of top campaign officials at Wexford, she took Dick Wirthlin aside and urged him to telephone Spencer, who had not been invited to the meeting, to see if he would be willing to come aboard full-time.

Spencer is one of those politicians—there are a handful in each party—who seem to have computers just behind their eyes. When a situation arises, they are already programmed instantly to recognize and assess the political ramifications of various courses of action. They can tell how other politicians will react, how the press is likely to behave, how the voters will respond. Big-time campaigns are rarely successful without someone like that at the elbow of the candidate, and Stuart Spencer was the obvious choice here. As Nofziger put it, "This gave us a full-time politician aboard and a very, very good one."

That Ron and Nancy Reagan were able to accept Spencer so readily tells something about their pragmatism, because there had been considerable strain in their relationship with him over the last few years. But their association went back a long way, and they knew each other well.

Spencer and his partner at the time, Bill Roberts, had first achieved some small national prominence working for Nelson A. Rockefeller and against Barry Goldwater in the California Republican primary of 1964. Although Rockefeller lost the race in the end, Spencer-Roberts Associates received high marks in the political community for both aggressive and imaginative work in their client's behalf.

Two years later they were the chief architects of the campaigns in which the neophyte Reagan first defeated George Christopher, then mayor of San Francisco, in a Republican primary and then the incumbent Democratic governor, Edmund G. (Pat) Brown, by a million votes in the general election. Four years after that, in 1970, they also directed his successful reelection campaign against Jess Unruh, the Democrat who had been known as the "Big Daddy" of California politics as speaker of the assembly during the 1960s.*

But after that 1970 campaign Spencer and the Reagans parted company, in large measure because of bad feeling between Spencer and Mike Deaver. Indeed, Spencer was convinced not only that he was being shut out by a palace guard around Reagan, but that Deaver was bad-mouthing him to other potential clients for his political consulting business.

Then in 1976 Spencer committed the ultimate sin by joining Gerald Ford's campaign as its top strategist. Beyond that, Spencer has an acid tongue, and the reports of some of his remarks about Reagan filtered back to his former candidate. When that happens with Reagan, a long-time associate once said, "he gets hurt a little bit, and his wife gets mad."

Now, however, all this was forgotten. Reagan doesn't hold grudges, and Spencer and Nancy Reagan had already put their differences behind them when Spencer had agreed in July to serve as a part-time consultant to the campaign. As far as she was concerned, bygones were bygones; what was important now was getting Ronnie elected. Deaver, the aide closest to both Reagans, was just as enthusiastic.

Spencer's presence on the plane did not, of course, solve all the campaign's problems. But it did give "the plane" somewhat more weight in the inevitable small contretemps with "headquarters" that develop almost every day in any campaign. And it put at Ronald Reagan's side someone who had been through one of these exercises before, with Ford in the fall of 1976, and someone from whom the candidate was willing to take advice.

The gaffes became rarer, but they did not disappear entirely. Indeed, a month later Reagan wandered into trouble in Ohio when he attempted to make common cause with blue-collar workers who blamed rigid antipollution standards for the problems of the automobile and steel industries.

At one point, for example, he told a group he had twice flown over the volcanic Mount St. Helens in Washington. "I'm not a scientist," he said, "and I don't know the figures, but I have a sus-

---

*Unruh is credited with that deathless definition: "Money is the mother's milk of politics."

picion that one little mountain out there in these last several months has probably released more sulfur dioxide into the atmosphere of the world than has been released in the last ten years of auto driving or things of that kind."

Predictably, President Carter's Environmental Protection Agency was right there to tell reporters that Mount St. Helens was producing 500 to 2000 tons of sulfur dioxide per day, compared to 81,000 tons of sulfur dioxide per day from man-made sources.

At another point, Reagan suggested that "growing and decaying vegetation in this land are responsible for 93 percent of the oxides of nitrogen abroad in the environment." EPA Administrator Douglas Costle quickly explained that Reagan had confused "nitrous oxide," the natural product of plant respiration, with "nitrogen dioxide," a regulated pollutant. (This was essentially a case of apples and oranges. Although there was no quarrel with Reagan's statement about oxides of nitrogen, he made it in the *context* of a discussion of government efforts to control man-made pollution and whether those efforts were justifiable when weighed against their economic effect.) And, at a time when Reagan's home town of Los Angeles was suffering a severe smog crisis, he put out a statement saying "air pollution has been substantially controlled." At Claremont College he was greeted by students chanting "smog, smog" and the single best heckling sign of the year—one affixed to a tree that said: "Chop Me Down Before I Kill Again."

On still another occasion, Reagan raised the possibility that some of those apparently noxious materials in the air "might be beneficial to tubercular patients." The breezes that blew off the oil slick on the Santa Barbara Channel around the turn of the century, he said, "purified the air and prevented the spread of infectious diseases." This was a vintage Reaganism, and one adviser speculated that he had probably read something about the Santa Barbara Channel "in one of these damned little magazines or periodicals" to which he was so devoted.

"He read it," this adviser said, "and it just fell into one of the crevices of his mind, and he went and dug the damned thing out and said it."

Reagan's abundance of misinformation in this important area

was appalling on the face of it, and reporters who had covered
him for years in California and on the national scene knew that
the problem was not limited to environmental matters. His previous campaigns had abounded in "horror stories" about the
excesses of government intrusion into the private lives of Americans. They had been duly reported, but Reagan would just smile
pleasantly or shake his head in disagreement with his critics, as
if matters of provable fact were things on which gentlemen certainly could differ in goodwill. It was maddening to reporters
and Reagan critics, but it was his special talent, and besides, who
could get angry at this benign, well-meaning, amiable man? Under other circumstances, Reagan's observations on the subjects
of air pollution and other environmental issues, not to mention
his hasty comments on military and foreign affairs, might have
become a critical factor in the election. Instead, a growing furor
over remarks critical of him made by Carter relegated the pollution flap to the category of comic relief.

But when Stu Spencer came aboard "Leadership 80," Reagan's campaign plane, the "killer trees" episode was no more
than a gleam in Reagan's eye. The imperative then, still early in
September, was to change the subject from the theory of evolution and Taiwan and the KKK—and, most of all, to stifle the
laughter before it became too destructive. Several factors played
a part in helping him accomplish that.

One, of course, was the new discipline and concentration on
the issues Reagan wanted to make the news of the day. His criticism of the leak about the Stealth aircraft in Jacksonville was a
classic case. With a topic so substantial on their platters, the re-
poters were less inclined to dwell on the Ku Klux Klan. There
were still protest signs and complaints from the other side, but
it was yesterday's news.

Then, by mid-September, Carter himself was straying into
trouble with his bitter attacks on the Republican candidate. In
Atlanta, speaking to a black audience at the Ebenezer Baptist
Church, the President accused Reagan of injecting "hatred" and
"racism" into the campaign by using "code words" such as
"states' rights" from the early days of the civil rights struggle.
With Reagan, this was something that simply would not play.

The Republican candidate might have been vulnerable to accusations of naïveté, ideological rigidity, or intellectual sloth, but there was no evidence he was a racist. "It was a tactical error," a Reagan strategist said. "It enabled us to get the focus off our mistakes." And Reagan was a master at playing the injured party for the network cameras, always mixing just the right quantities of righteous indignation with sorrow for the sinner who had strayed from the path.

Perhaps most important in liberating Reagan, however, was the beginning of the bargaining with the Carter camp over debates, and whether or not independent John B. Anderson would be included. As Jim Baker, Reagan's principal agent on this issue, said later: "The debate negotiations became a bigger story than the foot in mouth."

The League of Women Voters, displaying the righteousness of the politically pure, put Carter in an untenable position from the outset. The League first announced, unilaterally, that there would be three presidential debates—in Baltimore, Cleveland, and Portland, Oregon. A vice-presidential debate would be held in Louisville. John Anderson would be included if he attained an average of 15 percent support in the major national opinion polls.

Carter was prepared, even eager, to debate Reagan. He and those around him were convinced he could destroy the lightweight from California with his superior grasp of the complexities of government operations and policy issues. But the President and his advisers were equally adamant in their refusal to allow Anderson to participate. Although the poll figures were somewhat ambiguous, they seemed to suggest that Anderson would cut more deeply into Carter than into Reagan. And political professionals of all persuasions agreed the President would be taking too great a risk by giving the independent the respectability that would come from equal treatment in a debate.

It was also clear, however, that Carter would pay a price for denying him. A Harris Survey found that 69 percent of the voters wanted to see a three-way debate. Reagan was able to take a posture as the candidate willing to give the voters the broadest possible opportunity to see the entire field. And Carter was already on the defensive because he had refused to confront Ted Kennedy in debate during the contest for the Democratic nomination.

So the White House went through the motions of sending a team of negotiators led by Bob Strauss to discuss the debate. But Jody Powell complained bitterly about the imperious behavior of the League in taking so much on itself. It was even pointed out that the only Southern site chosen by the League had been set aside for the vice-presidential candidates rather than the main event (a specious argument in light of the fact the audience that mattered would see the debate on television). Jack Watson, who had replaced Hamilton Jordan as White House chief of staff when Jordan assumed command of the campaign, invited other groups to act as sponsors for a debate between the two major candidates by pointing out the League had no "franchise" to run it. The National Press Club, the *Ladies' Home Journal,* and CBS-TV's *Face the Nation* quickly came forward with offers, and Carter just as quickly accepted them. But the bottom line remained that there would be no three-way debate. "We just can't do it," Strauss said. "Whatever it costs, we'll have to take it."

Meanwhile, the President made things somewhat worse for himself than they might otherwise have been with his public displays of hyperbole and resentfulness. At one point, for example, he described his willingness to debate as "unprecedented" for an incumbent, although Gerald Ford had done exactly the same thing under the same circumstances four years earlier. Carter described Anderson as "primarily a creation of the press," conveniently forgetting that he had been given the same kind of press treatment as a dark-horse candidate in 1976.

"He's never won a primary, even in his home state," said Carter of Anderson on a campaign trip to New Jersey. "He ran as a Republican and he's still a Republican. He hasn't had a convention. He doesn't have a party. He and his wife picked his vice-presidential nominee." (This last thrust was particularly jarring coming from Rosalynn Carter's husband.)

When the debate between Reagan and Anderson finally was held on Sunday night, September 21, in Baltimore, it really wasn't a debate at all. The candidates did indeed disagree predictably on a whole range of issues—energy policy, the MX missile, taxes, abortion among them. But Reagan had no stake in trying to cut down Anderson; on the contrary, it was to his advantage to bolster the independent as a viable force in the campaign. And Anderson's first priority was establishing his own credentials as a candidate now that he had finally achieved a national forum. So each of the candidates spent most of the sixty minutes on network television giving excerpts from his standard campaign speeches.

In different ways, each could claim to be the "winner" later. In the first post-debate survey by ABC-Harris, 36 percent of the viewers thought Anderson had performed better, 30 percent favored Reagan, and 17 percent thought they were equally effective. But a subsequent Harris Survey and CBS-*New York Times* poll suggested that it was Jimmy Carter who had been the loser, no matter who won. Harris found that among those who had not watched the debate the matchup figures went this way: Carter 40 percent, Reagan 39 percent, Anderson 16 percent. Among those who *had* watched, they were: Reagan 42, Carter 36, Anderson 19. Also, CBS took a survey just before the debate and it came out: Carter 40 percent, Reagan 36, and Anderson 9. Just after the debate its poll found a reversal: Reagan 40, Carter 35, Anderson 9.

Reagan, however, won a great deal more that night in Baltimore than the figures could measure with any precision. The voters might have been hearing about a candidate with such a weakness for making "bloopers" that he would be too much of a risk in the White House. That, certainly, was the perception the Carter campaign was trying to build. But what the voters *saw* was one who was unfailingly good-humored, articulate, and apparently knowledgeable enough to qualify as at least a realistic alternative to the incumbent President.

And the campaign of John Anderson, although he might not have realized it at the time, had just reached its high point.

11.
Anderson and
the "Alienated Middle"

Almost from the very beginning John Anderson's independent campaign had been pointed toward a debate with one or both of the major party nominees that would give his own candidacy both national exposure and credibility. But now, his confrontation with Ronald Reagan at Baltimore over, it seemed that what he had done was make the "impossible choice" between Carter and Reagan appear less impossible after all.

To be sure, Anderson was still a factor in the campaign and would remain one until Election Day. His continued presence complicated efforts to bring Carter and Reagan face to face in debate. And in both of the major party campaigns there was concern about how many votes Anderson would draw from their candidates in critical states. Could he cost Carter the electoral votes of New York or Pennsylvania? Could his support be enough to deny Reagan Illinois or Wisconsin?

But in the days immediately following the debate in Baltimore, even many of Anderson's most devoted supporters were recognizing that he would not win the election. His candidacy had been a significant attempt to alter the shape of American politics, and it still might achieve that. But there were limits inherent in a campaign conducted outside the party structure that Anderson could not overcome.

Long after it was over we asked Anderson what he might have done differently. "It was such a textbook-perfect campaign," he said, laughing at himself, "that it's hard to tell."

"If there was one thing," he said, finally, "it would have been to be a little more adventuresome on some other issues and try to make sure that the distinctiveness of the candidacy was maintained." Then he added: "Operating against that was the idea that you didn't want to frighten people to death. You didn't want them to think you were just going to overthrow the system."

As well as anything, that summarized the independent campaign for the presidency in 1980. It evolved in the first place out of the "distinctiveness" of his candidacy—"the Anderson difference," his slogan said. It failed in the end because the voters did not find in the candidacy enough reason to abandon "the system" as it stood.

Even in its origins, John Anderson's campaign was unorthodox. It was motivated far more by his frustration as a politician than by the lust for power that is enough of a driving force for most politicians. He had spent almost twenty years in the House of Representatives, during which he had earned a reputation in Washington for both independence and intellectual honesty. Although he was a conventional conservative from the Middle West on many questions of fiscal and defense policy, he had broken with the pattern—and with many of his fellow Republicans—to cast key votes for civil rights legislation and to become a leading advocate of reforms in the rules of the House and in the financing of political campaigns. Typically, he had been one of the first Republicans in the House to recognize and say publicly that Richard Nixon was culpable on Watergate. But now Anderson had decided he had had enough. Like all politicians, he wanted to accomplish change. Now he had accepted the reality that he was never going to be able to do that in the House. So why not a last roll of the dice, a run for the presidency—at this point, the Republican presidential nomination—done *his* way?

The notion of running had been germinating for two years or more, at least within the Anderson household. In November 1977, when Anderson was facing a 1978 primary challenge from a fundamentalist minister, one of us had dinner with the Andersons at their home in Rockford, Illinois. At one end of the table John Anderson was railing about the seriousness of the threat to his congressional seat; at the other Keke Anderson, his wife, was talking about a presidential campaign in 1980.

To some extent, this idea was a natural product of a change in politics caused by Morris Udall's campaign for the Democratic presidential nomination in 1976. Although Udall had been defeated by Jimmy Carter, the successes he did enjoy had demonstrated that it was feasible for a member of the House to be a genuine possibility for the presidency. (Mo and Ella Udall, incidentally, were close personal friends of John and Keke Anderson.) It was also clear, however, that Anderson wanted to use a national campaign to make some kind of statement about what his party and politics should represent, even if he recognized that he was the longest of long shots in the Republican field. "I guess I just want to get it all off my chest before I close up the books," he told *The Washington Post* late in 1979.

More than any of the others in that early field (except perhaps Bob Dole), Anderson resisted the temptation to take himself too seriously. He joked about his reputation as a liberal or moderate in a party growing more conservative every year. "You don't have to be a Neanderthal to be a Republican," he would say, offering himself as the prime exhibit. He made sport of the light regard in which he was held by the press and political establishment because he lacked the trappings of a "serious" candidate. We encountered him one morning in December 1979 at a small gathering in the home of Arthur and Esther Nighswander in Gilford, New Hampshire, near Laconia. John and Keke Anderson had flown up from Boston on Air Winnepesaukee, he reported, and they were the only passengers on the eight-seat airplane. "The press would have thought," he announced, "that I had my own chartered plane"—then, in a tone of exaggerated discouragement, he added: "if there had been any press there."

He was, at that point, a candidate who could be relaxed because he was a candidate with nothing to lose. But when the campaign began in earnest in January 1980, that situation began to change. In his appearance at that first debate in Iowa January 5, he had set himself apart from the Republican pack as the only one who supported President Carter's decision to impose an embargo on grain shipments to the Soviet Union. And he was the most irreverent about the promises of the other Republicans (Ronald Reagan most notably) that they would balance the federal budget while reducing taxes and increasing defense spending. Asked how that could be done, he replied: "It's simple. You do it with mirrors."

In the weeks before the Iowa debate, Anderson had enjoyed a remarkably "good press" at the hands of newspaper writers. Most of them were based in Washington, and they knew Anderson as one of the most capable members of the House as well as one of the most determinedly independent. When voters across the country saw the Iowa debate on public television or excerpts from it on the network news programs, some of them began to see what the reporters had been saying. And if they missed it then, perhaps they caught up the following month when Anderson made a point of playing Daniel in the lion's den by showing up at a meeting of the Gun Owners of New Hampshire in Concord. There was excellent film for the networks in the enraged outburst from the crowd when Anderson asked them: "What is so wrong about telling the law-abiding public of this country we will license gun-owners?"

Meanwhile, Anderson had become something of a cult hero when Garry Trudeau devoted two weeks of the "Doonesbury" comic strip to poking fun at his shoestring campaign and the kind of people it attracted.

None of this helped Anderson very much in New Hampshire, where he finished far behind Reagan and Bush with less than 10 percent of the vote. In common with most of the other Republicans, he had made the mistake of thinking he could use New Hampshire, rather than Iowa, as a starting point in 1980. "I really, I guess, had pinned more hope than I had any rational right to do on my ability to somehow come out of the little state of New Hampshire with a more impressive total than I did," he said later. "Candidates do that, you know. You start believing your own arguments."

The new celebrity did help him, however, the following week, when he finished second to Bush in Massachusetts and to Reagan in Vermont, in each case by an eyelash. But his moment of hope was short-lived. Two weeks later he was beaten by Reagan in Illinois, a primary he had emphasized himself, 48 to 37 percent. And two weeks after that, he suffered what he called "the coup de grace" when he finished third in Wisconsin behind both Reagan and Bush.

The seed of the idea for an independent candidacy had been planted, however, even before the Massachusetts and Vermont primaries—by Tom Mathews, a professional direct-mail specialist who had made a reputation working for liberal candidates and organizations and, a decade earlier, in building Common Cause into an important force in American politics. At a meeting in Boston the night after the vote in New Hampshire, Mathews told Anderson he was talking to the wrong audience. As Mathews described it, he was addressing himself to the people in one room who were sitting on their hands while the message was evoking wild applause out of sight in an adjoining room. The people in that first room, he argued, were Republican primary voters; those in the second room were the ones who made up what Mathews called "the alienated middle." The direct-mail expert was not flying blind in saying this. A few weeks earlier he and his partner, Roger Craver, had sent out a fund-raising mailing of just under 50,000 pieces for Anderson and received an astounding response of almost 6 percent. A return of 1.5 percent is considered more than respectable in such cases, and similar mailings made for Ted Kennedy at the same time had yielded less than 1 percent. There was, Mathews argued, "something out there" for John Anderson, but it wouldn't be found in the Republican Party.

Understandably, Anderson was diverted by his success in Massachusetts and Vermont. But just a week after his loss in Illinois, he met in a suite in the Pfister Hotel in Milwaukee with Mathews, Craver, and several others: campaign manger Michael MacLeod and issues director Cliff Brown; the television producer Norman Lear and Stanley Scheinbaum, a longtime fund-raiser for liberal candidates, who had been raising money for him in California and elsewhere; and David Garth, the political consultant and media expert from New York. The topic, of course, was the efficacy of an independent campaign, and the hours of discussion grew heated and intense. MacLeod and others on the

Anderson staff resisted his leaving the Republican Party; the "outsiders" generally argued it was the only hope still left. "We were arguing over his political soul," Mathews recalled later.

Anderson remained uncommitted to the idea of an independent campaign, although by now he was sending even public hints that it was a possibility. At the very least he had recognized his limits within his own party. "I knew I wasn't making inroads in the Republican Party," Anderson said. "I just was not, even in my own state. I could not overcome that strong conservative Republican bias."

When he lost in Wisconsin the following Tuesday, he announced that he was going to California for a respite to think about the future. What was clear to some of those involved, however, was that Anderson never had focused up to this point on the possibility of the presidency but instead was still more interested in making a statement. "It was his *dernier cri,*" said Mathews.

The day after the Wisconsin primary Mathews flew to New York to see if Garth was willing to join such a campaign and, if so, what it would cost. (Garth was indeed willing, and it would cost about $35,000 a month.) Next Mathews contacted Arnold Siner of a prestigious Washington law firm, Arnold and Porter, to determine whether the firm would be willing to handle the problems of ballot access for Anderson and what they estimated it would cost. (The ultimate answers were that they would and it would cost something over $750,000.) On April 6 Mathews flew to California, tracked down Anderson at Malibu, and laid the whole idea out. "When do we button it up?" Anderson asked, and eighteen days later, before a packed house in the ballroom of the National Press Club, the "National Unity Campaign" was officially launched. "I will pursue an independent candidacy," he said.

The campaign was treated more seriously by the political community than any of its kind in more than half a century, and with good reason. At this stage, it was clear that the major party nominees would be Carter and Reagan, and both of them were laboring under heavy political burdens. The President's "approval ratings" in the opinion polls continued to rival those of Richard

Nixon at his lowest point. Reagan, despite his success in the primaries, at sixty-nine was viewed by many as too old, too conservative, and too much of a risk with the nuclear button. Pollsters such as Daniel Yankelovich were finding an astonishing reaction against the prospective choice in November.

Announcing his candidacy, Anderson said: "The obstacles pale when one considers that too many people in our nation are disillusioned with the prospective choices our party structures are offering." Mathews now was acquiring new evidence that the voters in the "alienated middle" would be extraordinarily receptive to an alternative. By early June polls began showing Anderson with as much as 25 percent of the electorate. There was much discussion of the possibility that no candidate might win a majority in the Electoral College and the election would be thrown into the House of Representatives.

The core of the independent candidate's support was made up, predictably, of the young on college campuses and the better-educated, affluent suburbanites who became known as the "brie-and-chablis set." The test for Anderson was clearly whether he could broaden his appeal by reaching out to blue-collar Democrats and members of minority groups who had the most reason to be dismayed by Carter's record on the economy, and the most reason to fear a conservative Republican administration as a replacement.

But several political realities stalled the campaign before it could gain any real momentum.

It became apparent immediately that although this was to be a "coalition" Anderson was going to find it difficult, if not impossible, to find any prominent political figures willing to coalesce with him. It was one thing for him, taking a last fling, and quite another for those who could see other steps up the Republican or Democratic ladders ahead of them—and the certain prospect that if they defected they would never be forgiven. Even Anderson's colleagues in the liberal-to-moderate Republican group in the House, the Wednesday Club, he said, "just couldn't find it in their own political self-interest" to join him. "I couldn't get mad at anybody for that," he said later. "Why should they throw themselves on the political funeral pyre for me?" The one Republican leader Anderson did pressure was Governor William G.

Milliken of Michigan, a highly respected moderate and a close friend with doubts about Ronald Reagan that were no secret. "I tried hard with Milliken," Anderson said. "I really worked on Bill Milliken." But after a lifetime as a Republican, even Milliken could not bring himself to break that connection.

The importance of such establishment supporters was not that they would bring voters with them, or even be capable of delivering any votes directly. Instead, their support would have been a signal to the press and to the public that other politicians were taking John Anderson's campaign seriously, and that they would do well to follow suit. "Initially," Anderson said, "you've got to build some kind of coalition [to run the government].... You don't impress people with ... your ability to build that coalition, nor do they see it as a realistic concept, unless you get a little coalition going in the campaign, and I didn't have that."

There was, of course, always the possibility that enlisting conventional politicians would offend and alienate some of the brie-and-chablis purists, but Anderson was willing to risk that. "A few old-fashioned political types, I don't think would have contaminated the campaign," he said.

In the end Anderson did enlist one of those types, Patrick J. Lucey, as his running mate for vice president. At sixty-two, Lucey was a former Democratic governor of Wisconsin who had served under Carter as ambassador to Mexico, then fallen out bitterly with the President and joined Edward Kennedy's campaign. Lucey, a veteran of more than twenty years in liberal politics, was a charming and intelligent professional, and he proved to be a more than respectable choice. But otherwise those who endorsed Anderson or enlisted with him were people whose public careers had passed the top of the curve—Milton Eisenhower, George Ball, Stewart Udall, and Mary Crisp, who had just been forced out as vice chairman of the Republican National Committee because of her failure to yield on her commitment to the Equal Rights Amendment and similar issues. And Anderson was reduced to appreciating and remembering small courtesies—the time, for example, when Republican Representative Jim Jeffords of Vermont had made a point of coming out to the airport to greet him when he arrived in Burlington.

Anderson also won the support of New York's Liberal Party.

But it was always obvious that the Liberals acted out of a great deal of self-interest and were trying to recapture some of the leverage they once had enjoyed in city and state politics. (In the end Anderson polled 441,341 votes on the Liberal line, for 7 percent of the state's vote, enough to have given New York to Carter if these voters had voted for him overwhelmingly against Reagan, which is questionable.)

Much of the late spring and summer was spent in gaining a place on the ballot in each of the fifty states. As George Wallace had learned twelve years earlier, that effort can be a time-consuming and costly business. But it appeared that both Anderson and his campaign strategists made this undertaking more costly in several respects than it should have been. For one thing, Anderson himself spent a disproportionate amount of time in states that were ordained to be lost causes for him in November— Oklahoma, North Carolina, West Virginia, and Idaho, for example. Anderson felt it was necessary to rally his troops in their circulation of petitions that would qualify him for a place on the ballot. But it was clear, too, that some of his managers in both Washington and the various state headquarters were beguiled by the unrealistic notion of using the ballot access operation to build an "organization" for the general election campaign. The result, in state after state, was that they labored to get far more signatures than were needed to qualify for the ballot, even allowing for the likelihood that many of them might be found invalid. For example, operating on the idea that numbers would be politically impressive, his supporters accumulated almost 150,000 signatures in Illinois when only 25,000 were needed. And even in conservative states where he was given no chance of winning, the same pattern was often followed. In Arizona, for instance, almost five times the required number of signatures were produced. All this yielded one-day stories in the state involved but nothing of any practical help for the general election campaign ahead. "You can't organize the state of New York, you can't organize California," Garth said later, "so how in the hell can you organize the country?"

One result, unsurprisingly, was that the ballot access campaign used up virtually all the money, some $2,500,000, available during the summer and left none for the equally important task of telling the country through advertising something about the candidate who was qualifying for the ballot. At one point, the campaign was supposed to be setting aside $250,000 a week from the returns on its direct mail so that David Garth would have one million dollars to spend on basic advertising in August. But when the time came, the money wasn't there, and the campaign was actually one million dollars in debt. As Anderson himself would say later, "I had a media expert without a media campaign." Late in August Anderson's advisers met in the Washington office of Mitchell Rogovin, the lawyer who had taken over the ballot-access program, and discussed the possibility of shutting down the campaign entirely. Instead they decided to realign the staff and give Garth full control. But by that time the opportunity to lay the foundation for the fall campaign had passed. And even if it had not, there was no cash on hand to begin.

"When we blew that money," said Garth, "we blew any real chance of keeping up there." It was not so much a question of the commercials enlisting supporters directly; rather, the advertising was needed to give his campaign credibility as a serious one, in the same category as those of Reagan and Carter. In the end the total media budget was only $1,400,000, enough for tests of two spots right after the Republican convention in July and a modest "blitz" during the final four days of the campaign. Even David Garth couldn't do much with that.

Anderson's problems were not all strategic and logistical, however. Now that he had become an independent candidate, he seemed to lose his way and forget "the Anderson difference" that had brought him to that point in the first place. The underpinning of his candidacy was the belief among his supporters that he was truly different—more honest, more independent, more candid, less fettered by convention than Reagan or Carter. Instead, he began doing things that made him seem more like the other politicians. Touring the states to support the ballot access campaign, he was talking more about the opposition and political mechanics than about his own ideas for the country. In July he made a twelve-day trip to the Middle East and Europe, which might not have caused even a ripple if he had not agreed to provide daily comment from those foreign capitals on the *To-day* program during the Republican National Convention in Detroit. The assignment was, of course, "exposure" of a kind Anderson could not afford any other way. But it cast him as somehow less than the "real" candidates, or at least "less presidential." A serious candidate for the presidency does not moonlight as a commentator on NBC. Moreover, the role projected an image of him as primarily a critic of the big boys rather than an alternative with his own ideas for solving the national problems. "That didn't do a hell of a lot of good," Anderson said of his trip abroad. "It didn't do much good and it probably did a little harm." Then, later in the summer, he held an attention-getting meeting with Ted Kennedy and seemed to suggest that if Kennedy captured the Democratic nomination, the need for his own candidacy might vanish. Both Anderson and Garth were convinced at this point that there was no realistic possibility at all that Kennedy would be nominated. What they were trying to do was exploit the situation by identifying Anderson as a possible recourse for those Democrats they expected to be defecting after the convention. They were trying to use Kennedy, but the episode came across as the crudest kind of media event. And what they discovered, very quickly, was that the Anderson and Kennedy constituencies were by no means the same. "An awful lot of individuals and people that were ready to vote for me," Anderson said later, "felt very passionately against Teddy." Moreover, they kept telling him about their disappointment in him "long after it died out in the press."

"I think it did hurt," he said. "I misjudged that. I blundered on that one."

For Anderson to prosper as an independent, he had to achieve a very delicate balance between being perceived as different from the others and being so different he was incapable of operating successfully in the political arena. In the Kennedy episode, he had appeared both manipulative and clumsy, the worst of both worlds.

Anderson did not spend the entire summer shooting himself in the foot, of course. By Labor Day he had produced a 318-page platform on which he and Pat Lucey would base their campaign.

It was a remarkable document for its specificity on a wide range of issues, from revitalizing mass transportation systems to strategic arms limitation to economic policy. But the platform came too late to make any impression on the public, and Anderson lacked the resources to use television to sell it himself.

One result of this was that it was still possible for his opponents, as they had done in the Republican primaries, to define Anderson on the issues largely in terms of a single proposal he had made—for a tax of fifty cents a gallon on gasoline that was designed to reduce consumption of imported gas and oil. The so-called "50-50 plan" was one Anderson had first advanced early in 1979, and there was far more to it than simply that additional tax. One crucial point was a provision for a 50 percent reduction in payroll taxes for Social Security to offset the additional levy on gasoline. Indeed, Anderson's tables showed that a taxpayer would actually get a net tax reduction so long as he drove fewer than 17,000 miles a year, well above the national average. But as George McGovern discovered with his $1000 "Demogrant" proposal in 1972, there are terrible risks in presenting complex plans, however innovative, in the forum of a presidential election campaign. It is too easy for the other guy to seize on the least attractive feature as political shorthand.

The case of one voter in Oregon illustrates the difficult problem Anderson faced in trying to explain himself to the electorate. Back in May we had written a column about Anderson's need to broaden his base. In it, we had described the typical affluent, well-educated suburban supporter of Anderson in these terms: "She drives a Volvo. When she attends a League of Women Voters coffee, she selects a prune danish on purpose. She thinks wine-and-cheese parties are 'great fun.' She doesn't think Ronald Reagan and Jimmy Carter are any fun at all." A few days later, after the column had been published by the *Portland Oregonian,* we received a letter from Nancy Murray of Lake Oswego, Oregon, a Portland suburb. "Do you know me?" she asked. Nancy Murray, it turned out, drove a Volvo, albeit one ten years old. She was president of the League of Women Voters, and had eaten a danish (although not prune) at the League's meeting the previous day. She had even been to a wine-and-cheese party earlier in the year, and she found nothing fun in either Reagan or Carter. So she was committed to Anderson. After the election we telephoned her, and she said she had indeed remained loyal to Anderson on November 4. "I felt I had to vote my conscience," she said, although she had begun to "feel comfortable" with Reagan during the year. But she had noticed that some of her friends who were originally inclined to support Anderson had drifted away to Reagan during the campaign as Anderson seemed to be more negative. "He needed to tell us," said Nancy Murray, "more reasons why he would be a better president."

That imperative of providing "more reasons"—one that Anderson, Garth, and Mathews all clearly understood—intensified the pressure on the independent to make the most of his one crack at a national audience, the debate with Reagan in Baltimore September 21. Although ABC had opted to stick with its movie, *Midnight Express,* the other two major networks would show the full sixty minutes live. Perhaps inevitably, however, it proved to be an hour totally lacking in memorable moments.

Reagan, of course, was primarily interested in exploiting the absence of Carter. And Anderson felt obliged to use his time for what he called "basic credentialing" on his positions. With Reagan following his own agenda and no Carter against whom to play, the independent candidate was never able to use the exposure to establish once again "the Anderson difference" that had sustained him early in the year. When the debate was over, the opinion polls found most voters thought Anderson had been the "winner" in debating points. But his standing in the presidential preference matchups did not improve and, in some polls, actually declined immediately while Reagan gained. "I felt I would get something more," Anderson said. "It wasn't enough for an independent candidate."

On the contrary, what seemed to happen was that the voters watched the debate and decided that, although Anderson had done well, Reagan had done well enough, too, to be more seriously considered. And it was the Republican nominee, not the independent, whom they saw as the "real" alternative to Jimmy Carter.

The morning after the debate Anderson flew to Chicago for a

lunch-hour rally downtown that was, by any measure, a success. But that night he arrived in Philadelphia for an appearance at a civic center auditorium that was, by any measure, a disaster. It was a Monday night, and the Eagles were playing football on one network and the Phillies were winning playoff baseball on another. Anderson's staff, for some inexplicable reason, had decided to charge three dollars for admission. The result was an audience of only about 600, almost all of them college students, in a hall in which chairs had been set out for 2500. Anderson was preaching not only to the converted but to an unimpressive number of the converted. The message for the press was clear: The debate with Reagan had ignited no fires in the electorate.

Anderson's stock in the polls began to decline rapidly. It was as if the voters had decided he had been given his moment at Baltimore but now it was time for the serious business of choosing the next president. The real world was intruding on the campaign again. It was clear that conditions both at home and abroad argued for rejection of Jimmy Carter, so the question now was whether Ronald Reagan would be an acceptable alternative.

Anderson was powerless to prevent this conclusion. Although he finally raised and borrowed another $1,200,000 for the advertising at the end of the campaign, his candidacy was clearly doomed. And he was no longer able to accept that fact with the equanimity he had shown back in those days as an unknown in New Hampshire. Now, by contrast, he grew strident, lashing out at Carter and complaining of his own fate. His frustration was apparent when he told a group of students at Yale early in October: "I am literally haunted, as we approach the end of this long, long democratic process of selecting a national leader, that somehow we have yet to really come to grips with all the very important issues."

In the final days of his campaign Anderson seemed to come to terms with his situation, and, as one adviser said, "he became authentic again." He would have some reason for satisfaction. By election time, enough Americans would have found something "distinctive" enough in his candidacy so that 230,000 made contributions to the National Unity Campaign, eight times as many as gave to Ted Kennedy, three times as many as contributed to the Democratic National Committee, and enough to suggest Tom Mathews was right and there had been "something out there" for John Anderson.

But in the days right after the debate in Baltimore, John Anderson was crowded off the political stage and began his slide in the opinion polls. How far he would drop was unclear, but what was unmistakable was a change in the shape of the campaign. President Carter, fearing Democratic defections, had been insisting all along that this was a two-man race. And now he made it so by turning the focus directly on Ronald Reagan.

12.
War, Peace,
and Meanness

Three weeks into the general election campaign, when Ronald Reagan had put his early missteps behind him, President Carter embarked on a cross-country campaign trip. After a brief stop in Springfield, Illinois, Air Force One took him to southern California. Reagan was heavily favored to carry his home state, but there were those in the Carter camp who had convinced themselves that the voters who knew Reagan best would want him least for president—if only the critical difference between being governor of California and president of the United States could be graphically and effectively delineated.

The concept was hardly a new one. In the California Republican primary of 1976, President Ford's strategists sought to tap the same lode—the fear of having Ronald Reagan's finger on the nuclear button. They ran a television ad that observed: "When you vote Tuesday, remember: Governor Ronald Reagan couldn't start a war. President Ronald Reagan could." The scare tactic didn't work: in fact, Lyn Nofziger, running Reagan's California primary campaign, ran Ford's commercial as a *Reagan* ad, so certain he was that it would inspire sympathy and support for the governor. He was right; Reagan clobbered Ford in the primary.

That recent history, however, did not seem to impress the Carter forces. Mickey Kantor, one-time campaign manager for Governor Jerry Brown now running the Carter campaign in California, was a determined optimist. He talked of an upset, and he based the hope in part on a survey by Pat Caddell that indicated Reagan had a 50 percent negative rating in the state. Californians, the survey was said to show, thought Reagan was a hip-shooter who didn't think things through, who didn't care about "people like us" and—most important—who would get the country into war. Also, voting in a primary was one thing. This was the general election—it wasn't that the winner *might* be the next president; he *would* be. And so a television ad strikingly similar to Ford's anti-Reagan ad in 1976 was prepared.

At the same time, Carter addressed another of his favored "town hall meetings," this one in the expansive gymnasium of North High School in Torrance, a Los Angeles suburb. Before taking questions, the President said he wanted to "make a few remarks about a subject of great importance to you." He went on: "Six weeks from now our nation will make a very critical decision. This decision will set the course of your lives and of our nation's life, not just for the next four years but for many generations to come."

Reporters traveling with the Carter entourage, finding themselves positioned behind a platform of television cameras, climbed up into the spectator sections on each side of the gym, squeezed in among the townspeople, and waited. Nothing of interest usually came from these opening remarks; if there was to be a story, it would come in the question-and-answer session that was to follow.

Carter continued. The election, he said, "will help to decide what kind of world we live in. It will help to decide *whether we have war or peace.* It's an awesome choice. ...." The reporters snapped out of their daydreams. Was Carter actually saying that the election of Ronald Reagan meant war? In some other context, the remark might have been dismissed, but not in Carter's first public appearance of the fall campaign in Reagan's California! The wire-service reporters jumped on it. And as if to make sure that precisely that reaction would occur, the President repeated the same warning two hours later before the California AFL-CIO convention in Los Angeles. "What you decide on that [Election] day," he said, "you and those who listen to your voice will determine what kind of life you and your families will have, whether this nation will make progress or go backward, and *whether we have peace or war."* Again, the words registered immediately on those in the audience who look for, and by their reaction determine, what "news" is. Almost at once the new stories were going out, and the television tape and film, depicting Carter's harsh allegation.

In the news business, there is a distinct application to the old question: if a tree falls in a forest and no one is there, does it make a sound? The fact is that Jimmy Carter was saying nothing that he hadn't essentially said before. This time, though, he had a particularly alert and conditioned press corps listening. The combination of where he said it, when he said it, and—most importantly—how he said it made the difference. And, most significantly for Carter's campaign in the long run, what had been intended as a tactic to criticize Reagan and encourage existing doubts about him backfired. In time, "the war-and-peace issue" led to what came to be called "the meanness issue"—to the very great detriment of the President's reelection prospects.

All this is not to say that the Carter campaign somehow stumbled unwittingly and unwillingly into the war-and-peace issue. It was a strategy that had been settled on and acted upon even before Reagan was nominated, and anticipated just as early by Reagan's strategists. Indeed, Richard Wirthlin in a campaign plan drafted in June had a chapter devoted to how Carter "would try to demonize us," as Wirthlin described it later. What went wrong—a critical blunder by Carter and/or his advisers—was that the President himself became the instrument for carrying out the negative campaign, at an ultimately severe cost to his one great political strength—his Mr. Nice Guy image.

Americans had, through the thick-and-thin of Carter's four years in office, maintained one belief about this particular President. They thought he was a very religious man of goodwill; that he was an honest, sincere, and fair man. If he had faults, they lay elsewhere. In the course of this campaign, however, doubts had begun to set in. Voters noticed that Carter had a penchant for sniping at his opponents. Sometimes it came in a context that won him more support, such as his press conference remark in advance of the New Hampshire primary that Senator Kennedy,

in criticizing him on the hostage situation, was making statements "damaging to our country." In the crisis atmosphere of
the time, most voters agreed.

But there was also the gratuitous slap at Cyrus Vance after he
had resigned as secretary of state over the hostage rescue mission, and there had been more than one dig at Reagan. Just since
Labor Day (when Reagan wrongly said Carter was launching his
campaign at the birthplace of the Ku Klux Klan), the President
had implied that his opponent didn't believe in nuclear arms
control or even peace. And in a speech from Martin Luther
King, Sr.'s church pulpit in Atlanta came an accusation that Reagan was practicing the politics of racism and hate. Reagan had
indeed used the phrase "states' rights," which *was*, as Carter
charged, a code phrase in the 1960s for resistance to racial inte-
gration in the South. And he did make that reference to the Ku
Klux Klan concerning Carter's kickoff campaign speech in Tuscumbia, Alabama. But it had been Patricia Harris, secretary of
health and human services in the Carter Cabinet, who had first
raised the KKK as an issue, when in early August she said,
"Many will see the specter of a white sheet" behind Reagan because the Klan had endorsed him—a comment that came *after*
Reagan had already repudiated the endorsement.

In a press conference two days after the Atlanta speech, Carter denied under persistent questioning that he had intended to
accuse Reagan of injecting hatred and racism into the campaign.
In fact, he said, he admired Reagan for repudiating the Klan, and
he claimed his own campaign had been "very moderate." The
press, he said, "appeared to be obsessed" by the issue and he assured the reporters, "I do not indulge in attacking personally the
integrity of my opponents."*

In any event, it was in this atmosphere that reporters, many
of whom had attended that press conference, went off to California with the President four days later. Their antennae for

---

*The next day, the Carter campaign launched a nationwide advertising campaign
in black newspapers that said, in part: "Jimmy Carter named thirty-seven black
judges, cracked down on job bias, and created one million jobs. That's why the Republicans are out to beat him."

conflict and contention, always well-tuned, were particularly
sensitive now. So when Carter made his two war-and-peace remarks about Reagan, they were likely to give them prominence,
particularly on television.

Ironically, some reporters for major newspapers, who had
heard Carter on the general subject before, thought so little of
the remarks that either they didn't mention them at all in their
stories or relegated them to a subordinate paragraph.* But Carter took care of that in a Los Angeles television interview the
next morning, when he remarked that Reagan had a "repeated
habit" of advocating use of force. "I think in eight or ten different instances in recent years," the President said, "he has called
for the use of American military force to address problems that
arise diplomatically between nations. I don't know what he
would do if he were in the Oval Office, but if you judge by his
past highly rhetorical calls for the use of American military
forces in these altercations, it is disturbing."

In all this, it should be noted that Carter was correct—Reagan
had called for the use of force on a number of occasions, from
sending an American destroyer in with U.S. tuna boats after a
seizure by Ecuador in 1975, to ultimata to the North Koreans
after seizure of the *Pueblo* and to the Cubans to get out of Angola. He also had suggested a blockade of Cuba to induce the
Russians to abandon their invasion of Afghanistan. But you don't
always get credit for being right in politics. Reagan, long antici-
pating that the Carter campaign hoped to "demonize" him, was
ready with a full store of anger, indignation, and appropriate re-
torts. "Every time you talk about national security and restoring
the margin of safety that for thirty years after World War II this
country had," he said, "there are those who say that's warlike,
that this is the fellow who wants to take us into war. I think to
accuse that anyone would deliberately want a war is beneath decency."

---

*As far back as June 6, speaking to Democratic state chairmen at the White House,
Carter said the November election would decide "who will be responsible for peace
or war." When reporters asked Powell if that was a suggestion Reagan might lead
the country into war, he winced and said, "Here we go again."

(After Reagan became President, in an interview with us in the Oval Office, he flatly labeled Carter's central campaign accusation against him as "pure demagoguery" and asked: "How can anyone say of another man in this country, or of another person in this country, that they would like to start a war? As I pointed out, there had been four in my own lifetime, and my own life was disrupted by being in the biggest of those, World War II. Now I never at any time claimed heroism about that because I never heard a shot fired in anger, which was also true of about fourteen million other people in the armed services that never got to the front line of combat. But I have sons. I thought it was pure demagoguery and, yes, it angered me.")

There was more on both sides, but that was the heart of the exchange. "The war-and-peace issue," which had been developing for weeks, now suddenly was in full flower, and alongside it, not yet up to speed but with the Reagan strategists coaxing it along, was "the meanness issue." Martin Anderson, Reagan's chief issues adviser, told Lisa Myers of *The Washington Star:* "Carter's biggest asset is the aura that surrounds the presidency. When someone starts tarnishing that office, people don't like it." Other Reaganites also came to their candidate's defense: "In no way has Governor Reagan been warlike," said Lyn Nofziger, "in no way has he advocated the use of force. The one reason he wants an adequate defense establishment is to maintain peace. There is bound to be a backlash from this constant slandering of the governor's motives and intentions." There was, indeed—if the Reagan strategists had anything to say about it.

What was going on here was a high-stakes contest of perception-shaping. Was Ronald Reagan the Mad Bomber? Was Jimmy Carter a meanie? To appreciate how much both sides wagered on getting the answers they wanted, it is necessary to emphasize again that there was general if unspoken agreement on both sides about one central fact: Carter could not run on his record and win. Given that premise, the war-and-peace issue was a classic political diversion. And the meanness issue was a classic political counter, designed to neutralize the diversion and return the public focus to Carter. The trick for Carter's campaign was to develop a negative image of Reagan without seriously damaging a positive image of the President. The trick for Reagan was to channel the voters' views into a perception that Carter was, after all, not so "presidential"—and not so congenial—and incompetent in his job, to boot.

Of the two tasks, Carter's was the greater. "We had to make Reagan the issue," one of his strategists said very frankly later. "We knew if we had to fight this campaign in the trenches, talking about the consumer price index and the Iranian hostages and the economy, we would not be in good shape. We had to make Reagan the issue. We knew the press wasn't going to. We thought you'd do a better job."

Reagan's task, by the same token, was to keep the public eye and mind on Carter's record and tell voters what they already knew about it—that it spelled failure in dealing with inflation and the economy generally at home and with the hostage situation abroad. The problem Reagan had, of course, was that his opponent was the President of the United States. There were many ways the incumbency could be invoked against him, but the one most feared, of course, was the power to affect events, particularly in the closing stages of the campaign—the "October surprise." Even in this area, however, Reagan's forces very early saw the opportunity to use that threat as a way to attack Carter's strength—his credibility, his honesty.

"We laid a strategy for it," Senator Paul Laxalt, the national campaign chairman, said later. "We learned in 1976 that the White House has awesome power in dictating events. There were any number of things that could be happening domestically, but we were less concerned about that, because it was apparent nothing dramatic could be done on unemployment or on inflation as we got into the last month. That left, obviously, some form of international surprise, and we knew what form that would take. That's why we started to condition the people in September." It was Wirthlin's strategy, Laxalt said, "that we should alert the American people to look out for the last-minute surprise, so that when it came they wouldn't really be surprised. It would appear to be a callous political plan."

In this effort, Laxalt said, Carter himself contributed heavily with his criticism of Reagan. "I think we finally established the climate in the country," Laxalt said, "that in order for him to be elected he would take any route. He would call Reagan a racist. He would call him a warmonger. He would take any route. He was that hungry for reelection. We had our people talking about it all over the country." Even Jerry Rafshoon acknowledged later: "They set us up on the 'October surprise.' "

If there was a basic failure in the implementation of Carter's negative strategy against Reagan, it was that his campaign could not prevent the President himself from being its point man, and hence risking the voters' turning against him personally. The Carter insiders foresaw this problem but could not handle it, for one main reason—the personality of Jimmy Carter.

The war-and-peace issue was not launched in that gymnasium in Torrance, California, at all, but in Madison Square Garden in New York on the night of August 14, when the renominated President warned in his acceptance speech that Reagan's election would mean "the risk of an uncontrollable, unaffordable, and unwinnable nuclear arms race" and an "alarming, even perilous destiny." There was nothing very unusual about this text, but Carter delivered the speech with all the stridency of a campaign stump harangue. Carter insiders were well aware that their man was almost always at his best in an intimate situation, when he was able to convey his ideas conversationally. When he had to address a large crowd such as this one, his tendency was to shout, and his voice would sometimes approach a screech. And so the effect was much more aggressive than might have been the case had he been talking to a smaller group.

The words on paper did not convey the harshness of Carter's tone. "He delivered it in a different fashion than I frankly had expected him to," Powell said later. "You could have said the same things in a different tone of voice and I think you would have had a different reading of the same words." In any event, Powell said, "it certainly had the result that we wanted it to have"—that the negative public attitude toward Reagan began to increase in Caddell's polls. Most of the newspaper stories and television reports of the speech ignored Carter's recitation of his administration's achievements and goals and focused on the assault on Reagan.

Going into the campaign in September, therefore, the line of attack had already been drawn. And in his nomination acceptance speech, Carter had served notice—whether by intent or not—that he was probably going to be the chief attacker. No one who had paid much attention at all to his public utterances leading up to the convention could have been very surprised. In April Reagan, speaking to a convention of the American Society of Newspaper Editors in Washington, had suggested that Carter's march up and down the hill over Russian combat troops in Cuba had encouraged the Soviets to go into Afghanistan, and that the hostages never would have been taken in Iran if he had been president. Carter had responded that Reagan had strange bedfellows. "I think the people in the Kremlin would agree completely with what Mr. Reagan has said," he told the same editors, "that the invasion of Afghanistan was not the fault of, nor the responsibility of, President Brezhnev and the Politburo, but was the responsibility of the President of the United States." And of the seizing of the hostages, he said, "I'm sure that same response would come from the terrorists who hold our hostages captive in the American embassy in Tehran. I think they would agree with candidate Reagan that this was really not their responsibility or their fault, but that the United States is somehow culpable."

By the time Labor Day rolled around, the negative approach was locked in place. Four years earlier, Carter's campaign slogan had been, somewhat arrogantly, "Why not the best?" Now, a Carter aide told Lisa Myers of the *Star*, it would be "At least not the worst."

Some of the Carter insiders had hoped at the outset that Carter could remain "presidential" throughout the campaign, leaving most of the hatchet work against Reagan to Mondale, other surrogates, and television commercials, thereby preserving and reinforcing his positive image. But, as one of the strategists lamented, "we couldn't get any ink for our surrogates"—meaning that Anderson's presence as an independent absorbed much of the news coverage (especially on television) that customarily was given to vice-presidential candidates. "So it had to be either Carter or the paid media. We did it with the paid media, but there had to be something out there that validated what we were put-

ting our dough on"—that is, Carter had to make a case against
Reagan first, and then the attack would be sustained in paid
commercials. "We certainly couldn't keep Carter from attacking
Reagan. Reagan attacked Carter. He called him incompetent, he
called him the most deceptive President in history. . . . More deceptive than Richard Nixon? Nobody asked him that. It was very
frustrating for Carter. It was very frustrating that the surrogates
were given the job. Fritz is not the most rough-and-tumble
[sort]."

Carter's strategists well knew about this frustration, and had
hoped to curb it. One, in fact, warned others in September:
"We'd better find a way to get a focus on Reagan, or he [Carter]
will."

"The strategy," he said later, "had been not to mention Reagan by name, to take the high road, to talk about the two futures
[under Carter or Reagan] and the stark differences between
them. The war-and-peace attack in California was contrary to
the expressed campaign strategy, but [Carter] did it because he
felt clearly it wouldn't be done otherwise. He felt Reagan was
not being examined carefully on his past and present record. We
would talk about [Reagan's record], and Mondale too, saying
things ten times worse than Carter [said], but they weren't getting covered. The President became, along with the rest of us,
frustrated and a little concerned this might become an up-or-
down referendum on [Carter's] four years, with Reagan on the
sidelines. And [Reagan] might just float in on a negative vote on
the Carter years. And so [Carter's] feeling was, 'If there's no other way of doing it, I'll do it myself.' That's why people in the
campaign would say, 'We better find another way to make the
Reagan record, or [Carter] will.' We never did, and he did."

The two war-and-peace remarks in California were also a result, another strategist said, of Carter's way of using verbal shorthand that put a harder edge on what he said than he might have
intended. He used the "shorthand that wire-service reporters
and television people are going to employ, by saying a couple of
code words," the adviser acknowledged. "He saved hours and
hours of editing time for Sam Donaldson"—a slap at the ABC
News White House correspondent whom the Carter insiders regarded as a special nemesis.

The President was criticized sharply in the news media as a result of his California attacks on Reagan, and for perhaps ten days afterward he seemed to be a bit more restrained. In a brief swing through the Midwest in the first week of October, he was careful to make his remarks on Reagan's positions relate to specific issues, such as his early criticism of Social Security, his opposition to the SALT treaty, federal aid to New York City and to the beleaguered Chrysler Corporation, and to Carter's newly created departments of energy and education.

For all that, however, by now the question of Carter's tone and manner had become a major problem. In an interview with the *Detroit Free Press* Carter was asked specifically about "the meanness issue—there is somehow a kind of mean side to Jimmy Carter that shows up in such issues as the Atlanta speech and the painting of Reagan as a warmonger." His reply was essentially what it had been earlier—that he always tried to be "very moderate in my campaign" and that although sometimes he might have made "some comment that's *misinterpreted* because of brevity, I've always tried immediately to correct misimpressions [italics ours]." Then he repeated his reference to Reagan's advocacy of the use of force in various international incidents, contrasting it with his own use of diplomacy. "I think that judgment, and that management of a crisis, that general inclination toward peace or peaceful settlement of a dispute or an attempt to settle a dispute by weapons, is a legitimate issue in the campaign," he said. "I say that, being cautious in my words, but also reemphasizing I'm not accusing Reagan of wanting a war. But I do know that in a troubled world, on the closest possible margins of decision—there is the option of the use of weapons or the commitment to try to resolve a dispute peacefully. That is a judgment the American people will have to make."

That was fair enough. Carter was being more careful, but he was not backing away from the general thrust of his campaign. Caddell's polls—and Wirthlin's too—were showing now that more and more Americans had doubts about Reagan's hard-line military views.

One reason the President could afford to be less aggressive against Reagan on the stump was that his negative advertising had begun to run on television and radio. One of the most effective was a man-in-the-street commercial in which Californians, selected from about one hundred who volunteered negative comments to Rafshoon's camera crews, said why they didn't want Reagan to become president. Perhaps the most pointed was from a Sacramento man who said: "As a governor it didn't really make that much difference, because the state of California is not going to be going to war with a foreign nation. . . . It was just amusing, but as president, it's scary." The commercial was run in major states, not just California, but it was essentially the 1976 Ford ad in the California primary all over again. This time, though, the ad seemed to be working. Wirthlin acknowledged as much.

The message, in fact, seemed to be reaching the word-of-mouth stage. Doorbell-ringing in Buffalo at around this time, for example, we came upon one Stan Sliwinski, who owned up to being uneasy about Ronald Reagan without really knowing why. "It's around," he said. "You hear it that Reagan is too much of a risk." Sliwinski said he had never seen any of the California man-in-the-street commercials and couldn't recall reading about Carter's war-and-peace remarks. "I'm a watchman and I work nights, so I don't see that much television," he said. "I read the paper every day but to tell you the truth, I don't pay a lot of attention to the political news. It's just something you hear people talking about. It's around."

If this concern about Reagan came at the cost of voters' positive feelings about Carter, Rafshoon was more than willing to accept the tradeoff. Other strategists, however, disagreed with him. Of the President's role as the chief attacker, one of the insiders said, "It was one of the major strategic mistakes of the campaign. It was a short-term gain at the expense of Carter's nice-guy image, and it became a pyrrhic victory. We thought he was relatively invulnerable to a meanness issue. We thought we were trading off in our area of greatest strength in exchange for a payoff on Reagan's greatest weakness. We thought it was a good deal." Or, as Caddell said later, he thought Carter rated so highly personally with the public that he could afford to spend some of that currency attacking Reagan.

Rafshoon and Caddell were wrong. Soon voters were making

remarks such as those of Mrs. Fred Lincoln, a nurse in Torrance, California: "I resented his inference that Reagan would send us into war. It is not a fair kind of thing to say." Wirthlin in his polling began to report more of the same; his findings squared, to be sure, with his own strategy, but he offered data to back them up. "What we see," he said, "has been without question a fraying of Mr. Carter's nice-man image. . . . Our image is very much intact, and in attempting to shatter it, theirs developed a few cracks of its own."

Those cracks soon widened appreciably. While Carter was touring in the Middle West, one of Reagan's political allies, the evangelist Jerry Falwell, caused a stir at a religious broadcasters' convention in Lynchburg, Virginia. (Falwell is the founder of the Moral Majority, an ultraconservative religious-political movement that seeks to rally faithful churchgoers, principally fundamentalists, to political action and financial support in behalf of right-wing candidates and such issues as opposition to abortion and to the Supreme Court's prohibition of prayer in public schools.) God, he told the broadcasters, does not hear the prayers of Jews and other non-Christians because they are not "redeemed in faith in Christ." Reagan visited the convention the next day, and when asked if he agreed with Falwell, said, "No, since both the Christian and Judaic religions are based on the same God, the God of Moses, I'm quite sure those prayers are heard." And then he added: "But then, I guess everyone can make his own interpretation of the Bible, and many individuals have been making differing interpretations for a long time."

Reagan clearly was disagreeing with Falwell, but at the same time he seemed to be saying that Falwell's opinion—criticized by Jews as anti-Semitic—was as valid as anybody else's, the Bible being as open to "differing interpretations" as it is. The whole exchange seemed like one of those one-day political tempests in a teapot—until two nights later in Chicago, when President Carter was addressing a fund-raising reception after a day of hard, aggressive campaigning. Earlier, in a backyard meeting at a private home in a suburb, Carter had started roughing up Reagan again. Asked about military preparedness, he replied that the question well illustrated the nature of responsibility in the presidency. "It's not a place for simplistic answers," he said. "It's not a place for shooting from the hip. It's not a place for snap judgments that might have very serious consequences. ... If you've got just a strong military and you're jingoistic in spirit, that is, you want to push everybody around and just show the macho of the United States, that is an excellent way to lead our country toward war." He again cited Reagan's advocacy of the use of force and concluded, "What he would do in the Oval Office, I don't know."

Now, at the fund-raiser, he picked up where he had left off on this same old war-and-peace theme. The audience had been rounded up out of a sense of duty to party by Mayor Jane Byrne, who personally and politically had no use for Carter and didn't mind anybody knowing it. As Carter spoke, people in the audience talked among themselves and gave only half-hearted attention to the President of the United States. He started out good-naturedly enough, but as he went on a stridency, a note of desperation and pleading came into his voice. As if he were forgetting that he had before him a pack of politicians and fat cats rather than a group of average voters, he launched into his standard anti-Reagan harangue. Their votes, he warned, would "literally decide the lives of millions of people in our country and indeed throughout the world. ... You'll determine whether or not this America will be unified or, *if I lose the election, whether Americans might be separated, black from white, Jew from Christian, North from South, rural from urban* [italics ours]." In the roped-off press section, jaws fell.

Carter now went after Reagan specifically by name, as a man believing "that the best way to control nuclear weapons is to start a nuclear arms race and play a trump card against the Soviet Union." He implored his fellow Democrats to help him, to appreciate as he did what was at stake. "This is my last campaign, the last political race that I will ever run," he said, with obvious determination. "I do not intend for it to end by turning the government of the United States over to people whose political philosophies and views about this country are directly contrary to everything in which I believe with all my heart and soul."

The audience, much of it dumbfounded through this monologue, finally burst into applause. But in the press section, there were only looks of disbelief as the words "black from white, Jew from Christian, North from South, rural from urban" sank in. News antennae vibrated wildly again, signaling that Jimmy Carter was back on the low road once more, this time outdoing himself.

Within minutes, Jody Powell came into the hotel press room looking thunderstruck. He knew he had a fire on his hands, and he tried to put it out. What must have happened, he said, was that the President, deeply offended by reports of Falwell's comments at the broadcasters' convention, was reacting to Reagan's failure to condemn or repudiate his preacher-supporter. This explanation at first seemed reasonable, except that one reporter present, Edward Walsh of *The Washington Post,* recalled that he had attended another Democratic fund-raiser in Washington two nights before Falwell made his statement, where Carter had made the same reference to the alienation of "Christian from Jew" as a consequence of a Republican victory. This night in Chicago, after the divisive line, Carter told his audience, "we must get our voice through to the American voters in a clear, undistorted way about the choice to be made on Election Day in November." To Powell's obvious dismay, Jimmy Carter had done just that.

The next morning, Reagan, campaigning in Ohio, was asked by reporters what he thought of Carter's latest remark. He was, predictably, a sorrowful, wounded bear. "I just have to say on this: I can't be angry. I'm saddened that anyone, particularly someone who has held that position, could intimate such a thing. I'm not asking for an apology from him. I know who I have to account to for my actions. But I think he owes the country an apology." This rather magnanimous response did not, of course, come out of the blue. Reagan was geared, Stu Spencer said later, to "aw, shucks it" every time Carter took a swipe at him. Reagan had a Mr. Nice Guy image, too, which he studiously concentrated on reinforcing even as Carter seemed bent on tearing down his own. And at the same time, Reagan continued to preach his gospel of "getting the government off your backs" and—as the nation was eventually to find out—meaning it.

(Reagan told us after his inauguration that Carter's Chicago remarks particularly angered him because the accusation that he would divide people on racial, religious, and geographical lines was "the kind of thing, when it's said about you, that it's almost impossible to answer. There are certain accusations that people can make, and they stick. Even if you go to court and come out proven innocent, people remember that; 'Wasn't he that fellow who was accused of this or that?' You can't go around saying, 'It isn't true. I like everybody.' " He argued that "long before there was any civil rights movement, and long before there was any Jimmy Carter turning around in that regard, I was one of those voices in the wilderness crying out against [racial discrimination]." He recalled playing football with a black teammate and, as a sports announcer in Iowa, "I was one of the few in the sports reporting field who editorialized against baseball's ban on [blacks]." He said the racism charge in the campaign was persisting into his presidency, contributing to the negative attitude of some black leaders toward him as a conservative, in spite of a record of appointing blacks in his administration as governor of California. But during the campaign, he said, "one of the strongest things going for [Carter] was an image of a nice guy, and he tarnished that a bit.")

If the question of Carter's "meanness" hadn't taken hold up to now, it surely did after this exchange. Wirthlin said later of Carter: "He came close to handing us the election that night." But in the Carter camp there were those who contended later that the matter had merely culminated that night in Chicago, and had been building for months, going back to before the Democratic convention. The fight over an "open convention," with intimations that Carter had used bully tactics, was one element, one strategist said. Greg Schneiders told of speaking on college campuses and finding that the first or second question always was on that general subject, which he had once assumed was mostly reporters' talk. "I had never seen an issue seep down from the press in Washington to the local level so fast," he said. "It was not that people would vote against him because they thought him mean. It was that it yanked the safety net from under him"—the feeling that whatever else, Jimmy Carter was a nice, honest man. For the first time, Schneiders said, "people were able to cast a vote against him without any guilt feelings. Previously, even when they had felt frustrated or thought he had failed, two things came back—that probably nobody could do any better, and he was a nice guy who was trying hard." And another adviser, putting it in the bridge-player's jargon, said: "Once he yanked out that stopper in that suit, obviously you could run that suit out, until finally they were saying, 'Good for the little bastard.'"

What's more, all this was happening while Reagan was minding his tongue. The plan had been to concentrate the first month of the campaign on building a "positive base" for Reagan, Wirthlin explained, and not on attacking Carter personally beyond hammering at his record. Even after the Republican convention the polls indicated that a full 40 percent of the electorate knew very little about Ronald Reagan and what he stood for, and that figure had to be whittled down. "Positive" media advertising showed him functioning as governor and used the simple technique of "the talking head"—a head shot of the candidate speaking straight out at the audience, a technique of which Reagan was a master.

With Reagan, Wirthlin said, "you don't need a lot of dramatic, well-structured kind of media." The simple head-shot ads were "almost a throwback," he went on, looking like something out of the early 1960s, but they did the job. "And it worked especially well when Carter came on as negative. We found that there was almost a role reversal. More people felt that Reagan was presidential than Carter, because Carter was down there in the trenches, talking about North being separated from South, and black from white, and Christian from Jew. And Reagan's response was not one of anger but of disappointment. That really helped us." (Not all of Reagan's strategists shared Wirthlin's view about the effectiveness of the television ads. Some found them amateurish and believed they contributed little to the outcome, for all the money spent.)

The Carter strategists could no longer ignore the fact that their candidate was going too far. Something drastic had to be done. And just as in the case of the retreat to Camp David more than a year earlier, it was decided to try to clear the decks and make a fresh start. The difference this time was that the President would accept some—but not all—of the responsibility for what had gone wrong. He would put the rest of the blame not on the American people but on Reagan and, more importantly, on the press and television news for failing to do their job in holding Reagan to account.

All along, Carter and his chief aides had felt that campaign coverage had been one-sided, that reporters were jumping on the President for his slightest misstatement while letting Reagan's rhetorical excesses and charges go unreported, or at least underreported. They were particularly incensed at the press treatment of the Republican nominee's suggestion that the threat of resuming the nuclear arms race be held out as a "trump card" in negotiation with the Soviet Union. As soon as this proposal came over the Associated Press wire, Rafshoon and Powell discussed how Carter ought to respond. They decided that the proposal in and of itself was so damaging to Reagan that the best course was for the President to say nothing.

"So I remember watching television that night, thinking 'God, I hope he handled it right,' " Rafshoon recalled later. "And there wasn't even a report. None of the networks carried the quote! . . . I could not believe it." Such complaints against the press, of course, customarily come from the strategists of candidates who are falling behind. The fact was, Reagan had been urging construction of new weapons systems as bargaining chips in negotiations with the Russians for some time. The criticism of the networks for not reporting Reagan's proposal to use nuclear arms control as a "trump card" was certainly valid, but even then there was hardly a news blackout, because newspapers and wire services did report it. But so keyed to television coverage were Carter's strategists—and Reagan's too—that as far as they were concerned, if it didn't happen on television, it didn't happen.

The idea, then, was to say that yes, maybe the President had been careless with words in the heat of the campaign, but it was only because the press had let the voters down on "exposing" Reagan. "When Carter injected the racism remark in Chicago," one of his strategists said later, "it was the unanimous feeling of the staff that this was going too far. But what we wanted was a surgical operation. We wanted to preserve the war-and-peace issue and cut out the other stuff, which was marginal [in its negative impact on Reagan]." Carter came to the same conclusion himself, so he agreed not only to back off, but to bare his soul and try to make a virtue of doing so.

The first step in this rather extraordinary presidential *mea culpa* came in a press briefing by Powell at the White House. He reported that the President's chief campaign strategists had made some fundamental decisions on how to accentuate the positive; on how to focus attention "on the very real differences between the candidates and the substantive nature of those differences" in the remaining weeks of the campaign. At the same time, Carter state coordinators around the country were advised, in one of a series of "talking points" issued to them from campaign headquarters almost daily, on what to say to reporters about the tone of the campaign. They were to acknowledge that the President had perhaps overstated things, but to make the point that the press had been giving Reagan "a free ride" and was not living up to its responsibilities.

Unfortunately for the Carter campaign, some reporters, touching base with several state coordinators on a single day, found themselves being lectured from precisely the same script, down to the exact words from the "talking points." And one state coordinator went so far as to call a press conference to say, in effect, that the President had screwed up but was going to mend his ways.

The pièce de résistance was an appearance by Carter himself on the same day, October 8, on ABC News with Barbara Walters. She had been negotiating with Powell for a presidential interview, and now the White House grabbed the opportunity. (Indeed, there was hope that if Carter did an interview with her, Reagan might also, and she might draw him into making some major gaffe on which the Democrats might capitalize. Nothing came of that, however.) The thought was that Carter's appearance would, in the words of one insider, mark "an artificial termination" of one troublesome phase of the campaign and force the news media to start another by putting Reagan more deliberately into its critical sights. This was the same basic reasoning that had led to the Camp David "malaise summit" fiasco, and it was about as successful.

"Mr. President," Walters started out, "in recent days you have been characterized as mean, vindictive, hysterical, and on the point of desperation"—hardly a soft pitch.

"Well," Carter replied, "those characterizations are not accurate, Barbara. I think it's true that when Mr. Reagan says I'm desperate or vindictive or hysterical he shares part of the blame that I have assumed. The tone of the campaign has departed from the way it ought to be between two candidates for the highest office in this land."

Walters: "Are you saying, Mr. President, that you've made some mistakes in personally attacking Mr. Reagan, and that now in the next few weeks you have to get back on the track again?"

Carter: "Yes, I'd say that. But there's enough blame to go around, and I think that the press sometimes has failed to cover major issues. Mr. Reagan has made some comments about me that probably are ill-advised."

Walters: "No more name-calling?"

Carter: "I'll do my best."

Walters: "Mr. President, are you apologizing?"

Carter: "I'm explaining. But sometimes human nature comes through. And when I feel extremely deeply about a subject, as I do the subject of arms control and peace and a strong defense, and see the crucial nature of it to the American people, it's incumbent on me, I believe, to express it. But I'll try to do it with more reticence in the future and stick exclusively to the issue itself."

Walters: "You talk about sometimes human nature coming through, Mr. President. Is it in your nature to be so emotional that you become mean?"

Carter: "I don't think I'm mean, Barbara."

Walters: "Well, you do strike out in this way. . . . A lot of people thought you were too calm over the years."

Carter: "Well, I know. Well, you get criticized both ways. I'll have to reserve the right when I feel deeply about a subject to express it as forcefully as I can."

Walters, noting that Carter had held a reputation as man who took the high road, asked him how he had wound up on the low road. "It's not a deliberate thing," the President replied, "but I am President of this country. Some of the issues are just burning with fervor in my mind and in my heart, and I have to sometimes speak extemporaneously, and I have gotten carried away on a couple of cases."

Carter again cited Reagan's opposition to the SALT II treaty. "This is a shocking and very profound departure from the policies of all presidents and this nation since Truman was in office," he said. "I watched with great attention that evening to the news broadcast. ABC did not mention it. CBS did not mention it. NBC did not mention it. And in my commitment to make that issue strong and to express the importance of it, maybe I went to excess. I'll accept the responsibility for that, but I'll do the best I can in the weeks ahead not to repeat that kind of personal involvement of the candidates in the race."

That, after all, was the nub of Carter's troubles—his inability to moderate his own words in the heat of political combat, and to avoid the careless shorthand that perhaps put a sharper implication on his comments about Reagan than he would have wanted. "We did the right thing after the Barbara Walters thing," one of the insiders said later, "sitting down and saying, 'Governor Reagan says this, Governor Reagan says that, I believe this, I believe that.' It's the old story, which we always try to do in our advertising. You draw your own conclusions from it."

While thus responding to the criticism, the Carter strategists insisted then and long afterward that it was grossly unfair. "The meanness issue was the most bogus issue of the campaign," one adviser said. He challenged anyone to give one example of any time in the four years of the administration that Carter as President had said anything mean!

Reagan, of course, remained the innocent, offended, but always benign bystander. Apprised of Carter's promise to do better, he said: "Well, I think that would be nice if he did . . . if he decided to straighten up and fly right, that'll be fine"—yet another application of what Greg Schneiders called "Reagan's natural inclination to play the more-in-sorrow-than-in-anger bit."

The complaint about the quality and focus of the campaign reporting was nothing new. Candidates always like to create the

impression that they are out on the campaign trail daily, dispens-
ing the wisdom of Socrates in profuse quantity, while the accompanying press corps occupies itself finding out and reporting
whether the candidate's socks match. This is utter malarkey.
Most candidates—Carter and Reagan certainly included in
1980—have only one or two set speeches, mostly long on slogans
and generalities and short on substance, which they make several times a day, six or seven days a week. When they have something truly new or significant to say, their press agents make sure
the reporters don't miss it. And the reporters for their part, looking hard for something new to write either to combat the bore-
dom or to get better play for their stories, are a ready market for
these tidbits of originality. In sum, if what a candidate says is covered too little, and the tone of his campaign or his personal foibles is covered too much, it's usually because he hasn't said
anything new or newsworthy; the kind of campaign he's running
is telling the voters more about him than what he's saying on
"the issues" does.

And so it was with Jimmy Carter. Just as his "summit" meetings at Camp David had drawn attention to the failures of his administration, by complaining about the press treatment he was
getting he gave the charges against him more currency than
they had before. As a result, when he resumed the campaign, his
words received even closer scrutiny by both press and public.
On October 9, his first day out after his *mea culpa*, the President
took care to make his criticisms of Reagan in the context of
specific positions, and he accentuated the positive. For example,
the point about national division that had gotten him into hot
water in Chicago came out this way: "I want to see the nation
united, North and South united, black and white united, rural
and urban united." But there was still trouble. At another town
hall meeting at the Grand Ole Opry in Nashville, a high school
student named David Magnum asked the President: "Why is it
that if you are the right man for the job, that you and your staff
have to lower yourself to the extent of slinging mud and making
slanderous statements [about] your rival, Ronald Reagan?"

It was all very frustrating to Carter, and adding to the frustration was another crucial difficulty—Reagan was still refusing to
debate him one-on-one as long as John Anderson qualified under

the League of Women Voters' criteria. So the President had no alternative but to carry the fight on the stump—and to watch his words. Of Reagan, he told the Nashville audience: "You have probably noticed lately that he is very cautious. He doesn't have town hall meetings like this. He doesn't have press conferences anymore. So I'll have to reserve the right, even though I'm going to be very careful to be both accurate and not attack him as a person, to spell out the sharp differences between me and him. And I'll try to do it in a way that will make you proud of me." Just why voters should be "proud" of the President for not engaging in personal attacks on his opponent, he did not say.

The very next day Carter was in St. Petersburg, Florida, saying, among other things, that Reagan's election would be "a bad thing for our country" and that he "would not be a good president or a good man to trust with the affairs of this nation in the future." As smears go, these certainly were marginal at worst. But with the heightened attention generated by Carter's promise to be an immaculate campaigner, they produced stories that the President was veering toward the low road again. On Carter's return to the White House, a reporter asked him whether he thought Reagan was "trustworthy," and Carter said he did. The difference between that and not being "a good man to trust" was not clear.

One other factor now compounded the President's task. Since Labor Day, the Carter campaign had been pressing its negative strategy by means of paid radio and television ads, as well as with the candidate on the stump; meanwhile the Reagan campaign had marshaled its financial resources. Much of its anti-Carter advertising was being withheld, and spending was modest for the pro-Reagan ads described by Wirthlin as designed to increase Reagan's "positive base." Now, at this critical juncture in mid-October, only three weeks from Election Day, the Reaganites began to reverse the two-to-one media spending deficit, outspending the Carter forces by roughly the same ratio down the homestretch. And given Carter's many personal comments about Ronald Reagan, it appeared safe for the Reagan side to attack Carter more aggressively in the media, especially since everyone knew the President's great vulnerability was his record.

That is exactly what now happened. Reagan, with Wirthlin's

polling data showing his campaign snapping out of an early October slump, began to go more on the attack himself. In a speech in Cincinnati on October 20, he actually turned the war-and-peace issue against Carter, charging that "his foreign policy, his vacillation, his weakness, his allowing our allies throughout the world to no longer respect us, [pose] a far greater danger of that unwanted, inadvertent war . . . than there is by someone in there who believes that the first thing we should do is rebuild our defense capability to the point that this country can keep the peace."

At the same time, Reagan also allowed himself to venture into the risky policy area of Iran and the hostages. With only two weeks left before election, and with concern about an "October surprise" foremost in the minds of his advisers, Reagan said he didn't understand "why fifty-two Americans have been held hostage for almost a year now." The next day, in Louisville, he stepped up the rhetoric: "I believe that this adminstration's foreign policy helped create the entire situation that made their kidnap possible. And I think the fact that they've been there that long is a humiliation and a disgrace to this country."

Trepidation in the Reagan camp over a possible "October surprise" was now rife. On October 18 Prime Minister Mohammed Ali Rajai of Iran had said in Tehran that he was "certain" the United States was ready to accept Iran's terms for release of the hostages. Reports grew that the Iranian parliament, scheduled to meet soon, would set definitive conditions for the Americans' release. Carter, campaigning in New Jersey and Michigan, tried to cool the speculation about a breakthrough—obviously he did not want expectations to build only to be dashed. But the Reagan campaign nervously watched and listened. Anxious about an "October surprise," worried because public doubts about Reagan had continued, and sensing that in spite of Wirthlin's encouraging polling numbers the campaign had hit a dead spot, Reagan and his key strategists had already come to a critical decision. It was time to debate Jimmy Carter, one-on-one.

13.
"There You Go Again"

On the night of October 14 Richard Wirthlin got the worst news of the entire campaign from his survey data: Jimmy Carter for the first time had moved ahead of Ronald Reagan, by 2 percentage points. "He had us that night closer than he ever came to us," Wirthlin said later. Up to now, the Reagan's media campaign had concentrated on building more favorable attitudes toward the candidate, and this strategy was not going down well with many of his most ardent supporters. They wanted Reagan, and his paid commercials, to answer Carter's "warmonger" and other charges in kind, rather than consistently turning the other cheek. "Going negative," Wirthlin said, "would have satisfied a lot of our True Believers, who were very critical of us during that period. They talked about 'the bland campaign.' " Something, however, now had to be done. Reagan's campaign, in the view of many of its insiders, had bottomed out.

Reagan himself sensed that his bid for the presidency, after having run in high gear for so many months, now seemed to be winding down. Early in the morning after Wirthlin had gotten the bad news, Reagan was riding in a limousine headed toward the airport in Sioux Falls, South Dakota, with Lyn Nofziger, his press secretary, at his side. Suddenly he turned to Nofziger and said: "I think it's about time we consider a debate." And the same day, aboard his plane, Stuart Spencer, after conversations with Nofziger and Deaver, was prepared to broach the same subject with the candidate. "Before I even got into it," Spencer said later, "he said, 'I'm going to have to debate that guy.' "

Those statements marked an abrupt change in campaign strategy. Until this point, Reagan and his chief advisers had been content with taking the position that he was willing to debate the President but unable "in fairness" to do so as long as Carter refused to include John Anderson. "My charter when I was given the debate-negotiating job," Jim Baker said, "was no debates if possible. If we could get out with one multi-candidate and one-on-one [with Carter], that would be super." And Nancy Reagan, whose views were critical in such matters, "was totally against debates," one insider explained, though presumably she had as much confidence in her husband's ability to handle himself as anybody.

A new factor, however, was changing the situation for Reagan, and fortuitously at precisely the time he was deciding that a debate with Carter was now in his best interest. As Election Day drew near, Anderson began to fall in the polls. The roughly 15 percent voter support that under the League of Women Voters' criteria had earned him a place in the first debate was slipping away. The League, in a board of trustees meeting in June at which the 15 percent yardstick was adopted, had also reserved the option of applying that yardstick at other times along the way. Thus, if any candidate failed to maintain 15 percent in the polls, he could be dropped from eligibility, or if any new candidate rose to that level, he could be added. (Realistically, of course, the only independent or third-party candidate who might be affected by this provision was Anderson.)

On October 14—the same day Wirthlin got the news that Carter had edged into a lead—the League made its move. It announced that its executive committee would shortly reassess Anderson's "significance" by examining polling data and "the whole picture." Reagan, hearing of this development and asked whether he would agree to debate Carter alone, was his usual cool self. "I'll meet that when it happens," he said. He stood by his earlier argument regarding Anderson, but added later that if Anderson "removed himself as a viable candidate, then that would remove the only reason why there isn't a debate."

Bob Strauss, speaking for Carter, announced simply, "Our position is clear and has not changed. We have accepted a one-on-one debate [by other sponsors]. Reagan has refused. I will try to force this issue. We will get him out to debate or we will make political capital out of [his refusal], to be very cold-blooded about it." If Reagan had had a Rose Garden, in other words, Strauss would have accused him of hiding in it. Strauss, as matters turned out, didn't have to apply any pressure. A new Gallup Poll showed that Anderson's support had been cut nearly in half—from 15 percent to only 8.

On October 16 the campaign had meanwhile reached one of its traditional mileposts—the Alfred E. Smith dinner in New York at which presidential candidates always meet in what is supposed to be a nonpartisan spirit of frivolity and goodwill. Carter began his speech in the appropriate vein by noting that the dinner's sponsor, Cardinal Terence Cooke of the Catholic Archdiocese of New York, in bringing the two presidential candidates together at the Waldorf-Astoria, had "demonstrated a power even greater than the League of Women Voters." But then he launched into a story about a twelve-year-old Jewish boy who had asked him the day before at a "town meeting" in Pennsylvania if he agreed with the evangelists who said God didn't hear the prayers of Jews. Carter used this story not only to allude to Reagan's embarrassment over Jerry Falwell, but also to trumpet his own peace-making achievement with the Egyptians and Israelis at Camp David: "I said I was sure that God heard all our prayers, Christian, Jewish, and Moslem, because thirteen days later we had an agreement." The audience seemed underwhelmed. Reagan was by far the bigger hit, pointing out to the audience that "it is not true that I was at the original Al Smith dinner" and getting a laugh with a line about looking younger "because I keep riding older and older horses."

The next morning, in Reagan's suite at the Waldorf-Astoria, the decision to debate was confirmed. Reagan's performance in the informal proceedings the night before had strengthened the hand of those who favored a debate, but by now they already were in the clear majority, and above all, Reagan wanted to go ahead. One of the strongest advocates for debating from the very start was Paul Laxalt. "When the surveys started to come down in October," he said later, "there was no one happier than I when it was apparent that Anderson was dropping well below the viability point. So I personally was delighted when it beoamo clear that we could have a head-on-head [against Carter]. I felt the warm Irish nature would come through, especially on the tube, and he [Reagan] was well able to handle the issues."

Others, however, were not so sure. Some of those who had been in Ford's campaign in 1976, Laxalt said, "felt he might fall into an Eastern European gaffe type thing"—like Ford's observation during a debate with Carter that Poland was not under Soviet domination. That mistake had cost Ford dearly, stalling his closing rush against Carter for a full week. "They'd been through it, so they were gun-shy," he said.

Laxalt, though, held that "in those few days we were pretty much dead in the water. We needed an event, a big event, and I think the debate broke the logjam." Doubts about Reagan's ability to stand up to Carter and avoid serious errors were brushed aside by those who knew him best, most notably Laxalt. "I felt the governor could handle himself on matters of substance," Laxalt said, "and would clearly defeat Carter in style. He'd demonstrated that he was always given to the light remark at the right time, he was always gentlemanly, and by contrast Carter would be uptight and computer-like and grim. And the tube picked that up." On radio, he said, Carter might do better, just as Richard Nixon did against John Kennedy in their first and critical 1960 debate. "But radio doesn't pick up the looks, the frowns, and all the nuances that the camera does. It was a rerun of 1960—the cold professional as opposed to the warm Irishman."

Of all Reagan's advisers, only two, Wirthlin and Bill Timmons, spoke out against debating. (A third, the media specialist Peter Dailey, had been opposed but changed his mind.) Only two days after Wirthlin's data had shown Carter 2 percentage points ahead of Reagan, new figures indicated Reagan had bounced back strongly, to 7 percentage points ahead. Wirthlin thought it was safe simply to do nothing to disturb that lead, and Timmons, with his solid organization that he believed Carter could not match in place across the country, was willing to ride with it.

"The risks were so great," he said later, "because we were going to win [the election anyway]." Timmons made a lengthy argument to Reagan and the inner circle. "I wanted to make sure the governor knew what was out there politically. The things I talked about were direct mail, saving our media money [$5 million for the last days], we had a lot of [radio and television tapes] in the can." Timmons reviewed the whole volunteer and field operation, which included distribution of five million pieces of literature and hundreds of thousands of yard signs, a "fantastic" door-to-door canvass operation, and the placing of literally millions of phone calls to most Republican precincts in the country and some Democratic.

"Also," Timmons told Reagan, "if you debate one-on-one and John Anderson's not there, it will in my opinion drive him off the map and you run a grave risk of destroying any credibility he may have." Timmons felt it was in the Reagan campaign's interest to keep Anderson viable as a candidate, because he would drain away "somewhere within the five and ten or twelve percent mark" from the Carter vote.

Timmons argued too that a debate staged only a few days before election only encourages the less dedicated, more uncertain voter. That, he said, was not in Reagan's interest, because "the Reagan vote is a dedicated, hard-core loyal vote that is going to go through snow, wind, sleet, and hail to vote. The marginal voters are likely not to be our votes." Moreover, he speculated that Reagan could easily dodge the debate with Carter since he had already debated several times and had made himself known as the candidate who wanted a debate. "I don't think we would have been criticized at that late date," he said, "for saying, 'Stick it in your ear, Jimmy. You had your chance. You're failing, your campaign is losing, and now this is a desperate attempt.' "

It is notable that all these rationales for not debating were advanced by the campaign technocrats—the organization expert and the pollster—supremely confident as they were in the effectiveness of their techniques and measurements of public opinion. The intuitive politicians, on the other hand, concerned about the less measurable but nevertheless important dynamics of the campaign—the sense of a lack of "movement"—were much more willing to roll the dice. The candidate himself was an intuitive politician; it was very likely he had made his decision even before all of them met, and had listened to the two oppos-

ing views only as a matter of courtesy and diplomacy. He had decided to go ahead anyway, he said, "because the American
people deserve a debate."*

An acute awareness of the manner in which actual events had
intruded on the careful plans of the professionals and media
technocrats, and how they might intrude once more in the final
weeks of the campaign, dictated the wisdom of this choice. Concern about the "October surprise" continued unabated within
the Reagan camp, and the governor's strategists reasoned that if
the Carter administration were to effect some remarkable breakthrough in the Iranian crisis, it would help the President's campaign most if it were to occur two to three weeks before Election
Day. If anything like the release, or a promise of the release, of
the hostages happened, it was imperative that Reagan have
some means by which to counter the political blow to his efforts,
to address the American people under circumstances that would
give him maximum public attention. A debate, Jim Baker said,
"would give us a way to answer anything that might come up
and it would obscure pre-surprise leaks or announcements of a
surprise." As Drew Lewis observed, "We can't run out the clock
when we don't have the football." Also, Reagan needed an opportunity to demonstrate that he was not an ogre on foreign policy, and the debate was ideal for that purpose.

The amount of thought that Reagan's advisers gave to the
prospect of the "October surprise" and to coping with it suggests
the thoroughness of his campaign. "Carter had a window of opportunity," Wirthlin said, "if the hostages were to come home.
. . . So we developed the concept of 'October surprise' early. All
of us talked about it. . . . There wasn't much we could do directly
if the hostages [came] home, but to talk about how the hostages

---

*One puzzling question at this juncture, however, was why Reagan's popularity
had improved so quickly and so resoundingly in Wirthlin's polls in only two days.
Wirthlin thought it was because voters hadn't liked Carter's Christian-against-Jew
formulation in Chicago more than a week earlier. "You look for a major event [like
that] to take five to eight days to work its way through the electorate, mainly because
of secondary coverage," Wirthlin said. He meant that not simply the immediate reporting of what Carter had said, but the subsequent analysis and critical comment
about it in the press over the next several days, had taken its toll.

had been used in Wisconsin [on the day of the Democratic primary] in a rather political fashion to hype the vote there. We were concerned that the same thing might happen [again]. I did a lot of research on it. We did an historical study, 'The Impact of Crises on Presidential Vote.' ... And against that historical study we also ran some ongoing research that led us to the conclusion that had the hostages come home about the 20th of October, it would have given Carter ten points. And that kind of momentum is pretty hard to overcome."

The Reagan camp's concern grew in the next few days, as the campaign entered that window of which Wirthlin spoke. Sure enough, reports were heard that the American government was indeed on the verge of some imminent breakthrough. "There was talk about the hostages coming home," Wirthlin recalled, "hospital beds being prepared in Wiesbaden, planes set at Andrews Air Force Base to fly equipment, and so on. At that point we created a campaign within a campaign."

Every morning between 6:00 and 6:30 at the Skyline House in the Washington suburb of Falls Church, Virginia, where many of the Reaganites had apartments, a small group of men met. They assessed the latest hostage information and rumors, and planned what to do, in paid ads especially, if the "October surprise" became a reality. In the group, in addition to Wirthlin, were Ed Meese, William Casey, Pete Dailey, and Admiral Garrick. They set aside some $200,000 for radio ads, reserved television time, and prepared tapes for possible use. (They never were used.) Also, Ford and Kissinger were readied to go on various talk shows. "We were building all the contingencies that we could possibly think of," Wirthlin said, "enabling us to change the nature, thrust and scope of our campaign very dramatically right up through Monday night [before the election]. ... We were not going to simply lie down and take another Wisconsin passively."

As for Reagan, Wirthlin said, "he had the sense that we were as prepared as we could possibly be." Any breakthrough had to be late enough in the campaign, they reasoned, so that Carter wouldn't have to endure any second thoughts after the euphoria had died down, the voters asking, Why were they captured and held in the first place? "It would have to be sometime from the

18th to the 25th," Wirthlin explained, "but as you got past the 25th—and our data showed this when we raised the hypothetical issue of the hostages returning—the amount of political cynicism about that event [would] increase to some extent."

On the Carter side, there was no great eagerness to have the President face Reagan. "We always knew," Pat Caddell said, "that we had to run a campaign, given the baggage we were carrying, that was candidate-oriented, that forced people to do what they traditionally do, which is to make a judgment on the presidency based on the best person, weighing all the doubts. That is the only way Carter could win. And we had Reagan pretty much in that posture until we hit the debate. You knew the monkey [of Carter's record] was there. . . . What you did not want . . . was [for it to be] the sole thing that was on people's minds. What you wanted to do was to turn their attention to some other issues. . . . This is one advantage the incumbent has. And that was the whole reason not to want to have to debate."

Then why *did* Carter debate? One reason was that his strategists felt their man was being hurt too much by the appearance that he had been dodging. Carter's continued refusal to debate on the grounds that Anderson should not be included was beginning to sound suspicious, and having insisted all along that he was willing and eager to debate Reagan one-on-one, it would have been politically damaging to keep dodging once the League eliminated Anderson.

"We felt we were boxed in," one Carter insider said later. "What would you all have written if Carter had said no? You would have handed us our head. . . . There was no way out."

There had been a time, back in August, when the President had looked forward to debating Reagan—not once, but several times. At the White House, Reagan was viewed at bottom as a know-nothing who would blunder if given enough opportunity, just as Ford had done in 1976. The longer the exposure, the more rope that was fed out to him, the better chance that he would hang himself, the Carter strategists reasoned. "If we hadn't had the Anderson thing," said one Carter man, "we would have had three debates, and who knows?"

But of course Anderson's continued presence in the race, and

Reagan's insistence that he be included in any debate, worked against the likelihood of multiple Carter-Reagan debates. As time grew short, it became clear to everyone that the best that could be hoped for was one debate. Election Day was now less than three weeks away. The fact that only one debate could be held made the Carter strategists much less enchanted, and they conceived a plan to sabotage the whole matter so that there would be no debate at all.* The idea, as some of its architects explained later, was to set a deadline they believed that Reagan, because of assumed disagreements within his own camp, would be unable to meet. "We figured that kind of pressure probably would keep them from accepting," one of the Carter men said. "We had heard they were divided, and by putting pressure on them, and making it seem more like we needed the debate, we thought they would be more likely to reject it." But just as the Carter people got ready to spring this offer, the League shut off that road by reporting that Anderson was no longer eligible and a two-way debate could now take place.

From the outset, on Reagan's side, the thinking was that the later the debate took place, the better. Jim Baker even proposed that it be held on Election Eve, as a way of giving undecided voters the best opportunity to make up their minds. But the Carter camp, still hoping that Reagan would make mistakes, thus saving the day for the President, rejected this timetable, obviously feeling there would not be enough time to capitalize on the effect of any blunder and to alert the electorate to its implications. (The professionals on both sides well remembered that after Ford's mistake in the third 1976 debate, polls taken immediately afterward indicated that many voters believed that he had "won" the debate, and only after the television and newspaper analysts had spelled out the nature of his error—and some had deplored it as an indication of his naïveté—did voters take the

*The idea of a vice-presidential candidates' debate fell by the wayside too. The Reagan people thought that a Bush-Mondale debate would be given undue prominence at that juncture, and they had very real doubts about Bush's ability to hold his own, given his performances in the primary debates and the great success Mondale had achieved in his 1976 debate against the Republican vice-presidential nominee, Bob Dole.

view that Ford had "lost.") Carter's negotiators, led by Strauss,* also argued that if Reagan were to make a serious misrepresentation or misstatement of fact, there would not be enough time after an Election Eve debate to set the record straight.

Later, after the debate, Reagan's strategists crowed that they had snookered the Carter side into a late debate by seeming not to want it themselves, when the fact was they wanted it desperately. "We needed a way to reassure the country about our candidate," Baker said, "and they gave us an audience of one hundred million voters on prime time to do it."

Some of the President's men conceded ruefully that they had, indeed, been taken. "That late debate was the worst thing that happened to us in the campaign," one of them said. "When we wanted to debate Reagan, I think they very smartly suckered us into the late debate." Once hooked into it, he went on, "we needed to minimize the damage." The President would have to do well just to cut his losses, this aide said, and Reagan "had everything to gain."

The Republican nominee, for his part, was not thinking negatively about the approaching exercise. "If I'm going to say I'm better than him," a Reagan aide recalls him saying, "if I want to walk in his shoes, I should debate him." And Stuart Spencer, when we asked him whether Reagan might be intimidated about standing before the same cameras with the President of the United States and the "Leader of the Free World," just smiled. "He doesn't see him as the President," he said. "He sees him as a little shit."

Spencer went on: "I've seen him do it so many times. He rises to the occasion. So much in a debate is style, and he has style and class. And he's dealing in his medium. If they [the Carter side] have any idea they're going to psych this guy out with the President of the United States, they're going to be surprised. And if he [Reagan] stays even in the debate, and I have every reason

---

*Strauss frequently had to break off the talks to check with the White House, and the Reagan negotiators needled him about being kept on such a short leash. "You know," he cracked at one point, "I'm pretty close to the President. I follow him into the bedroom. But Jody follows him into the bathroom."

to believe he will, and the hostage thing doesn't break, I think he's going to win this thing [the election]."

Although Carter's strategists talked after the election about how the debate had been an exercise in "damage control," there was ample indication before it that they still hoped the President would show Reagan up as a boob. They insisted on ground rules that would permit sufficient rebuttal time to enable Carter to challenge Reagan on misstatements of fact and to hold him accountable for whatever he said. But other debating opponents had tried to do that against Reagan and almost always failed. That "warm Irish nature" of which Laxalt spoke usually carried the day. When Carter reviewed the tapes of Reagan's performance during earlier debates, he was "impressed," one of his advisers acknowledged later, at his opponent's slickness.

The preparations on both sides for the debate, set for October 28 in Cleveland, were similar and by now virtually traditional. Thick briefing books on the key issues were prepared and studied.* Tapes of earlier debates were run for Carter at Aspen Lodge at Camp David and for Reagan at Wexford. Advisers in each case stopped the tapes and commented on what had been said and how, like football coaches going over game films. And stand-ins for the opponents—Republican Representative David Stockman of Michigan (who was to become Reagan's director of the Office of Management and Budget) playing Carter for Reagan, and Sam Popkin, an associate of Pat Caddell's, playing Reagan for Carter—participated in dry-run "debates," with staff aides posing as panelists. Here the Reagan side had the edge in verisimilitude: Stockman, though only thirty-four years old, has gray hair like Carter's and is of roughly the same height and build. Popkin, however, is big and bulky, in his forties, and nobody is likely to mistake him for an elderly Irishman. But he had mastered Reagan's familiar responses, and the Carter team

---

*The newspaper columnist George Will, who after the election raised eyebrows in Washington by giving a dinner for the President-elect and who wrote a column in defense of "friendship" between "journalists and politicians," was among those who helped Reagan prepare for his debate with Carter. He said later he had submitted material on the SALT treaty for Reagan's consideration.

judged that their preparation, at Camp David and again at the President's hotel the day of the debate, was superior to what they had done in advance of the three debates with Ford in 1976.*

Yet, one of the advisers said afterward, Carter "wasn't as relaxed as we had hoped." Why was that? Why, indeed, was he so tense as the actual debate started and, as many thought, through most of its ninety minutes, not only when he was responding but as he watched Reagan give his answers? "Reagan is an actor," this aide said, with some frustration. "Reagan has spent forty years being told what to do on camera when the other person is talking. You've got to remember that directors teach you that one of the biggest things isn't just when you deliver your lines. It's what do you do when the other people are delivering their lines. Reagan was a study in a studied performance."

Observers in the auditorium in Cleveland saw Carter's stiffness as soon as he walked onto the stage, before the television cameras were on. He arrived first and stood at his stage-right podium. When Reagan strolled on, he walked over and extended his hand to the President, who seemed startled at the gesture. The first question went to Reagan, which on a coin toss was the President's choice—in the belief, aides said later, that Reagan for all that was said might well be nervous. And he was, somewhat, but he quickly settled down and was his relaxed self the rest of the way.

In response to this first question, about criticism that he was "all too quick to advocate the use of lots of muscle, military action, to deal with foreign crises," Reagan moved swiftly to counter it. "I'm only here to tell you that I believe with all my heart," he said, "that our first priority must be world peace, and that use of force is always and only a last resort when everything else has failed—and then only with regard to our national secu-

*To the very end, Carter relied essentially on the same tight little band of loyalists—Jordan, Powell, Rafshoon, Caddell, Eizenstat, Kirbo, and Rosalynn Carter. Although his campaign chairman, Strauss, was his chief negotiator in arranging the debate, and although Strauss flew to Cleveland aboard Air Force One and stayed at the same hotel, he never was brought into the debate strategy and preparations and never saw Carter in Cleveland until after the debate was over.

rity. . . . To maintain that peace requires strength. America has never gotten in a war because we were too strong."

And then, dispelling any notions that he might be intimidated by the President, Reagan added: "We can get into a war by letting events get out of hand as they have in the last three and a half years under the foreign policies of this administration of Mr. Carter's, until we're faced each time with a crisis." Carter for his part used his rebuttal time to repeat his allegations that "habitually Governor Reagan has advocated the injection of military forces into troubled areas when I and my predecessors, both Democrats and Republicans, have advocated resolving those troubles and those difficult areas of the world peacefully, diplomatically, and through negotiation."

The debate proceeded in that fashion, each candidate using whatever questions were asked to recite his standard positions on the issues, from the rate of inflation and the general state of the economy to proposed tax cuts, urban decay, the hostages and nuclear arms control. Like the campaign itself, the debate centered essentially on two issues—economic policy and national security. Other issues that have been important in other years— the decay of America's cities, law and order, social welfare—receded to secondary significance. As the discussion droned on, Reagan seemed to become more and more relaxed, in contrast with the sober, even at times menacing, Carter. As one of the President's advisers said later, "the most damaging thing was that in all the cutaways [on television] Jimmy looked like he was about to slug him."

Carter had been determined to make the matter of nuclear arms control—and proliferation—a means of emphasizing the sharp difference he had with Reagan, and to reinforce the argument that Reagan's election would jeopardize peace. He repeated what he had already said so often on the stump: that Reagan had said the spread of nuclear weapons "is none of our business," and he reminded the listeners of Reagan's opposition to the SALT II treaty. But Reagan blandly ignored these criticisms and said he would negotiate another nuclear arms limitation treaty with the Russians that would not give them the advantage he claimed SALT II would have extended.

Having the final rebuttal on the arms control question, Carter
said he would try to "put into perspective what we're talking
about." Then, to the puzzlement of everyone, he went on: "I had
a discussion with my daughter Amy the other day, before I came
here, to ask her what the most important issue was. She said she
thought nuclear weaponry and the control of nuclear arms." And
then, with no further explanation, the President went on to describe the terrible destructive force of nuclear arms. Before he
could explain his reference to Amy, if indeed he ever intended
to, the time had expired for his answer and the debate went on
to other matters.

Bob Strauss and Hamilton Jordan were watching the debate
on television. "Oh, no," Jordan groaned.

As the debate went on, President Carter repeatedly pressed
Reagan to explain his earlier statements opposing Social Security
or his actions as governor of California on such matters as air pollution. Each time Reagan would simply respond that Carter was
misrepresenting his positions—just as he had done throughout
the campaign. He was dodging the substance of the issues under
discussion and deflecting Carter's thrusts, but he was doing so
with style. Finally, when Carter accurately pointed out that Reagan "began his career campaigning around this nation against
Medicare," Reagan looked over at him, forlornly, shrugged his
shoulders, and said, simply, "There you go again." When he had
opposed Medicare, he explained, he really favored an alternate
piece of legislation; this was true—he had supported a much less
comprehensive bill backed by the American Medical Association. But polls later indicated that it wasn't his defensive answer, but the simple expression of an innocent wronged, that
most voters remembered from this exchange.

In their summations, Carter concentrated on reminding the
television audience of "the stark differences that exist" between
himself and Reagan, and he returned again to the question of
Reagan's reliability in world crisis by speaking of his own cool-
headedness. In areas of possible combat in the previous four
years, he intoned, he had responded "with moderation, with
care, with thoughtfulness." He did not mention Reagan, but few
could miss the point.

Reagan, in a brilliantly simple conclusion, posed some basic questions to the audience: "Are you better off than you were four years ago? Is it easier for you to go and buy things in the stores than it was four years ago? Is there more or less unemployment in the country than there was four years ago? Is America as respected throughout the world as it was? Do you feel that our security is as safe, that we're as strong as we were four years ago?"

Then, just as simply, he said: "If you answer all of those questions yes, why then I think your choice is very obvious as to who you'll vote for. If you don't agree, if you don't think that this course that we've been on for the last four years is what you would like to see us follow for the next four, then I could suggest another choice that you have." These key comments in the summation had been carefully composed by David Gergen, one of Reagan's speechwriters, and Reagan had committed them to memory. The other choice about which Reagan spoke, of course, was the same one he had been peddling as private citizen, public official, and candidate for more than a quarter of a century. "We don't have inflation because the people are living too well," he said in one of his debate answers, alluding to Carter's 1979 "malaise" speech. "We have inflation because the government is living too well." And concluding his closing statement, he made the same old repetitious pitch: "I would like to have a crusade today, and I would like to lead that crusade . . . one to take government off the backs of the great people of this country, and turn you loose again to do those things that I know you can do so well, because you did them and made this country great."

In a few moments it was over. Well-wishers from Carter's inner circle walked up to the stage to congratulate him. Reagan's advisers came up to him, too, but he broke away from them and stepped over to shake Carter's hand. The President had dropped something and was stooping over to pick it up. He did not seem to see Reagan until he was straightening up, and again seemed somewhat nonplussed by the gesture. He did not know it immediately, but he had just been had.

Carter's assistants naturally insisted that the President had "won," and they rushed out to an adjacent hall where some hundreds of reporters were writing their stories, to argue why.* Reagan's aides did the same, until the scene resembled a cattle show. But Reagan's strategists, even as the debate had been progressing, had been getting an instantaneous reading on the public's reaction. Wirthlin's polling operation in Washington was connected to two hundred television sets in private homes in Portland, Oregon, that were equipped with rheostats, enabling viewers to register how they felt as the answers were being given. "They were hooked live to my group in Washington," he said, "which then interpreted the answers to me [by phone in Cleveland], and I was apprising Ed Meese [on another phone], who was sitting within earshot [offstage] of the governor, as to how people were reacting." It went like this, Wirthlin said: "The positives are now building. Good positive response to that answer. . . . People are really turned off. . . . Not much happening in terms of either response, positive or negative, during this statement."

This whole exercise was a kind of ultimate in public-opinion technology. Voters were pushing a button at one end of the continent, the impulse was being transmitted instantaneously to the other, then phoned at once to a monitor not more than five feet from the debaters. There was no way, of course, for Meese to tell Reagan the results until after the debate was over. So the whole hookup was little more than a toy, and its use in a sense summarized the relationship between the new political technology and what was really happening in the campaign.

The consensus of most commentators was that the confrontation between the two candidates had been a wash. Neither candidate had scored any telling forensic blow nor, just as important, had he committed any horrendous blunder that would make a difference one way or another in the election. But that consensus missed the lessons taught in other political de-

---

*Afterward the Carter strategists tried to peddle to reporters the notion that the President had won because he had delineated "the stark differences" between himself and Reagan. "Talking points" were sent out to state campaign coordinators to make the same argument to visiting reporters, and many did—often using exactly the same phrases, unwittingly revealing that they were spewing out the campaign line dictated from Washington.

bates of fairly recent history—in 1960 between John Kennedy and Richard Nixon and in 1976 between Carter and Ford. In both of those, one candidate, previously judged as having less experience than the other, needed only to prove that he could hold his own. Also, Reagan was a challenger, and, like Kennedy and Carter before him, as long as he was not chased off the stage in disarray, he figured to benefit. And in Reagan's case, since Carter had spent all fall describing him as a dangerous man to have his finger on the nuclear button, all he had to do was be his benign self. "Since he didn't walk out on stage and act like Dr. Strangelove," one of Carter's media advisers said, "it was a boost [for him]. . . . I thought we won the debate [on substance]. We got our Democrats, we got our blacks, but I knew we'd lose the debate just because Reagan was the challenger. Reagan didn't push the button. We kept waiting for him to push the button."

In an effort to cut through the Reagan style, this Carter adviser said, "we wanted him [Carter] to really drive home the idea that, 'All the things Governor Reagan says sound nice, but when you're President they don't happen quite this way. He's a good guy, but—' And the truth of the matter was, people wanted to see who was a good guy. A good guy wasn't going to nuke the world."

For Reagan's part, this Carter strategist went on, all he had to do was "put himself on the level of the President of the United States." For an old actor like Reagan, it was duck soup. "Goddamn it," Carter's man said, "the guy is an experienced actor. He's been up against Errol Flynn. He's been up against bigger stars than Carter. And at the end, he did a commercial. Everytime you can stand up there and do a commercial in one take, you're okay."

The polling data that now were coming in to both campaigns suggested that Reagan's style had carried the day over Carter's substance. A national sample of five hundred voters polled the same night by Bob Teeter for Wirthlin had Reagan carrying undecided and independent voters by about two to one. Among another 1500 voters in Arizona, polled by a local group, the number of voters concerned about Reagan's militaristic views didn't decrease, but those who thought he had come across as warm and compassionate increased. Also, as Wirthlin said, "Carter took some real negatives, especially on his Amy statement. It was viewed as contrived."*

After the election, Carter's advisers declined to say how the "Amy statement" had come about. But one report, which they would not deny, said that the President had suggested in one of the preparation sessions that he wanted to mention her, and his advisers unanimously counseled against it. Another side speculated that Carter "was trying to raise the specter of our children and our children's children" being imperiled by the threat of nuclear proliferation and war. "It was," he said, "a little of the 'daisy' commerical." (This was a reference to a devastating anti–Barry Goldwater television commercial that had been run in 1964, produced by a master of negative political advertising, Tony Schwartz of New York, for Lyndon Johnson's campaign. It showed a little girl picking a daisy, and then a mushroom nuclear cloud. It was judged in such bad taste—though effective—that it was taken off the air.) In any event, whatever Carter's reason for mentioning Amy, it was a mistake. The next day, a reporter for one of the television networks actually interviewed the child in her schoolyard and she acknowledged that yes, she did think the spread of nuclear weapons was a big problem. The ridicule had already started.

We traveled the country all through the last week—the East, Midwest, South, and Southwest—and jokes about Amy were epidemic. For Reagan, the master performer, Carter's remark was a target of opportunity for good-natured humor. When a crowd in Milwaukee, for example, began to chant "Amy, Amy," Reagan responded by saying: "I know he touched our hearts, all of us, the other night. I remember when Patty and Ron were little tiny kids, we used to talk about nuclear power." The ridicule even reached the point that a former quarterback now working as a television broadcaster, Roger Staubach, got into the act. Covering a Dallas Cowboys–St. Louis Cardinals game and discussing

---

*Bill Timmons, who had argued so strongly against Reagan's debating, nonetheless contended even after the election that it had been a major political mistake for Reagan to take part. "I think it was a risky thing to do that we got away with," he said.

the Cardinals' inability to throw the long pass successfully, Staubach said: "I was talking to my daughter Amy about it. She said St. Louis' biggest problem was the bomb."*

Carter advisers were chagrined that the remark about Amy generated more comment than Reagan's flat assertion that nuclear proliferation was "none of our business." They had him on tape saying it and later used the remark in a commercial. But everybody knew how old Ronnie was about saying such things. Still, the hope was that the debate would produce only "an afterglow" for Reagan that would die off in a few days, and that something would happen to enable Carter to make up the lost ground.

That something, indeed, already seemed to be in the works. On October 29, the day after the debate, the Iranian parliament at last agreed to hold a public session in Tehran on the fate of the American hostages. Perhaps the month of October would yet produce the long-awaited surprise after all.

*The remark lit up the CBS switchboard with angry calls, including one from a flack for the Carter-Mondale campaign committee. Staubach, incidentally, endorsed Reagan, but he does have a daughter named Amy.

14.
"Well, Mr. President, It's Gone"

Like most politicians of long experience, Fritz Mondale gives great weight to "the feel" of a campaign, and in the days immediately after the debate in Cleveland this one didn't feel right. Most of the reporters traveling with him on his campaign plane told him they thought President Carter had "won," but the Vice President himself was less certain. He had been impressed by Reagan's ability to project himself as both confident and optimistic and by his skill at deflecting—"rather effectively," he thought—the thrusts Carter made against him. "I had a very uneasy feeling," Mondale said later.

The opinion polls tended to agree when voters were asked who had "won" the debate or "performed" better. Louis Harris had it Reagan 44 percent, Carter 26. The Associated Press figures were Reagan 46, Carter 34, and CBS had Reagan ahead, 44 to 36. Comparisons of CBS polls taken just before and just after the debate showed that the number of voters concerned that Reagan "would get us into war" had declined rom 43 to 35 percent. That number was still three times as many as those voicing the same concern about Carter, but the result did seem to indicate some lessening of the principal fear about the Republican candidate. Similarly, studies by the University of Connecticut Institute for Social Inquiry immediately before and after the debate found that more voters described Reagan as "forceful" and fewer thought of him as "rash," an important distinction in politics. Taken together, the data from several sources seemed to say that the challenger had made himself appear at least acceptably "presidential"—an absolute essential when voters are weighing the risk of turning over to a newcomer the authority to wage nuclear war. Reagan might still be a risk but he was at least now an acceptable risk.

Also immediately clear after the debate, even before the opinion technicians took the national temperature, was that the event had changed the dynamics of the campaign. The view in Carter's camp was that the debate had interrupted whatever progress the President was making in putting the focus on the choice between the two candidates. And with the election now only days away, too little time was left for that objective to be gained again.

There was, however, more to Carter's dilemma than that. The war and peace issue—"Tolstoy," the reporters called it—was now less credible if credible at all, and Reagan had less need to be on the defensive. On the contrary, he seemed to have regained the initiative with his basic question in the debate about whether voters were better off than they had been four years before. At just the wrong time for Carter, the campaign was becoming once again a referendum on his four years of stewardship. Campaigning in East Texas on the day after the debate, for example, Reagan told an audience at Texarkana that Carter's administration had been "a tragicomedy of errors."

"In place of confidence," he said, "he has given us ineptitude. Instead of steadiness, we have gotten vacillation. While Americans look for confidence, he gives us fear."

With so little chance to rebuild his case against Reagan, Carter had no choice but to concentrate on the traditional attempt to rally his own party, and to persuade those potential Anderson supporters not to "throw away" their votes on Tuesday. But, inevitably, he was also obliged to defend his own record, and the best he could do here was tacitly concede his failures and plead that he had learned from them—at least to the point that he would be preferable to an unknown quantity. To an audience at St. Louis, two days after the debate, Carter put it this way: "I've been President now for almost four years, and I've made thousands of decisions, and each one of those decisions has been a learning process for me. Every decision I make leaves me better prepared to make the next one, and what I've learned has made me a better president and will make me a better president in a second term."

By this time his description of the "two futures" that were being offered in the election had to be targeted toward those "weak Democrats" whom Caddell's polls had shown were defecting from the Carter column. "Think about the prospects in your life if you wake up Wednesday morning with a Republican president in the White House," he told such a group in Brownsville, Texas, that last Saturday.

The signs that Carter was in serious trouble were obvious not only in what he was saying but in where he was saying it. In these final days of the campaign both candidates were spending most of their time in states that should have been part of Carter's base as a Southerner and Democrat—Reagan because the opportunity was there for breakthroughs, Carter because he could not feel confident they would not slip away. On Friday, October 31, for example, Reagan campaigned in four states—Pennsylvania, Illinois, Wisconsin, and Michigan—that were properly considered "battlegrounds" and well within his reach. But both Pennsylvania and Michigan, where Bush had beaten Reagan in the primaries, should have been "safe" for the Democrats by now. Meanwhile, Carter was in Mississippi, South Carolina, Tennessee, Florida, and Texas, all of them "must" states for him but still requiring his attention. Indeed, the fact that the President felt obliged to go into South Carolina, Tennessee, and Mississippi was a certain sign of his vulnerability; none of these states should have been a question for him at that point in the campaign.

There were other, subtler indications of the direction of the political wind. Mondale, for example, began to hear a lot of questions from local reporters suggesting that the new flurry of activity over the hostages might be another attempt by the White House to exploit it politically—"Is this another Wisconsin caper?" As the Reagan camp had hoped, the "October surprise" was stirring old skepticism. "What I heard," Mondale said after the election, "was a series of negative, cynical questions suggesting a different public mood. I do know something sour hap-

pened. You could feel it in the last four or five days. It just turned
on us. The last two days you could just cut it with a knife."

Meanwhile the Reagan strategists were doing what they could
to help things along. This was what they called "Peak Week,"
and the efforts to reach voters, either directly or through advertising, were at their most intense. The Reagan managers saved
$5 million of their $15 million-dollar media budget for the final
ten days, and it was giving them heavy exposure. There was
good reason, too, to think they were reaching a peak. At a meeting with the campaign deputy directors in Arlington Friday
morning, Wirthlin had outlined a "worst-case scenario" under
which Reagan would capture 310 electoral votes. The "best-
case" simulation had now reached 380 votes, but Wirthlin, fearing excessive optimism, remained silent on that one.

Within the Carter entourage there was some inevitable self-
deception. Shortly before dinner on the last Friday night, Jody
Powell came into the bar of a Holiday Inn in downtown Houston
to have a drink with some reporters. Standing at the bar we began idly comparing notes, drawing up lists of states whose electoral votes might be expected to be decisive the following
Tuesday. What was soon apparent was that Powell still considered some states "possible" for Carter that had been long since
written off to Reagan by independent and Democratic, as well
as Republican, assessments. Florida's 17 votes, for example, were
a lost cause for Carter and had been for ten days. So were the
17 in New Jersey. And if the 26 electoral votes in Texas were still
considered a promising target—if they weren't, why was Carter
there?—it was a measure of the desperate situation of the President's campaign.

The mood was quite different in Reagan's headquarters. The
following morning we called Paul Manafort, the coordinator of
the campaign in the Southern states, back in Washington and
found him scarcely able to accept the figures and projections on
the South. Reagan was indeed either even with Carter or leading
him in Mississippi, Tennessee, and South Carolina, and there
were indications that North Carolina and Alabama, parts of the
core of Carter's base, were within range. The Republican lead in
Texas was solid, and in Florida it was so substantial that Reagan

was running ahead even in Miami and Dade County, the most liberal parts of the state. "If we can carry Dade County," Manafort said, laughing, "hell, we could carry Massachusetts."

On Reagan's plane, too, the mood was increasingly confident. That final Friday night, flying in from Milwaukee to Grand Rapids, Michigan, we encountered Wirthlin waiting on the airport tarmac. He was smiling, and his grin broadened when we asked him whether he thought Reagan could sweep the large Midwest states. He said yes, but begged off saying more until he had a chance to go over his latest polling figures with his candidate. It was later that night he told Reagan he was going to be elected—barring, of course, the feared "October surprise."

The next day, Saturday, campaigning with Gerald Ford in Michigan, Reagan was buoyant. When hecklers in Battle Creek shouted "Bonzo! Bonzo!" at him—a reference to the monkey who was his co-star in the movie *Bedtime for Bonzo*—Reagan smiled and quipped: "Well, they better watch out. Bonzo grew up to be King Kong." And he thoroughly enjoyed Ford's bare knuckle attacks on Carter. The former President outdid himself, zestfully flailing at the man who had narrowly driven him from the White House four years earlier.*

Aboard the campaign plane the frivolity continued. Reagan performed with glee his customary stint of rolling oranges down the aisle on takeoffs. He bantered with photographers aboard about the number of pictures they had made of him in the act, and he joked about Carter's attempts to depict him as a warmonger who was insensitive to domestic needs. When the photographers reminded him he would finally have to autograph all those pictures for someone or other, he assured them that would be no problem. "You know," he said, "after you've canceled Social Security and started the war, what else is there for you to do?"

---

*In Grand Rapids, Ford's home town, Ford poked fun at Carter for having referred to it a few days earlier as Cedar Rapids. The mistake was the kind, of course, for which Ford himself was famous. Carter, he told the crowd, was "as screwed up in his geography as he has been in his economics. Let me just say in front of all of you, this is the most wonderful community in all the forty-eight, er, fifty states." The audience, including Reagan, roared. Good old Jerry. Laughing himself, Ford did his best to recover. "I voted for Hawaii and Alaska," he said, "and I'm proud of it."

Reagan also cheered on the other featured performers on his campaign plane as they did their specialty on takeoffs. Standing single file at the front of the press compartment, a pair of television technicians in their stockinged feet would respond to shouts of "Surf's up!" by placing beneath them those slick laminated airline cards that tell passengers what to do in an emergency. Then, as the jet lifted off the runway at an exceedingly sharp angle of climb, they would whiz down the aisle, employing expert body English, amid shouts of encouragement. They got up such speed that two reporters at the rear of the plane had to stand ready in the aisle to break their ride (the surfers having no drogue parachutes attached to them).*

The contrast between the moods on the Carter and Reagan planes proved to be an accurate forecast of the election, but at this point, just before Carter broke off the campaign to deal with the developments in Iran, his entourage was not without hope, because the two candidates were acting on essentially conflicting information. The day after the debate, October 29, surveys done by both Wirthlin and Caddell had shown Reagan leading by about 15 percentage points. But over the next four days their data diverged. Wirthlin, "tracking" public opinion by doing five hundred interviews a day and computing a three-day "rolling" average (thus, on Friday, October 31, his figures would be based on data compiled on October 29, October 30, and October 31), was finding was a steady Reagan gain—to a lead of 7 points on Thursday, 9 on Friday, and 10 on Saturday. By contrast, Caddell had taken a national survey of 1200 interviews immediately after the debate and another of the same size on Saturday—and found that Carter had gone from 5 points ahead to essentially even.

Just how this discrepancy developed between the two later be-

---

*For all his relaxed mood, Reagan never was one to abandon his old-fashioned sense of decorum. On one flight we were sitting on the sofa in the front compartment of the plane, discussing the campaign with Stuart Spencer. Reagan was going over some papers at a table just across the way. Suddenly, he got up to go to the rest room and, as he did, an alert stewardess strode out of the galley and into the toilet, and busily began to tidy it up for the candidate. He did not see her enter, and she left the door ajar. He was halfway inside when he encountered her. His jaw dropped, he backed out quickly, wheeled around, and, in a stage whisper with eyes wide, said to Spencer: "She's in there. And she's left the door open!"

came the topic of an intramural controversy among pollsters. Caddell pointed out that his figures tended to agree with those of most, although not all, of the public polls. Moreover, his numbers were consistent with the "internals" in his data—meaning the more detailed findings about the voters' attitudes toward the candidates and issues. But Wirthlin's figures generally agreed with those of other private pollsters, and were consistent with other surveys of the trends in major states.

In terms of the campaign, however, it didn't really matter that Wirthlin and Caddell disagreed. Once again, outside events were controlling the campaign. It was at this juncture that, as noted earlier, the belated "October surprise" arrived, and the President dashed back to Washington from Chicago while Reagan slept in Columbus. Again, Jimmy Carter dominated the news on this final Sunday of the campaign. He was the President caught up in crisis, ending a day of tension and doubt by going before the American people on television to report once again on the hostage crisis.* The outcome in Tehran was still in doubt, but the development did inject enough uncertainty into the final hours of the campaign to encourage Carter to perservere to the last moment in the hope that victory could yet be achieved. And Ronald Reagan, for his part, could only follow the same themes he had been using—and avoid involving himself in the situation in Iran.

So it was that on Monday morning, November 3, less than twenty-four hours before the polls would open, Jimmy Carter was flying to Akron, Ohio, to begin a last frantic day of campaigning across the country and back again in a final attempt to save his presidency.

This final-day cross-country journey on Monday was not in it-

---

*The timing of Carter's television statement was a commentary on the effectiveness of Reagan's strategy of conditioning voters to look for a calculated "October surprise" by the incumbent. Ideally, Carter would have waited until prime time on Sunday night, eight or nine o'clock, to assure the largest possible audience. But his political advisers remembered the suspicions raised by his appearance the morning of the Wisconsin primary in April. So they decided the President could not afford to delay, lest it appear this latest development concerning the hostages was no more than another political ploy. As soon as arrangements were made, he went on the air—breaking into the broadcasts of professional football games.

self unusual. In the age of jet air travel, presidential candidates usually spend the last day of the campaign following the sun from east to west, trying to squeeze out those extra hours of political opportunity in as many media markets as possible. But even considering that custom, the President's schedule was a measure of his desperate position—from Washington to Akron, then to St. Louis for an appearance across the Mississippi River in Granite City, Illinois, then on to Springfield, Missouri, then back to Detroit,* then west again to Portland and Seattle and finally back to his home in Georgia in time to vote the following morning.

The schedule was frenetic enough in itself to make it plain this was a candidate struggling to earn a reprieve from the judgment he feared the electorate was making. But talking to reporters on Air Force One out of Washington, Jody Powell was putting a good face on the situation. The President and his advisers, he reported, thought he was going to win by recapturing some of those voters who had been flirting with the idea of casting their lot with John B. Anderson, particularly in the critical industrial crescent that runs from New York and New Jersey west through Pennsylvania, Ohio, Indiana, and Illinois to Wisconsin. "Their views," the press secretary said of these Anderson sympathizers, "are closer to the President's than to Reagan's." Thus the trip was intended to "call home the Democrats" to their leader at the eleventh hour. Democrats, of course, always talk about voters "coming home" on Election Day, if only because there are so many more of them than there are Republicans.

Ronald Reagan also was flying west on this final day. He had begun in Peoria, spending much of the morning making a television tape for a half-hour broadcast that night. Now he was flying on for stops in Portland and San Diego before returning to his base in Los Angeles. But there was no pressure on the Republican challenger; the only imperative was avoiding any last-minute misstep, particularly about the sensitive hostage situation.

While the two principal candidates thus were visibly conclud-

*For an appearance that was scheduled even as the President was airborne from Akron to St. Louis, replacing a stop in Los Angeles canceled at the same time.

ing the 1980 campaign, playing out their roles as if all might be decided on their final east-to-west odysseys, their professionals were privately arriving at identical conclusions: short of a miracle, Ronald Reagan was going to be elected the next President of the United States.

In a room on the top floor of the Century Plaza Hotel in Beverly Hills, two polling associates of Dick Wirthlin—Vincent Breglio and Richard Beal—were reading printouts from their computers on the final surveys made for Reagan by Wirthlin's firm. The results were staggering. The new projections showed Reagan with 50.6 percent of the popular vote, Carter with 40, Anderson with 9.8. The projections of the electoral vote showed at least 360 for Reagan, 90 more than needed, even in "worst-case" simulations, and more than 395 in others. Incredibly, there was a rout in the making.

Breglio and Beal were elated. Bursting with the news, they were frustrated because there was no one to tell. Wirthlin was on the plane with Reagan, in the Middle West, and the suite across the hall reserved for Reagan's use when he arrived late at night was empty. Finally they poured out the news to two Spanish-speaking hotel maids who appeared at the door to clear away some of the computer paper. "It's a landslide, it's a landslide!" they said, and the maids smiled and nodded, agreeable but uncomprehending, at the two excited men.

Across the country, at his apartment in the Watergate complex in Washington, Robert Strauss had reached essentially the same conclusion, although as much on the strength of his political antennae as on the hard data of the pollsters. Pat Caddell's results on Sunday had shown a 5-point lead for Reagan, although the figures were not conclusive; there was a chance the election "might break back" before Tuesday. Quite beyond that, however, Strauss had been watching the television networks' treatment of the developments in Iran and Carter's final statement, and he had been talking to other politicians. He was convinced that the flurry over the hostages had not only failed to help Carter but might have crystallized the feeling in the country that things in general—not just Iran—were out of Jimmy Carter's control.

"I was convinced that these things were flying around out

there, it was all flying around out there," he said later. "It was almost like putting together a montage of things. You just had them all separated, all these different colors. You need an artist to put them together to make them look pretty on the map. The thing that pulled these together was the hostage thing the last day. No question that Sunday was the magnet that finally pulled it all together. Reagan had not really been able to do that. He began to do it with the 'Are you better off now?' [in the Cleveland debate], which was a great line. It was the beginning of pulling it together. For the first time people were sorting it out. But it still needed something, and that was the absolute spark when we [Carter] went on television that day. . . ."

Strauss decided to call his children, Susan, Bob, and Rick, and prepare them for the news. "It's all over, kids," he told them. "I know how wrapped up in this [you are] and I don't want you to think it's going to give me a stroke. Don't worry about me, I know it's happening, and when it happens tomorrow night, forget about it. Go about your business."

Beginning that last day the President was clearly weary—his sleep had been broken repeatedly both Saturday and Sunday nights—and he seemed somewhat subdued. As he was reboarding Air Force One in Akron, a reporter asked whether he expected to win, and Carter replied, "I think we will." Sam Donaldson, the irrepressible correspondent of ABC News, noted the conditional optimism, so Carter added: "But I feel good about it." That, of course, was vintage Carter. It was what he always said in such circumstances—that he "felt good" about a political situation. What he had been told then, of course, was that he was trailing but not out of reach. A more definite indication would come twelve hours or so later, when Caddell's organization completed another full national poll, taken that same day between 4:00 p.m. and midnight Eastern Time.

So Carter persisted, but said nothing about the hostages. In midafternoon, after the stops in Akron and Granite City, there was a rally at the airport in Springfield, Missouri. Anyone who stopped to think about it might have wondered, of course, what Jimmy Carter was doing in Missouri on the final day of a campaign. Missourians have determinedly voted Democratic in

presidential elections, and the state should have been "safe" for
Carter long before this point. That Missouri was not spoke volumes about his situation.

The speech at Springfield was typical of those Carter had been
giving in these final days of the campaign, particularly in its emphasis on the history and traditions of the Democratic Party as
a rationale for voting for him. Inevitably he cited Franklin Dela-
no Roosevelt and Harry Truman, Lyndon Johnson and John Kennedy, and he closed each speech with a quotation from Robert
Kennedy. Repeatedly he spoke of "Democratic issues"—Social
Security and the minimum wage, TVA and REA, Medicare and
collective bargaining. "You've seen many four-year periods
come and go, many campaigns for president come and go," he
said, "and Republicans always run like Democrats. But once
they're in office, in the Oval Office, they govern like Republicans, and by the time their four years is over, after they have
misled the people enough to get elected, they never have done
anything worth remembering, and they never have said anything worth quoting."

At another point, he said: "There is no way that Republicans
can win an election in this country. There's only about thirty
percent of them. What costs the Democrats the election [are]
Democrats who forget history and who forget how their own
lives and the lives of their families, and the lives of people you
love, are affected by the outcome of an election. That is a very
important thing for us to remember during these last few hours
before election time."

Such rhetoric, of course, was predictable coming from a
Democratic candidate at this stage, not unlike what Hubert H.
Humphrey and Lyndon Johnson had used at the same point in
their campaigns. But coming from Carter, it never rang quite
true. For all his history as a Democrat in Georgia, he had never
been truly involved in the party at the national level before he
began running for president. So he was trying to identify himself
with traditions of which he had never been a part.

There was also substantial irony in the fact that while Carter
was calling Democrats to arms, other Democratic candidates
were finding him a heavy burden. This was particularly true of

those embattled Senate liberals who were being assailed by their right-wing opponents on the failures of the administration as well as their own political sins. Few imagined at this point that the Senate would be lost to the Republicans, but no one doubted there would be heavy casualties.

As Air Force One zigged back to Detroit, Powell continued to show the flag of hope, if not optimism. Caddell, he told the reporters, had done a survey with a "small sample" (actually, the size was 1000) on Sunday that showed Reagan ahead by "one or two points" (actually, the margin was five). But the important thing, he said, was the finding that although Reagan held a "big lead" in the far West and the Rocky Mountain States, the President was leading in all other regions of the country. Pressed on whether he expected Carter to hold the crucial South, Powell replied: "I believe the South is going to be there. What Reagan got there right after the debate was the softest of any place in the country. I have faith in the good judgment of the home folks."

This comment, of course, was another telltale sign of the true dimensions of Carter's weakness. Politicians who are in trouble always talk about how the other guy's support is "soft" or "a mile wide and an inch deep." The implication is that it is made up of voters still subject to persuasion at the last moment.

At Metropolitan Airport outside Detroit, the message from Carter was much the same. He seemed obsessed with Reagan's temerity in quoting Roosevelt during his acceptance speech at the Republican convention almost four months earlier. "Every election year," Carter said, "shortly before the voting comes, the Republican candidates begin to act like Democrats. They try to mislead the American voters with highly financed campaigns from rich people. But all of you know that you have never heard a Republican candidate for president quote a Republican president. They all quote John Kennedy or they all quote Franklin Roosevelt, and there's a reason for it, because once Republicans get in the Oval Office they govern like and act like [Republicans]. They don't do anything to be remembered later. They don't say anything to be quoted later. We want to keep a Democrat in the White House for the working people of this country."

It was dark now in the East as Carter left Detroit and flew toward the Pacific Northwest, where his strategists were convinced there was still that outside chance he might pick off the six electoral votes in Oregon and the nine in Washington.

The crowd at Portland was emotional, as crowds tend to be in the final rounds of prizefights and political campaigns, cheering the combatants simply for their willingness to see it through to the end. As the President made his way to the speaking stand, voices called out, "Give it to 'em, Jimmy!" and "We love you, Jimmy!" and "Go, Jimmy!" On the platform Carter tore a Band-Aid off the back of his right hand, which was now red with the cuts and scratches of thousands of handshakes. And, despite his fatigue, he seemed to some almost ebullient.

"Now I'm also glad to come to Oregon," he said, "because you're a state that loves trees. Now Ronald Reagan has provided a lot of opportunity for jokes about trees. But there's nothing funny about Ronald Reagan's candidacy, nor is there anything funny about what he stands for. You know that very well here in Oregon. And here in your state, you might very well hold the key to this election. All the poll results I've seen show that here in this state the issue is in doubt, the outcome of the election hangs in the balance with just a few votes one way or the other making a difference. That's why I've crossed this continent tonight, to make my last appearance here and a little bit later in Seattle before I fly back home to vote in Plains."

The independent candidacy of John Anderson was a particular target here, because Oregon was considered a strong state for him,* just as it had been for other candidates with maverick images in the past—Eugene McCarthy in the Democratic primary of 1968, Jerry Brown in the Democratic primary of 1976, and McCarthy again as an independent presidential candidate in 1976. It was essential that Carter confront that special challenge.

"Tonight I want to say a word directly to those Oregonians who might still be considering a vote for John Anderson," he said. "On many of the key issues . . . issues like energy conservation, equal rights for women, protecting our air and water, and above all, the overriding issue of nuclear arms control and pre-

---

*Anderson polled 10 percent of the vote in Oregon.

venting the spread of nuclear weapons to countries that don't have them—on all these central issues you and I are basically in agreement. It would be a tragedy if a split among those of us who are committed to these goals resulted in handing over the White House to those who oppose these directly. I know what I'm talking about because here in Oregon, in 1976, the Gene McCarthy candidacy got 40,000 votes and as a result the Republicans won this state by just 1700 votes.* So tonight I appeal to all of those who support Mr. Anderson. Consider the consequences of a Ronald Reagan Republican victory. Vote for Fritz Mondale and me, not just for his sake and mine but for your own sake and for the sake of the goals and ideals that you and I share."

Carter finished speaking at Portland just before 10:00 p.m. Pacific Standard Time, just before 1:00 a.m. Eastern Standard Time—just as Pat Caddell, restored by a nap, arrived at his office in downtown Washington to look at the figures from his final national survey. There was no one in the waiting room, but Caddell could see seven or eight members of his staff silhouetted in his own office, sitting silently and waiting for him.

"How bad is it?" he asked Paul Maslin, one of his principal assistants.

"Ten," Maslin replied.

Caddell examined the figures. Reagan had 46 percent, Carter 36, Anderson 9.5, and 8 percent were still undecided. The data were consistent, he said later, "clear across the board" of demographic groups. "Your most critical groups in the electorate," he said, "they were all gone." Carter's lead among those "weak Democrats" had fallen from 9 percentage points to 3. The story was the same elsewhere—among Catholics, among independents, among white women and white men, even among upper-income voters who had been most suspicious of Ronald Reagan. It was a disaster.

Caddell quickly telephoned Hamilton Jordan. "I hate to wake you up," he said, "but it's all over. It's ten points and it's getting worse." Then he patched Jerry Rafshoon into a conference call. The three went over the figures and decided to meet at the

*Actually it was fewer than 1000.

White House in the office of Jack Watson to consider how to
break the news to the President and to discuss what might be
done, if anything, to lower the margin.

By this time, 2:00 a.m. in the East, Air Force One had arrived
at Seattle for that final campaign rally. Jordan, Caddell, and Rafshoon reached Powell there while Carter was speaking. Jordan
was sitting at Watson's desk and the other two were on extension
telephones, and they could hear Carter's voice in the background.

"We got the last survey," Jordan said, "and it looks like we're
going to lose, and it could be really bad."

Then Caddell went over the figures and the four men—the
very innermost of the inner circles around Jimmy Carter
throughout his time on the national political stage—discussed
what could be done. They were seeking a way, as Caddell put it,
to "shake things up" when the President appeared in Plains election morning for what would be his last crack at the "free media" in the 1980 campaign.

None of them imagined Carter could save himself, but there
were still things to discuss. The margin on congressional voting
had slipped 6 percentage points in the final survey, and Caddell
was concerned about the possibility Congress might slip away
from the Democrats, too. At the very least the Senate was in
jeopardy. And Jordan was understandably worried about the dimensions of the defeat and the outlook in the Electoral College.
Because the trends ran so uniformly across the board, Caddell
said, Carter might be lucky to win even 35 or 50 electoral votes.
"If we can lose by five [points nationally] instead of ten," Jordan
said, "it would be a lot better." Powell said he would tell Carter
the news, and they hung up the telephones. Jordan, the young
Georgian who had been the principal architect of Jimmy Carter's career in national politics, was clearly shaken. "Hamilton
was just white," Caddell remembered long after the fact. "He sat
there and he was just white."

Ironically, out in Seattle, the President was enjoying one of his
most successful rallies of the long campaign. Although the crowd
was not an overwhelming one, probably fewer than 2000 people,
it was infected with that last-round enthusiasm. And because the

people were packed inside a hangar to escape the ubiquitous Puget Sound drizzle outside, the cheers and the sound of the bands reverberated so that the turnout seemed much larger and even more enthusiastic.

Carter himself, down to the final rally on the final night, seemed liberated—even insouciant. The campaign was over, for better or for worse, and there was nothing more he could do except give this one last speech. When someone held up a sign that read "Jimmy, You Blew Your Four Years," the President blew him kisses, twice. And when someone else advanced on the platform holding aloft a sign that read "Carter's Maternal Grandmother Was a Mulatto," he ignored it. He spoke for twenty-six minutes and was interrupted twenty-three times by applause and shouts of "yes, yes" and "no, no" in reply to his rhetorical questions.

There was nothing intrinsically remarkable about the speech. It included the same appeal to potential defectors to John Anderson, the same call to Democrats to "come home" to their party, the same derision of Ronald Reagan and Republicans who behaved like Democrats at campaign time—and then some blurring of the reality of the Carter record. But some rush of adrenalin seemed to make the President more forceful and articulate than he usually seemed to be when faced with a large audience.

"I'm proud to be a Democrat," he said, "because I believe in the heritage and mission of the Democratic Party. It changed my life. It's changed the life of my mother. It changed the life of my father. The Democratic Party has given my children a better chance for a better life. I believe in the heritage and mission of Franklin D. Roosevelt. I believe in the heritage and mission of Harry Truman. I believe in the heritage and mission of John Fitzgerald Kennedy, and I believe in the heritage and mission of Lyndon Baines Johnson, and I believe also in the heritage and mission of Hubert Humphrey. Every great advance, every single great advance in our nation, in the private lives of our citizens for the last half-century, from collective bargaining to the minimum wage, from Social Security to Medicare, every single one of them has been made possible by Democrats over the opposition, over the opposition of Republicans." If there was something out of place in Jimmy Carter wrapping himself in this "heritage and mission of the Democratic Party," this last time at least it didn't ring false.

Powell, carrying the burden of the news from Washington, came into the hangar while Carter was speaking. Reporters and staff members who noticed him were struck by the look on his face. His mouth was set in that small public smile that had become so familiar over the last four years, but his eyes were bleak.

Greg Schneiders, who had left the White House staff early in the campaign to go into the consulting business with Rafshoon, was one of those who saw him. "Jody came in, and it seemed to me from the look on his face that he must have gotten the figures," he said later. "He was smiling but he didn't look happy."

"Have you heard anything?" Schneiders asked.

"Yeah," Powell replied.

"Is it bad?"

"Yes."

"How bad?"

"Pat says it's gone."

For Powell the knowledge of that polling data put a different context on the scene. He listened while Carter told the cheering crowd: "The issue of this election is so close nationwide that what you do personally might be the difference between victory and defeat. It might be the difference between a good life for you and those you love and a challenge to the things in which you believe so deeply." And he watched and listened, too, when Carter, the speech over, walked along the crowd shaking those last hands while the loudspeaker blared a recording of his campaign song from 1976, "Why Not the Best?" Randy Lewis, a young assistant, had arranged especially for it to be played for this final moment.

"It was very emotional," Schneiders recalled. "He was working his way down the stage, and he was taken aback by this and the crowd reaction."

As the record played, however, Powell walked out of the hangar into the drizzle, puffing on a cigarette and looking off into the middle distance. "We can't talk about this to anyone," he told Schneiders. "We still have congressional races to worry about."

"Maybe we'll be surprised tomorrow," Schneiders said.

"That's always possible," Powell replied. But it was clear he didn't believe that, and his duty now—as it had been so often in all his years with Jimmy Carter—was to break the bad news to the boss.

As they all prepared to leave, Powell told one of the reporters in the pool assigned to ride Air Force One that Carter "might have a drink when he gets back on the plane. I expect he's probably due for a Scotch or vodka and tonic tonight." Carter himself told Helen Thomas, the veteran White House correspondent of United Press International, that "I feel good" about the political outlook.

On the plane Powell walked back to the galley to get a drink, then forward to the staff section, where he found Carter in his shirtsleeves talking with several members of the staff—domestic affairs adviser Stuart Eizenstat, speechwriter Rick Hertzberg, appointments secretary Phil Wise, personal secretary and assistant Susan Clough. Powell didn't want to break the news to this group, so he waited, but then Carter decided he would invite the pool reporters to join him for a talk. Powell, fearing that Carter might say something embarrassing because he still didn't know the figures from the poll, insisted the conversation be off the record. Then the press secretary waited while Carter, seated at a table in the front cabin, picked at a turkey-and-ham club sandwich and chatted with the reporters for almost forty-five minutes. When they asked him how the election looked, he said what he always said: "I feel good about it."

Before the conversation ended—it was now nearly 4:00 a.m. Eastern Time, and the plane was somewhere over Kansas—Jordan and Caddell called again, reaching the airborne Powell over the White House communications radio. Powell went into Carter's private cabin to take the call. He still hadn't been able to inform the President, he explained. But while they were talking, Carter came into the cabin. Powell turned away from the telephone and told him he had Caddell and Jordan on the line.

"What did they find?" Carter asked.

"They say it looks bad," Powell replied. "It's probably all over."

"Just let me talk directly to Pat," Carter said, taking the phone. Then to Caddell, in what the pollster later remembered as "a happy, 'up' voice," Carter asked: "What's happening?"

"Well, Mr. President," Caddell replied, "it's gone."

Carter made no reply. The pollster added some of the detail: the margin was going to be substantial, perhaps in the range of 7 to 10 points. They needed to decide what the President should say when he arrived at Plains. "At that moment," Caddell recalled, "it was like the air went out of the whole conversation. It was the worst thing I did in my life."

Finally Carter said, "You all talk to Jody and work something out. I think I'll take a nap." He handed the phone to Powell.

Air Force One touched down at Robins Air Force Base in Georgia at 6:45 a.m. in a heavy fog. As Carter walked toward the helicopter that was to take him to Plains, the reporters called out their questions. Anything from Iran? "No," he replied. What about the election? The President shrugged and walked on.

At Plains the chopper landed near the softball field on which Carter had shown himself in 1976 to be such a determined competitor. He kissed his wife, and they got into a limousine for the drive down to the polling place at Plains High School. There they were steered into the principal's office for a few minutes while the poll workers dealt with thirty or so other voters already in line. "We've got to get these people voted," Powell joked, "so they can go down to north Florida"—presumably to vote again. Then Carter and his wife emerged, and the reporters called out the usual inane questions about how they would vote. "Well, I've made up my mind," the President said. "I just talked to my wife and I'm going to vote the same way she does."

By now it was becoming increasingly clear that the news was bad, and that he knew it. Carter looked tired, his eyes red, and, under the pancake makeup, his skin was blotchy. He seemed dispirited as he left the high school but he made a point of stopping to talk to the reporters who were roped off out of his path. To Sam Donaldson, that was enough of a deviation from the normal pattern to signal that something was different, and probably bad news.

Was he going to win? "I hope so," Carter replied. "We'll see ... I always think I'll win." When Curtis Wilkie of *The Boston Globe,* a longtime Carter watcher, reminded him he had not used his favorite expression from 1976, Carter paused and, half-heartedly, added: "Okay, I don't intend to lose. Right on."

Then he went to the old railroad depot, to the same place he had spoken to his friends and neighbors just four years earlier, at almost exactly the same hour of the morning. But in 1976 the occasion had been a joyous one, a moment of great expectations and unlimited hope, the climax of what may have been the most stunning triumph over the odds in modern American political history. Now there was the bitterness of defeat, a judgment by those whom he had served that they would prefer someone else, and it was a very different occasion indeed.

"The same setting, many of the same people, everybody up for twenty-four or thirty-six hours," Schneiders said. "In 1976 he had made a very moving statement to his neighbors, what it all meant to him. But this time he got up there and gave a stump speech—a defense of the administration, Panama, deregulation, all that. It was inappropriate.

"He probably went beyond the point where he could make a heartfelt statement without breaking down, but this way he could put his mind and mouth on automatic pilot. He knew the polls were open and he would be on television and he was thinking like Jimmy Carter—one more shot. It was very disconcerting to many of the press people. They felt it fit in with the whole 'mean Jimmy' phenomenon. 'Here he is with his own people, the campaign over, when he ought to try to say something meaningful to them, and here he is still campaigning.' And he was."

The speech, however, was more than that. It was both his rationale for losing and a kind of apology for doing so.

For more than two years, ever since it had become apparent he was in political trouble, Carter and his advisers had sounded one theme: He had faced the tough issues, made the hard choices that other Presidents had avoided, and he had paid the political price for doing so. That had been the rationale all along and would be the explanation for his defeat, and now he used the rationale to justify himself to those who had gathered at the depot on Election Day.

"I've had now a chance to serve for four years the greatest nation on earth and the greatest people in the world," he said. "We've made some very difficult decisions and every time I've made a judgment in a time of crisis or a time of solitude about the future of our country or the future of your lives, I've done it with the memory of my upbringing here in Plains, the fact that I'm a Southerner, the fact that I'm an American. I've offered my life, as many of you have done in time of war, to preserve freedom and to preserve the things in which we all believe."

"We've made some difficult decisions. Some of them have not been politically popular. Some of them have been highly publicized. Some of the crises with which I've dealt, you've never known about them because they didn't develop into something that affected your life or the lives of the people around you."

Some of his decisions, he said, had "aroused the displeasure of others," and some had been "politically costly" and still others had "aroused the animosity" of his critics. He mentioned energy, the Panama Canal treaties, his success in keeping the peace.

Near the end, however, it was clear Jimmy Carter was being overcome by the emotion of the moment and the knowledge that this speech was a kind of farewell. His throat seemed to tighten and his eyes filled.

"Many people from Plains, from Americus ... from around this area have gone all over the nation to speak for me and shake hands with people, to tell them that you have confidence in me and that I would not disappoint them if I became President. I've tried to honor my commitment"—his voice broke, he paused and dropped his eyes—"to you." Then he added: "God bless you. Thank you. Don't forget to vote, everybody."

15.
"The Real World Is All Around Us"

It was shortly before noon on Inauguration Day and President Carter and the man who had defeated him, Ronald Reagan, were riding together to the Capitol, where Reagan was about to be sworn in as the fortieth President of the United States. That last ride from the White House up Pennsylvania Avenue is never an easy one for a man who has lost the presidency, and it was particularly trying for Jimmy Carter. The Iranians who had plagued his last fourteen months in power were now extracting one final hour of uncertainty, one more pound of political flesh from the departing leader of the nation they called "the Great Satan."

Release of the fifty-two American hostages held for those fourteen months had appeared likely for several days now. Carter, in fact, thought for a time he might as his last act as President fly to West Germany to greet them at the United States Air Force Base near Wiesbaden. But as one obstacle after another developed, that hope had dissolved. Now he was reduced to the chance that at least they might be released in the waning minutes of his rejected presidency.

Carter had spent most of his final night in the Oval Office, where he had toiled for more than a year to achieve the hostages' release. Passing the last hours with him were his Vice President, Fritz Mondale, his old friend Charles Kirbo from Atlanta, and the two young Georgians who had been closest to him all along, Hamilton Jordan and Jody Powell. Meanwhile, all

307

across Washington the Republicans had been celebrating their ascendancy at parties and dinners; sampling the hors d'oeuvres at Bill Timmons' reception at the F Street Club, eating steaks at Mel Krupin's restaurant on Connecticut Avenue. Ronald and Nancy Reagan had spent most of a carefree evening at the Capital Centre, a huge sports arena in suburban Prince Georges County, Maryland, where an inaugural gala produced by and starring Frank Sinatra was held in their honor.

In the White House that night, however, there was no cause for celebration. Members of Carter's staff were still cleaning out their desks and taking down their pictures while moving crews loaded filing cabinets of the departing President's papers into vans lined up in the driveway. The President himself could only wait, powerless to hurry the process along.

The only hitch in the release of the hostages now was an arrangement for the transfer to an escrow account in London of the Iranian assets held in American banks since Carter had ordered them frozen at the outset of the crisis. It was, Powell reported at about 1:00 a.m., an "itty-bitty hangup." Two hours later, the chief American negotiator, Deputy Secretary of State Warren Christopher, called from Algiers reporting that the procedure had been agreed upon. And two hours after that, at about 5:30 a.m., a group of American bankers working on the transfer reported that the money, some $8 billion dollars, had been deposited in the Federal Reserve Bank. At 6:47 a.m. the Fed sent a teletype message that assigned the money to the escrow account at the Bank of England, and at 8:17 a.m.—with less than four hours of Jimmy Carter's term remaining—the Central Bank of Algeria certified that the money was indeed in that escrow account.

Still the Iranians delayed, and Jimmy Carter waited. During the morning there were frequent reports of alarums and excursions in Tehran, all of them maddeningly inaccurate or premature. About 11:00 a.m. one wire service quoted a Tehran airport policeman as saying two Algerian jets had taken off with their precious cargo of fifty-two Americans, but that report proved to be unfounded. At 11:36 a.m. another news agency sent a bulletin: "Hostages freed." That wasn't true either. As Carter rode toward the Capitol with Reagan, he took one last telephone call in the limousine. The Algerian planes, a White House aide monitoring the situation glumly informed him, were still sitting on the tarmac outside Tehran.

The scene at the Capitol was magnificent. For the first time the Inaugural platform had been constructed on the West Front of the building, facing Washington's most majestic panorama—the long, open mall broken only by the Washington Monument, then running on to the Lincoln Memorial. As Carter and Reagan took their places and the preliminary ceremonies unfolded, thousands strained for a view, and as they did, the same brief words of inquiry wafted through the crowd: "Are they out?" That was all anyone had to ask; everyone knew, of course, to whom "they" referred.

As Ronald Reagan began taking the oath of office at 11:57 a.m., Jimmy Carter sat just behind him and to his left, and his face conveyed a measure of this final presidential agony. He was somber, unsmiling, and at times he closed his eyes tightly, as if in prayer. Not even he, the President of the United States for these final seconds, knew the answer to that same question: Are they out?

Reagan, only now acquiring responsibility for the hostage crisis and unmarked by the long ordeal, delivered an Inaugural address of optimism, as all new Presidents do. His only reference to the trouble in Iran was the briefest of oblique warnings: "Our forbearance should never be misunderstood. Our reluctance for conflict should not be misjudged as a failure of will. . . . Above all we must realize no weapon in the arsenals of the world is so formidable as the will and moral courage of free men and women. It is a weapon our adversaries in today's world do not have. It is a weapon that we as Americans do have. Let that be understood by those who practice terrorism and prey upon their neighbors."

The Carter presidency was now history, and the Reagan presidency had begun. Inside the White House, Reagan transition officials, watching television for the exact moment at which national power changed hands, began at once rearranging the furniture in the Oval Office. Pictures of Democratic presidents were quickly taken down and replaced with those of Republicans. A new nameplate was affixed to the back of the President's chair in the Cabinet Room. Still Jimmy Carter waited, sitting disconsolately on the platform through Reagan's address, as sunshine bathed the scene. At the end, the old President shook hands with the new, and as Reagan entered the Capitol for a lunch of celebration, the deposed Carter left for Andrews Air Force Base and the trip home to Plains. Not until well after he was airborne for Georgia did Carter learn that the hostages had left Iranian air space and at last were free.

The delay of the hostages' release until Carter was no longer President was a final cruelty for him. Even many of those who most wished to see him leave Washington felt some sympathy now at his having to endure what was perceived widely as a last gesture of contempt from the people the new President had called "barbarians."

In a sense, however, it was grimly appropriate that there be this kind of ending to a crisis that had had so much to do with Carter's defeat and Reagan's election. It could not be said that the crisis in Iran *in itself* had defeated Carter. The abysmal state of the economy, and Carter's inability to cope with it, certainly were major contributors as well. But there can be no doubt that his failure to obtain the hostages' release by Election Day summed up for many Americans a general weakness and ineffectiveness they were not willing to reward with four more years in the presidency.

Exactly why one candidate wins and another loses a presidential election is always difficult to say with any precision. The voters make their decisions on the basis of a whole complex of factors: national and parochial issues, the personality and character of the candidates, voters' own personal situations, peer pressures, information and misinformation from the news media and advertising, sometimes simple impulse. Not even the most sophisticated opinion poll can sift out all of these elements and assign them relative weights, although that task is among those the new technocrats of politics always strive to accomplish.

Moreover, such an analysis is even more difficult when one candidate wins a landslide, because so many currents run together to form the national consensus. And what Ronald Reagan won on November 4, 1980, was by any definition a landslide of those who expressed a choice: 51 percent of the popular vote to 41 percent for Carter and 7 percent for John Anderson, and a plu-

rality of more than 8 million votes.* Reagan won 489 electoral
votes to only 49 for Carter, sweeping 44 states to only 6 for Carter—his Georgia, Mondale's Minnesota, and four Democratic
strongholds: Rhode Island, Maryland, West Virginia, and Hawaii,
plus the District of Columbia.

The landslide flowed across the congressional and gubernatorial elections as well. Reagan's Republicans captured control of
the Senate for the first time since the Eisenhower landslide of
1952, with a net gain of twelve seats. In the House of Representatives they picked up 33 seats, putting them within range of a
takeover in 1982 or 1984. And Republicans won a net of four
new governorships.

Why did all this happen? And why were the results such a surprise? We have talked much here about the "October surprise"
the Reagan campaign feared Carter would spring. In the end,
however, it was Reagan and the Republican Party who produced
a November surprise—not simply victory, but a political triumph
of such overwhelming proportions that it assured a sea change
in American politics and in the conduct of national policy.

Certainly an explanation must start with the two overriding
political realities of 1980 that held the professionals in the elections business at their mercy—held them "hostage," as the developing cliché put it. Of these two realities, one—the hostage crisis
and the patriotic fervor it triggered—at the outset was working
for the incumbent Carter. The other—the sick economy and his
failure to heal it—was working against him. And so, during most
of the primaries, he used the reality that was working for him to
divert attention from the one that was damaging to him. To a
large extent the strategy worked. Carter was helped, of course,
by the personal problems that mired the campaign of his principal opponent for the Democratic nomination, Edward Kennedy. Meanwhile, on the Republican side, Reagan after a stumbling
start fastened onto the reality of Carter's poor presidential record. With his own identification as a strong leader who would
change things, at home and abroad, he easily captured his party's
nomination and united his party at the same time.

*Again, however, as in 1976, the turnout was barely more than half the number
of Americans old enough to vote. What this meant, as with Carter in 1976, was that
for every voting-age American who cast a ballot for Reagan, three did not.

By the time the fall campaign began, both of the two realities were now working against Carter. The economy was in worse shape. And not only were the hostages still in captivity; a failed raid ordered and then aborted by Carter had made any rescue all but impossible. In a nutshell, the Carter record, which even his own professionals acknowledged could not be a vehicle with which to seek reelection, was even less defensible. And so, the only hope was to divert the voters' attention from what Carter was, toward what Reagan was, or might be.

As the general election campaign got under way, there were two dominant public perceptions about the candidates themselves. One was that Reagan was a dangerous man who, voters feared, might by intent or blunder take the country into war. The other was that Carter, for all his shortcomings, was a decent, honorable man. But Carter, stripped by now of any major positive reality to help him, decided with his professionals' agreement to try to worsen the negative perception of Reagan. And in doing so, unwittingly, he eroded the one main positive perception the voters still had of him.

In the end, both the reality and the perception of Carter were negative. The economy continued out of control and the last-minute flurry over the hostages—the belated "October surprise"—served principally to point up Carter's ineffectiveness. Not only that, but because his earlier actions like the "Wisconsin primary press conference" had encouraged the public to be skeptical about his motives, his credibility plummeted. Jimmy Carter couldn't get things done, he wasn't such a nice man after all, and he seemed willing to resort to almost anything to hold onto his job. That latter idea was helped along by Reagan's aides harping on an approaching "October surprise." But they never could have made much progress with that strategy had Carter himself not given birth to the skepticism, first by his exploitation of the hostage crisis, then by his personal attacks on Reagan. Reagan's strategists did not dream up the "October surprise"; they just gave the growing skepticism a catchy name and conditioned the voters to think the worst of Jimmy Carter.

There was much more involved in Ronald Reagan's landslide victory, however. The campaign is only one of two principal elements in any election. The other, at least equally important factor is the context in which the election is held. What usually produces a landslide is a context that is decidedly favorable to one candidate, together with a campaign that takes full advantage of the winning candidate's personal qualities and political skills to exploit that context, and to capitalize on the loser's vulnerabilities. From the beginning it was clear that the context in which the campaign of 1980 would be conducted was hostile to the incumbent President, and hospitable to Reagan or some other Republican challenger. By virtually every measure the economy was in far worse condition than when Carter assumed responsibility for it from a Republican, Gerald Ford, four years earlier. Carter could, and did, argue that there were reasons for this condition—most notably America's continued dependence on foreign oil. But whatever the reason, the economic indicators were inescapably poor. Similarly, the international situation seemed much more threatening than when Carter took office. The signal accomplishment of his presidency was the tenacious effort he made to bring Egypt and Israel together in a peace treaty. But what the country also saw was a disintegration of the United States' own, more easily identifiable self-interest in the Persian Gulf, and increased Russian adventurism in Africa, Cuba, and Afghanistan that Carter seemed powerless to prevent.

Issues aside, the political framework was decidedly disadvantageous to Carter as a Democrat. The party had seemed to lose its ability to produce new or innovative approaches to national problems at a time these problems were growing more serious and the burden on taxpayers increasingly oppressive. The dialogue during the primaries between Kennedy and Carter, and the platform adopted by the Democratic convention in New York in August, seemed to many voters to be little more than rehashed New Dealism. The contrast with the Republicans was striking because, under the leadership of chairman Bill Brock, they had amassed huge amounts of money with which to fashion a clear Republican identity on issues.

To some, that contrast had been apparent long before the general election campaign. In March 1980, for example, the pollster Peter Hart told the Democratic House and Senate campaign committees: "One thing which is not working for Democrats is some basic, simple set of ideas of what this election is all about.

Republicans have their issues and their agenda. Democrats do not. They may have a program, but they have not articulated it to the public. Individual Democrats can win by one strategy or another. But Democrats generally . . . cannot count on winning a majority without presenting the public with some articulated message."

Much of the responsibility for that failure, of course, could be assigned to Carter. A president by definition is the leader of his political party and, as such, is the one person most responsible for giving the party a clear identity. But Jimmy Carter had come full-blown to the national stage as a presidential candidate, with no history of fighting in the political trenches alongside other Democrats. The great battles over civil rights, the war in Vietnam, Richard Nixon's appointments to the Supreme Court, Watergate—all these were matters Carter had experienced only through the newspapers and television.

Moreover, Carter was a singularly self-involved politician. He gave his trust only to those for whom he was the entire political universe. He did not see politics as the shared enterprise it is, and he viewed the Democratic Party far more as a vehicle for himself than as an institution to which he had some obligation. That fact was bluntly apparent on Election Night, when he conceded defeat an hour before the polls closed in the West Coast time zone, despite warnings from his staff that this action might mean that some Democratic voters waiting in line would give up and go home, to the detriment of other Democratic candidates.

Regular Democrats around the country, and in Washington, were furious, and none more than Speaker of the House Thomas P. O'Neill, Jr. They were convinced Carter's timing had cost the reelection of at least one prominent Democrat, Representative James Corman of California, who lost by less than two voters per precinct, and probably other good Democrats as well. "I'm sitting here," O'Neill told us later in the speaker's office, "and my men are tumbling and falling. My men are checking the returns, and pollsters are coming in and saying, 'You're hitting an avalanche.' I get a phone call from Frank Moore [Carter's chief of congressional liaison]. He says, 'The President ten minutes from now is going to say he's conceding, and he wants you to come down.' I told him, 'I can't, and he's doing the wrong thing.'"

O'Neill, to drive the point home, then told us of the time in 1958 he was campaign manager for the winning candidate for governor in Massachusetts, Foster Furcolo. Just before being interviewed on network television, he was told that Furcolo was winning by a landslide and that the Democrats were also winning handily in neighboring Connecticut. So O'Neill proceeded to report, at about seven o'clock in the East, that the Democrats "were sweeping the country." Some years later, when he was in Congress, O'Neill said, a colleague from California came up to him and said, "You elected me to Congress. We had national television on [in his campaign headquarters] with our tails between our legs. Then you come on and tell about a tidal wave." The news, the Californian said, had such an impact on the West Coast that he won easily.

Some opinion polls and analyses disputed the conclusion that Carter's early concession had been costly, but in any case it underscored his lack of sensitivity to the political interests of other Democrats.

Still another essential element in the context of any election is what the news media, for want of a better term, call "the national mood"—the collective wisdom, collective opinion, or collective predilection of the voters at the time. Before, during, and after the campaign of 1980 this mood was defined as "a conservative trend" that had been running in the country during the 1970s. There was some obvious truth in that observation; more voters were describing themselves as "conservative" than in the past, and more conservative candidates were winning elections.

That trend was not surprising in light of what was happening economically in the country. The American middle class was expanding broadly, but its financial gains were being compromised by soaring property taxes and, with rising inflation, by the average taxpayer's "creep" into higher income-tax brackets. The expanding middle class was feeling squeezed, making its members more sensitive to government spending and inefficiency—and, in many cases, less sensitive to the old social welfare programs from Washington. In this mind set, most welfare programs were apt to be reduced to "giveaways" and their recipients to "chiselers"—expressions that were congenial to the rhetoric of Ronald Reagan and other conservatives.

But there was also much evidence that voters rarely think of themselves in terms of ideology except when confronted by politicians, pollsters, or political reporters who do think in such terms. For example, measuring "the national mood" by using the criteria of issues usually thought of as "ideological" yields an inconsistent picture. In 1980 the opinion surveys found, for instance, majorities for "liberal" positions on some social issues—favoring the Equal Rights Amendment and gun control, opposing a Constitutional amendment forbidding abortion—and for "conservative" positions on others—the death penalty, limiting the rights of homosexuals. Similarly, most voters favored more spending for national defense—a cornerstone of conservatism—and also favored national health insurance—a litmus test for liberalism.

What seemed far more pervasive than ideology in the electorate of 1980 was a pronounced practicality. If there was a single strain running through a variety of groups, it was the conviction that government in general, and the federal government in particular, was not doing anything to make people's lives better, despite the higher taxes most were paying.

In that climate incumbency obviously is not an advantage. On the contrary, incumbents are seen as part of the problem. If they have the answers, why haven't they demonstrated it by their actions? Jimmy Carter himself was a product of that kind of thinking when he was elected in 1976—a determined "outsider" boasting of his lack of Washington experience. How else could you explain the voters' willingness to risk electing someone with such limited credentials?

That reaction was even more obvious in the 1978 election, when voters turned out of office a whole clutch of liberal Democratic senators—William Hathaway of Maine, Thomas McIntyre of New Hampshire, Wendell Anderson of Minnesota, Dick Clark of Iowa, Floyd Haskell of Colorado. Each of them had been obliged to run on his "experience," and that was the wrong identification for success. Again in 1980 the same was true when the Republicans seized control of the Senate by defeating, among others, several liberal Democratic senators well-respected *in Washington*—George McGovern, Gaylord Nelson, Birch Bayh, and John Culver, most notably.

Ronald Reagan was perhaps the ideal candidate to profit from, or to represent, this new popular imperative. Over his sixteen years in the political arena he had established himself as, more than anything else, a determined critic of activist government. In hundreds, perhaps thousands, of speeches, radio broadcasts, and newspaper columns year after year, the staple of his presentation was his rich fund of "horror stories" about the foibles and failures of bureaucrats and the elected officials who supposedly controlled them. This record does not suggest, of course, that Reagan lacked identification as a conservative. On the contrary, he espoused all the positions of prime importance to the right— in his policy toward China and Cuba, on national defense, on government spending and balanced budgets, in his opposition to abortion and to ERA. What made Reagan so attractive to the voters of 1980, however, was his ability to express their own frustrations at the failures of government to function with more efficacy. And if in the bargain he turned out to be a personable fellow who communicated a certain warmth and good humor, so much the better. Simply representing the direction in which the country wanted to turn was all that was really required to make him at least an acceptable alternative to Jimmy Carter, if the judgment on Carter could be focused squarely on his record of failure.

In the campaign of 1980 it was always clear that the general election would be just such a referendum on Carter, unless he and his managers could accomplish two things—first, convert the election to that choice between "two futures" about which he had spoken in Madison Square Garden and, second, create and embellish a perception of Ronald Reagan that would make him unacceptable to the voters.

But the President was in no position in 1980 to make promises for the future that would be believable. He had sent too many conflicting, even contradictory, signals to the American people over the four years for them to have confidence that he would be a forceful, consistent personality guiding the nation in a second term. In his first two years, he had been meek, willing to

turn the other cheek at the failures of those on whom he was de-
pending. A wisecrack by Bob Strauss during that time became a
widely circulated and widely accepted axiom in Washington:
"The trouble with this administration is there's no penalty for
fucking up." Then, with the firing of the Cabinet members after
the Camp David "malaise summit" of 1979, Carter had tried to
present himself as a changed man who had finally lost patience,
but it didn't take.

Jimmy Carter never managed to convey the image of optimism and confidence that Americans seem to want in a president. Sharing a drink with one of us at the White House in the
summer of 1979, he said of inflation and the role of OPEC prices:
"You know, there's nothing we can do about that." Facing the
evidence of the Russian brigade in Cuba a few weeks later, he
insisted that the situation was "unacceptable"—and then was
obliged by reality to accept it after all. Throughout the election
campaign he continued to send these same uncertain signals.
One day he would smear Reagan, the next promise not to do it
anymore, then go right out and do it again. The opinion polls at
the outset found that people saw him as a decent and sincere
man. But as the campaign wore on they saw him increasingly as
manipulative, even devious.

When his attempt to "demonize" Reagan failed—Reagan's
cool, relaxed, "presidential" demeanor in the debate in Cleveland had buried that effort once and for all—Jimmy Carter was
politically naked. In other times and other elections, he might
have relied on advertising and other stratagems of the new political technology to construct a more favorable image of himself.
But in the campaign of 1980, when the voters were focused on
the dominating news events of the day rather than on the carefully crafted commercials that ran just before and after the relentlessly bad news, that political diversion was impossible.

Strauss described the helplessness and frustration of the professional campaign strategist this way: "Let me tell you something. With all the politics in the world, I could have been gone
the last ninety days of that campaign. . . . It didn't make a goddamned bit of difference whether we were here or not, coming
to work at six o'clock or working until midnight. The truth of the

matter is, I think, things are going on out there. People aren't paying attention to anything that's being done, and I'm pretty sure I was right on that—that it was the events.... I think I could have stayed in bed the last ninety days and he [Carter] would have got exactly the same number of votes he had, give or take two.... I said, 'The real world is all around us.' "

What the eleventh-hour flurry of activity on Iran represented that final weekend of the campaign was only a last chance that reality might salvage something for Carter. But the overriding fact was that he had destroyed all his credibility by then, as President and as candidate. Imprisoned by his own excesses, he even had to shy away from waiting for prime television time to make his statement on the hostages that last Sunday night, his strategists fearful that he would be accused once again of manipulating the crisis to save his political skin. Carter and his men had good reason to entertain such concerns, because skepticism now pervaded the electorate. In Cleveland on the day after the debate, a widow named Millie Stein came out onto her back porch and told us: "I think Iran is going to decide who the next president is. What I think might happen is, Iran wants Carter to be president because he seems to be able to be pushed around easily. If they think Reagan will be president, they'll release the hostages quickly. It will be like a flash the last day. We're in the grips of another country."

Wirthlin, comparing a poll taken on September 30 with another the final weekend, found that the number of voters who thought that Carter might for political purposes control the timing of the hostages' release had risen from 19 to 44 percent. Even after the election, a survey taken for the *Los Angeles Times* found that one voter in five thought Carter had "held back so they [the hostages] could be released at election time"—although, of course, they had not been. These postmortems do not mean that at the last moment the voters turned against Carter because of his handling of the long crisis. On the contrary, some polls even showed an increase in approval of the President's performance in the final days. But the last-minute attention to the crisis did crystallize all those doubts—across the board—about his ability and leadership. As Bob Teeter, the astute Republican pollster, put it, "The hostage thing threw light on Carter's greatest failing. He took a last cut and missed by about eight miles."

When the election was over, the proprietors of most of the major national polls were dumbfounded because they had missed so widely the size of Reagan's victory. The Gallup Poll had shown a margin of only 3 percentage points three days before the election, and the CBS, *New York Times,* and *Newsweek* polls had indicated an even closer race. Only Louis Harris among the public pollsters had pointed to the decisiveness of the victory, and he had Reagan leading by only 5 percent. The result was that a "big bang" theory evolved, circulated by Pat Caddell among others: that is, that a disproportionate number of voters decided at the very last moment to go to the Republican candidate. The pollsters understandably were more interested in explaining why they were wrong than in why the election turned out as it did. But Reagan won by a landslide, not because the bottom fell out of Jimmy Carter's credibility as an effective president on the final weekend, but because that credibility had been eroding steadily, and his failure on that final weekend merely completed and confirmed the erosion.

What was clear was that the voters, inundated with bad news day after day all year long, had indeed come to see the election as a referendum on Carter, and had rejected him in overwhelming numbers. That fact was underscored in the "exit polls" of voters leaving the polling places. One taken by ABC News, based on a very large sample, found two-thirds of those who had voted for Reagan saying they would have voted for Anderson rather than for Carter, had those two been the only available choices. The disillusionment with Carter did not mean, either, that there was a lack of genuine enthusiasm for Reagan, because indisputably there had to be enthusiasm in a victory of such proportions. But even in the triumph, doubts about the Republican candidate were not by any means resolved; ABC also found one-third of its sample still thought Reagan "might get us into war."

The more important, extensive reservations about Jimmy Carter had finally been confirmed by the "barbarians" in Tehran and by his inability to cope with them. To the very end, past the election and through the two last, sorrowful months of Carter's term, those doubts never could be dissipated. All the goodwill and hope that poured out toward him only four years earlier, when after his own inauguration he had captured the imagination and the hearts of millions of television viewers who saw him walk, beaming, with his wife at this side down Pennsylvania Avenue to the White House, was now directed toward the man who had defeated him.

As Ronald Reagan now told other millions of television viewers where he intended to take America in the next four years, what they heard in his Inaugural speech was, of course, the same promise he had been preaching for more than two decades. "In this present crisis," he said, "government is not the solution to our problem; government *is* the problem. . . . It is my intention to curb the size and influence of the federal establishment. . . . It's not my intention to do away with government. It is rather to make it work—work with us, not over us; to stand by our side, not ride on our back. Government can and must provide opportunity, not smother it; foster productivity, not stifle it."

The words were all too familiar, and so the country should not have been surprised in the immediately ensuing days and weeks that the new Republican President meant, indeed, to bring about a sharp break with the past, particularly in the areas of social welfare and federal regulation. Jimmy Carter had been right in his plaintive warnings of the last frenetic days of the campaign—that Ronald Reagan's election would mean "stark differences" in how America was run. But those other plaintive warnings of Reagan the reckless adventurer in the nuclear age—and the "meanness" with which they were sounded by an "unpresidential" president—had drowned out Carter's alarum about a new social revolution at the gates. It was too late for such second thoughts now. The people had spoken, and said they wanted a change. Perhaps the change they wanted, and expected, was primarily the removal of Jimmy Carter from the presidency. But in victory, the winner always claims a popular mandate; he always reads the vote for him as a demand for the changes he wants to make, and a landslide vote emphatically reinforces such a reading. And so Ronald Reagan saw himself not merely as the vehicle for expressing public disenchantment with the incumbent, but as a man with a mission resoundingly endorsed by the American people to take the reins from Carter and set a new national course.

"I'm sure in any election there's a certain amount of voting against," Reagan told us later as President. "But I have to say that as the campaign went on, I was seeing evidences of acceptance of our proposals, support of the things we were advocating. . . . I know that the people who normally would not be Republican voters were the ones that I would meet at a rally [and] the things I had said we would do, they wanted."

The transfer of power in this country is unfailingly a scene of high drama and poignancy, no matter what the circumstances. Reagan himself took note of its inspirational nature in his Inaugural speech. "The orderly transfer of authority as called for in the Constitution," he said, "takes place as it has for about two centuries, and few of us stop to think how unique we really are. In the eyes of many in the world, this every-four-years ceremony we accept as normal is nothing less than a miracle."

But seldom has that scene of authority transferred been more poignant than at high noon on the breezy January day when Jimmy Carter, tight-lipped and distracted to the very end by events half a world away, relinquished the presidency of the United States.

Reagan, now the beneficiary of all the goodwill and hope, eagerly assumed the office he had pursued for so long. In the Carter experience, however, there was a clear warning to the new President—a warning of how events he could not foresee on this bright Inauguration Day might color and perhaps dominate all the plans he had for the country. And there was a reminder as well that from this day forth, he too would be judged, beyond all else, by one paramount standard. Ronald Wilson Reagan, like the President he had just succeeded, would be judged not on what he had said as a candidate or on how well he had said it, but on how he dealt with the realities that confronted him in the Oval Office.

Index